Fertile Visions

Thinking Cinema

Series Editors

David Martin-Jones, University of Glasgow, UK
Sarah Cooper, King's College, University of London, UK

Volume 10

Titles in the Series:

Afterlives: Allegories of Film and Mortality in Early Weimar Germany by Steve Choe
Deleuze, Japanese Cinema, and the Atom Bomb by David Deamer
Ex-centric Cinema by Janet Harbord
The Body and the Screen by Kate Ince
The Grace of Destruction by Elena del Rio
Non-Cinema: Global Digital Filmmaking and the Multitude by William Brown
Sensuous Cinema: The Body in Contemporary Maghrebi Film by Kaya Davies Hayon
European Cinema and Continental Philosophy by Thomas Elsaesser
Limit Cinema: Transgression and the Nonhuman in Contemporary Global Film by Chelsea Birks

Fertile Visions

The Uterus as a Narrative Space in Cinema from the Americas

Anne Carruthers

BLOOMSBURY ACADEMIC
NEW YORK • LONDON • OXFORD • NEW DELHI • SYDNEY

BLOOMSBURY ACADEMIC
Bloomsbury Publishing Inc
1385 Broadway, New York, NY 10018, USA
50 Bedford Square, London, WC1B 3DP, UK
29 Earlsfort Terrace, Dublin 2, Ireland

BLOOMSBURY, BLOOMSBURY ACADEMIC and the Diana logo are trademarks of
Bloomsbury Publishing Plc

First published in the United States of America 2021
Paperback edition published 2023

Copyright © Anne Carruthers, 2021

For legal purposes the Acknowledgements on p. ix constitute an extension
of this copyright page.

Cover design: Eleanor Rose
Cover image © Rooney Mara and Casey Affleck in *Ain't Them Bodies Saints*,
Dir. David Lowery, 2013 © Sailor Bear/ DR / Collection Christophel / ArenaPAL

All rights reserved. No part of this publication may be reproduced or transmitted
in any form or by any means, electronic or mechanical, including photocopying,
recording, or any information storage or retrieval system, without prior
permission in writing from the publishers.

Bloomsbury Publishing Inc does not have any control over, or responsibility for, any
third-party websites referred to or in this book. All internet addresses given in this book
were correct at the time of going to press. The author and publisher regret any
inconvenience caused if addresses have changed or sites have ceased to exist, but can
accept no responsibility for any such changes.

A catalog record for this book is available from the Library of Congress.

ISBN: HB: 978-1-5013-5857-9
PB: 978-1-5013-8131-7
ePDF: 978-1-5013-5855-5
eBook: 978-1-5013-5856-2

Series: Thinking Cinema

Typeset by Deanta Global Publishing Services, Chennai, India

To find out more about our authors and books visit www.bloomsbury.com
and sign up for our newsletters.

For my parents
Theresa and Joe

CONTENTS

List of illustrations viii
Acknowledgements ix
Notes on text xi

Introduction 1

1 Challenging the pregnancy genre 15

2 Phenomenologies and pregnancy 35

3 Narrative negotiations in *Juno, Gestation/Gestación* and *Stephanie Daley* 55

4 Internal landscapes and biotourist narratives in *The Milk of Sorrow/La teta asustada, Ain't Them Bodies Saints* and *Apio verde* 89

5 The recollection-object, breaching the threshold in *Up, The Bad Intentions/Las malas intenciones* and *Birth* 125

6 Pregnant embodiment as *mise n'en scène* in *Arrival* and *Ixcanul* 155

Conclusion 175

Notes 179
Filmography 199
References 203
Index 216

ILLUSTRATIONS

3.1–3.6	*Juno* (2007) 60–69
3.7–3.14	*Gestation/Gestación* (2009) 72–78
3.15–3.18	*Stephanie Daley* (2007) 82–85
4.1–4.7	*The Milk of Sorrow/La teta asustada* (2009) 100–106
4.8–4.14	*Ain't Them Bodies Saints* (2013) 108–114
4.15–4.17	*Apio verde* (2013) 118–121
5.1–5.10	*Up* (2009) 130–137
5.11–5.16	*The Bad Intentions/Las malas intenciones* (2011) 140–145
5.17–5.23	*Birth* (2004) 147–153
6.1–6.9	*Arrival* (2016) 161–167
6.10–6.15	*Ixcanul* (2015) 169–173

ACKNOWLEDGEMENTS

My thanks go to Sarah Cooper and David Martin-Jones, series editors for Thinking Cinema, and Katie Gallof commissioning editor for Bloomsbury who have all been wonderfully supportive, understanding and encouraging at every stage of writing. I would also like to thank Tarja Laine who recommended the series as a home for my work. Each chapter of the book has been developed in conference presentations or in research seminars. I would like to thank the organizers of *Cognitive Futures in the Humanities* at Durham University (2014), the *Ethics of Storytelling* at the University of Turku (2015), *The Pregnant Archive* at Birkbeck University (2017), *Nature, Nurture, Future* with Sunderland University and the Thought Foundation (2017–18), *Film-Philosophy* conferences at Lancaster University (2017) and the University of Gothenburg (2018). I am also very grateful for research and travel awards from the Research Centre for Film, the School of Modern Languages and the School of English at Newcastle University, and the Fran Trust at Foundation Scotland. I was delighted when Erica Teichert and Rachell Sánchez-Rivera from Cambridge University invited me to join a panel on reproductive justice at the Latin American Studies Association (LASA) annual conference in 2019. Thanks to Rachell and Rebecca Ogden who invited me to speak at Kent University in 2020 as part of their seminar series on reproductive justice where the staff and students offered fantastic perspectives on reproduction and Latin American cinema. Thanks also to David Sorfa who gave me permission to include material from my 2018 article 'Temporality, Reproduction and the Not-Yet in Villeneuve's *Arrival*' published in *Film-Philosophy* Vol 22 (3): 321–39 in a substantially reworked form for Chapter 6. I am also very grateful to Erin Duffy at Bloomsbury for keeping everything on track.

I have been incredibly lucky to have friendship, advice and encouragement from Suzanne Moffatt, Julie Cupples and Kevin Glynn, and I thank Kevin for suggesting this book's title. Thanks go to Suzanne, Gerard Reissmann and Gez Casey for reading and checking draft material, and to Rebecca Knight who read an early draft and gave perceptive comments, critical suggestions and all-round encouragement. I would also like to thank Julie Roberts for being so helpful over the last few years. Thanks to Francesc Morales Brucher from Efecto Morales Film in Chile and to Esteban Ramírez from Cinetel in Costa Rica. Stacy Gillis and Guy Austin from Newcastle

University provided much needed scholarly and personal support. I would also like to thank Stacy for setting up a writing group in the School of English where writing time became a collaborative and social activity (thanks Caroline Rae, Chiara Pellegrini Giampietro, Joey Jenkins) and where much of this book was written. My colleagues in film and Latin American studies at Newcastle University have listened to my work in progress and spent time with me challenging my ideas. I would particularly like to thank Antonia Manresa, Gary Jenkins, Lydia Wu, Alba Griffith and Philippa Page. And to Julián Daniel Gutiérrez-Albilla for encouraging me many years ago to write a book. Kate Stobbart and Tessa Holland have always been amazing as have Emma Dooks, Ruth Bently, Jane Hanlon, Barbara Convery, Fiona Reed and Julia Fisher.

My children Rita, Harry and Joe have always been brilliantly supportive and all-round gorgeous. And thanks to my parents Theresa and Joe for being good life role models, especially my mother who was the first in her family to go to university. They both paved the way for my love of books, reading and learning. Thanks to my brothers Michael and Phil who have calmly watched the writing process throughout the many months of the 2020 lockdown. Finally, thanks to my husband Guy Pilkington, a film fan who has supported me throughout and has always put everything into perspective, and perspective means everything when you are writing a book.

NOTES ON TEXT

This book uses the spelling *foetus* rather than *fetus*, but original spellings will be included in quotations. The titles of films will be given in English and Spanish where appropriate. All film titles will be shortened throughout the text. The titles for films in Spanish always use a capital letter for the first word followed by lower case for the rest, for example, *La teta asustada*; I will follow this convention in all titles given in Spanish. The book uses a small number of screengrabs from each film as an integral part of the academic critique. The subject of pregnancy means that the book includes references to pregnancy loss and abortion.

Introduction

Imagine these film scenarios: a scientist doubles over as if in pain and then catches a glimpse of a child she does not know; a musician takes the scan photograph of his unborn baby and looks beyond it to the teenager who is pregnant with the child that he will adopt; a dying woman describes what her unborn foetus saw through her body during a civil war; and an ultrasound scan reveals an unviable foetus that is considered a child. All the narratives relate to pregnancy, reproduction and the reproductive body. A critical analysis, therefore, might begin with a discussion about the pregnant body, the unborn child or the foetus. But this approach becomes complicated when the temptation is to rely on a discussion about women's bodies, stereotypes of femaleness, personhood of the foetus or ephemeral notions of the reproductive body as otherworldly, monstrous or abject. This book argues that considering the uterus as a narrative space offers an alternative way of closely analysing these filmic texts. Exploring the properties of the uterus as a frame for on-screen and off-screen narratives, the analysis will provide a counterpoint to how pregnancy and reproduction have become so inextricably linked to notions of femininity, maternity and the maternal-foetal connection. Although the uterus is interchangeable with the womb in a medical sense, analyses of pregnancy and reproduction often rely on understanding the 'womb' as a conceptual location in which the foetus is a separate entity. This separateness, paradoxically, creates a narrative space. It is this off-screen narrative space that will be crucial to this analysis of overlooked moments of pregnancy and the labouring body in film. The approach offers a timely reconceptualization of pregnancy and reproduction by prioritizing the uterus in its *affectiveness* and centrality as a frame and narrative space, rather than its gender specificity.

That is not to say that the book considers pregnancy or reproduction as non-gender-specific or gender-free. These concerns, however, are not the focus of this critical discussion. Rather, the analytical framework engages with Sobchackian notions of the frame to offer a new route into close textual analysis of images of pregnancy and the reproductive body, and the details of this theoretical and conceptual framework will be outlined in Chapter 2. The analysis means that it is possible to approach a film like *Roma* (2018, Mexico) by director Alfonso Cuarón not only for the representation of pregnancy and the way it adds to the narrative or to character development, but also to examine specific imagery in the film. In a remarkable mise en scène construction about twenty minutes from the end of the film, pregnant bodies in labour are filmed in a static shot outside a hospital. The main character Cleo (Yalitza Aparicio) is helped to the hospital entrance by the family driver, and they are followed by her employer's mother. The long shot emphasizes the size of the hospital entrance which towers over the human figures at the bottom of the frame. Pregnant bodies, many being held by companions, walk out of the hospital into shot, or move across the front of the frame circling their own small area of space. It is an extraordinary shot, akin to a landscape painting in the way that size and perspective are framed. The brightly lit hospital entrance prevents the scene from being read as purely dystopian. Importantly, despite the sound of Cleo's rhythmic breathing and the sound of children crying, there is no sign of distress. Medical staff in white scrubs walk quickly in and out of the frame, some deep in conversation. Other non-pregnant bodies move around or give physical support to the labouring bodies in the frame. The scene, which lasts less than twenty-seven seconds, shows the natural progression of the labouring body. This is in sharp contrast to the sequences that follow where Cleo gives birth in a painful and distressing part of the narrative. In a film that invites social, political and cultural analysis, this short textual moment of framing labouring bodies as normal and as multiple may be overlooked.[1] It is an easy image to miss because the sequence is brief and because little importance is attached to its role in the narrative. It is crucial, however, if the film is assumed to have a pregnancy narrative, that images of corporeal normality are given some analytical attention. The analysis in this book thus offers additional critical strategies for discussing *all* of the images of pregnancy in this film.

When investigating pregnancy in contemporary films, it is an impossible task to try and catalogue all films with a pregnancy in the narrative. First, there are simply no effective search terms that can accurately find out where a pregnancy appears in a film. Second, films that have pregnancy or reproduction as part of their narrative do not always fall easily into an established corpus, and this is a crucial point. It is not effective or even possible to group films according to a 'pregnancy genre' or to a 'pregnancy narrative' once the supporting structures of representation or generic conventions are removed. This will be addressed in Chapter 1 which investigates how pregnancy and reproduction appear in domestic drama films – the focus of the book. Pregnancy, however, has not been ignored by critical film scholarship. As Lucy Fischer (1996) suggests, there have been many references to the maternal–infant relationship in film where the image and the acoustics of cinema have been likened to being in the womb or where the dream-like quality of viewing is compared to the infant at the breast. She argues that attention should return to the mother and that analyses should focus on the 'maternal register' (31). This suggests that there *is* a maternal register that it is being ignored. Thinking of a maternal register, however, encourages analyses of pregnancy and reproduction to remain in the realm of representation of the mother and conceptualization of the foetus. Thinking of a uterine register, rather than maternal, can challenge or offer more depth to some of the more established notions about maternity or the maternal-foetal connection in film theory and critique.

The book argues, therefore, that pregnancy and reproduction must be considered in a more meaningful way than just an extended discussion of gender and maternity or merely as an aesthetic or convenient narrative device. One way to do this is to make new connections between different kinds of films. The films that have been chosen for analysis – *Juno, Gestation, Stephanie Daley, The Milk of Sorrow, Ain't Them Bodies Saints, Apio verde, Up, The Bad Intentions, Birth, Ixcanul, Arrival* – are examples of contemporary films that address pregnancy in some way. Some of the films, such as *Juno* and *Stephanie Daley*, are more recognizable as films about pregnancy; others such as *Ain't Them Bodies Saints, Up, The Bad Intentions* and *Arrival* would be unusual in a corpus of films about pregnancy. Importantly, the films chosen do not have a clear thematic or generic link until they are placed alongside each other and when the uterus is thought of as a narrative space. It is the way that the book brings these films together that offers a different way to understand the subject of pregnancy and reproduction. For example, *Ixcanul* (2015, Jayro Bustamente, Guatemala/France) has a cultural and geographical specificity to its narrative as it concerns a young woman from a poor family in Guatemala who is promised in marriage to her father's boss but is already pregnant by her boyfriend. When this film is placed alongside *Arrival* (2016, Denis Villeneuve, USA), a drama about a linguistics expert and her encounter with aliens, the route to an effective analysis is challenging. Chapter 6 places these two films in dialogue with each other by thinking of the uterus as a frame and narrative space to discuss how pregnant embodiment can be read as absence, presence and temporality. Repositioning the uterus as a frame and a narrative space in close textual analysis encourages any discussion about pregnancy to tackle crucial questions about spectatorship and narrativity *before* examining gender or context.

Importantly, the concerns raised about pregnancy and reproduction in this new corpus of films are not inconsistent with global concerns about reproduction in other national cinemas or other geographical areas. The fact that the Americas can be understood as a specific geographical area and understood as separate nations means that there will always be an argument for it to be included as part of area studies or global studies. This book provides a framework for close analytical study of pregnancy that begins with cinema from the Americas. It should be emphasized that this is a place to start. The broader argument is that the female body has been subjected to scrutiny and represented metaphorically in film in many cinemas because of its capacity for human reproduction. Yet there is no analytical framework to discuss the aesthetics of pregnancy beyond gender, maternity or the foetal-maternal connection, and this limits close textual analysis and theoretical discussion. The analytical framework, therefore, can add depth to any discussion of pregnancy and reproduction in other global or small nation cinemas and will be helpful for any close textual analysis that is geographically, politically or historically more specific. Moreover, as the book refers to the pregnant body and the pregnant person rather than just the woman, there is space for rethinking gendered bodies in how pregnancy is lived or experienced with a view to returning to questions of nation and gender.

Above all, the theoretical discussion crosses disciplines and draws on feminist theories of the body, the foetus and the scan, and phenomenology in film studies. This means that it offers a unique contribution to the critical medical humanities as well as notions of affect and spectatorship in contemporary film analysis. Throughout, I position the uterus as a narrative space phenomenologically by engaging with Vivian Sobchack's (1992) notion of the gentleness of the frame and how the frame provides a '*premises* for perception', Kim Sawchuck's (2000) investigation into the internal body as bioscape, Laura U. Marks's (2000) notion of the recollection-object and Eugenie Brinkema's (2014) notion of *mise-n'en-scène*. Reading for form, I bring film analysis into dialogue with Julie Roberts's (2012a, b) work on the foetal ultrasound and the collaborative quality of narratives around the pregnant body, Charlotte Kroløkke's (2010, 2011) essays on biotourism and the foetal scan, and Janelle Taylor's (2008) broader discussion on the theory of ultrasound bonding. Although the foetal scan has been understood negatively for the way it fragments the pregnant body and isolates the foetus, it is this quality of embodied separation, emphasized by the scan, that allows the uterus to become a narrative space. Although scholarship on the foetal ultrasound has offered the complexity of discussion that is crucial to my discussion of the uterus, the foetal scan itself is not my main focus. My critical aim is to understand how pregnancy creates multiple narratives, not how the scan operates. Nevertheless, my analysis draws on empirical data from the scan primarily to investigate other ways of thinking about imagery and the internal body: in short, other ways of looking at and into the body through the uterus.

The uterus: *See* womb

The uterus as a term in film studies is virtually non-existent, and I have been constantly redirected in my research to look instead for the 'womb'. The womb is often considered as a metaphorical or symbolic location, which suggests that it is more significant – or perhaps just more interesting – than the uterus itself. The womb represents the pseudo-homestead when maternity functions as a metaphor – both positive and negative – for nature and community on the one hand, and protector and carer on the other. As Barbara Creed (1993) suggests, the womb is often considered as a monstrous part of the body as well as a useful mise en scène aesthetic in cinema. So, it is the womb, not the uterus, that has a long history in narrative cinema whereby it functions as a location for emerging aliens, false offspring and comedic bodily growth. The 'uterus' is almost non-existent as a search term in film studies, as I have said, and a quick search for the uterus reveals short films, TV episodes and action movies with a mission to 'abort'.[2] Despite Creed's influential work, she does not refer to the important question of language when describing the internal body. In the index to her book, there are thirteen separate entries for 'womb', two references for 'uterine iconography' and no reference for the 'uterus'. In Kelly Oliver's (2012) work on pregnancy in Hollywood cinema, there are sixteen separate entries for 'womb' and none for 'uterus' (232). When 'abortion' is added as a search term, more filmic texts appear such as the documentary *The Silent Scream* (1984, USA) by John Duane Dabner, a purported science information film that argues that the foetus screams in utero during an abortion procedure. The term also uncovers Pedro Chaskel's black-and-white documentary drama *Aborto* (1965) from Chile, a public-information film that advocates family planning to avoid back-street abortions. A quick search for 'abortion' will unearth documentaries about the legal status of reproduction *and* horror films about the monstrous foetus.

The difficulty of finding the uterus in film searches should be no surprise as it reflects the way in which the uterus has been historically, scientifically and medically misunderstood. In early documented medicine, the physiology of the human uterus was once confused with the uteri of dissected animals, which led to misunderstandings about procreation and reproduction. This allowed the female reproductive body to be labelled as animal-like. Physicians through medical history, as Cheryl L. Meyer (1997) explains, have been perplexed by the uterus and have produced many theories about how this reproductive organ functions. In the fourth century BCE, Hippocrates suggested that the uterus wandered around the body attaching itself to other organs which then caused hysteria in women – a condition that could be solved by intercourse or impregnation. In the second century CE, the physician Aretaeus added that the wandering uterus could be attracted and repulsed by a variety of smells. The movement of the uterus, he deduced, could be controlled by the right use of odours which could align the uterus in the body and prevented 'hysterical suffocation' (Meyer 1997: 2). This ability of the uterus to move freely around the body is reflected in how the human uterus was imagined as consisting 'of a number of cavities exhibiting angulation and horns, its lining studded with "tentacles" or "suckers", like an animal within an animal' (T. Chard and J. G. Grudzinskas 1994: 2, note the use of the term 'animal' rather than human). Conversely, in the second century BCE, as Meyer explains, the Greek physician Galen argued that the uterus was in fact stationary. Galen did, however, believe that hysterical suffocation existed. Hysterical suffocation, he explained, was caused by the uterus retaining male and female bodily fluids and the cure again was intercourse.

The uterus, then, is a compelling embodied space, which explains my reason for appropriating the critical history of the foetal ultrasound. The discourse around the foetal ultrasound highlights how the materiality of the uterus can become lost while looking inside it for the foetus. The scan provides a screen to look at images inside the uterus and in turn replaces the internal frame of the uterus. The technology itself has a rich history in the way that came from military sonar equipment and was developed for medical diagnosis, as Malcolm Nicolson and John E. E. Fleming (2013) explain in their history of the ultrasound scan.[3] The technology was developed for medicine as a positive contribution to the health and well-being of the maternal body. The introduction of the foetal ultrasound scan, they explain, meant that 'the uterus [was] no longer quite the mysterious object it [had] previously been' because 'the ultrasound beam [. . .] allowed the medical gaze to breach the "iron curtain of the maternal abdominal wall"' (178).[4] In fact, the scan uncovered the foetus rather than the uterus. The uterus remained a mysterious object when viewing the foetus. More importantly for my discussion, the technology was experienced differently by scan technicians as equipment that relied on feeling as much as on visualizing. As Nicolson and Fleming say, 'the fact that the image on the monitor followed the motion of the probe as it was moved across the abdomen increased the visual and proprioceptive feedback for the operator during the scanning process. Conceptualization of the abdominal contents was therefore facilitated. The need to wait for a photographic image to develop was removed' (2013: 231). This connection or mediation between the technician and the technology helps to understand how narratives are developed from experiencing this technological imagery as to how it feels or how it looks. It is a process of what Karen Barad (1998, 2007) calls intra-action which expresses connectivity, and I will return to this notion throughout the book. The origins of the scan as a visualizing, observing and diagnostic tool in medicine have also, paradoxically, established its association with an emotive and subjective spectatorial response, which is important to this book. The history of the foetal ultrasound depends on the history of scanning itself from the United Kingdom (Scotland), the United States, the Netherlands, Germany, Australia, Japan.[5] This transnational history reflects the cross-pollination of medicine globally.

The Americas

Beyond the historical and geographical beginnings of the scan as a technology, it should be noted that medical practices and beliefs about the body and reproduction are not limited to the Western or to the modern world. Humoral medicine and its associated beliefs, for example, were thought to have been brought to Latin America by Spanish and Portuguese colonial medics. As George M. Foster (1987) explains, there is also compelling evidence to show that humoral medicine was developed independently across the continents of Europe, Asia, Australasia and the Americas (355–93). He argues that similar – though not identical – beliefs based on the Elements (earth, water, fire and air, but more specifically, the properties of wet and dry, hot and cold) can be traced to ancient Greece, India, China and Australia. In addition, as Patricia J. Hammer (2001) suggests, the lack of written pre-Hispanic records, compounded by differences across cultural beliefs, social structures and language, means that physiological concepts are difficult to compare (243). Hammer, for example, notes the existence of the *madri*, in the community of Cororo in the Bolivian Andean Highlands, which is considered to be a marker of femaleness and reproductive potential (248–51). The *madri* is understood to be an organ that is not attached and can move around the female body but is located in the abdomen. Hammer explains that this is, in fact, the abdominal aortic artery which, when depressed, produces a strong beat and is described by the *madri* expert in the community as a 'heart-lung' only found in a woman. As Hammer explains, it is likely that the *madri* is a concept that is more widespread than this community as, in personal communication with another ethnographer, she finds a similar notion in pregnant immigrants from Mexico who call the female pulse the *tipte* (250). I mention this because a full examination of the transfer of beliefs across continents is beyond the scope of this book, but it suggests that caution should be applied in any discussion on pregnancy, the pregnant body and reproduction if it assumes or presumes any medical, national or regional specificity.

The Americas of my title refers to the United States, Canada, South America and the Caribbean. This is an area that has many cultural and historical crossovers, but has traditionally been divided, for academic study, into north and south with corresponding linguistic allegiances. This tradition emphasizes the differences across the region rather than the commonalities. It also splits the central region of the Caribbean, for example, into linguistic groups based on colonization. The book establishes a new corpus of films, but I do recognize that their disparate nature demands discussion. There are commonalities in relation to pregnancy and reproduction that I think mark the Americas out as distinct, particularly the constantly shifting political influences that affect reproductive rights and access to reproductive services. The Southern Cone countries, including Central America and the Caribbean, have broadly conservative attitudes to pregnancy and reproductive rights and, according to the Guttmacher Institute which monitors reproductive rights worldwide, 'more than 97% of women of childbearing age in Latin America and the Caribbean live in countries where abortion is restricted or banned altogether.'[6] In North America, restrictions are placed on reproductive rights in individual states across the United States, with delaying tactics a common strategy in accessing abortion services.[7] The targeted regulation of abortion providers (TRAP) along with limits placed on insurance for abortion remains widespread, despite constant campaigning against such measures.[8] State laws as opposed to central government directives may insist that people referred for terminations undergo compulsory ultrasound and/or counselling. These delaying tactics can have two important effects: seeing the foetus on the ultrasound screen (presuming positive bonding) may make a person change their mind about having a termination, and delaying the legal process may take the pregnant person beyond the gestational viability for a legal termination. Significantly, in Canada reproductive rights are part of the medical rather than the legal system, and abortion is freely available. Termination of pregnancy in Canada, however, must also be carried out, as it is in the United States, by regulated clinics and not all cities have these clinics. The location of services such as abortion clinics in sparsely populated areas means that such services are not necessarily accessible. This undermines the idea of these services being freely available. Although there continue to be shifts in abortion laws and reproductive rights across the region, the fluctuation of reproductive rights and the (in)accessibility of reproductive services, including abortion, remain a concern globally and specifically across the Americas.[9] Given that progressive political and economic attitudes towards pregnancy are inextricably linked to the accessibility of services, it is clear that reproductive rights in the Americas remain fragile and are constantly under the threat of being diminished. This legal vacillation demands an urgency to finding new ways of thinking about pregnancy and reproduction across the Americas.

In addition, the concerns around access to healthcare and reproductive rights in relation to abortion are extremely complex across the region. The issue in the United States, argues Linda J. Beckman (2016), is 'contentious, convoluted, and unpredictable' because of competing ideologies about the role of motherhood and the personhood of the foetus (102). As Beckman points out, although abortion has been declining across the United States for the past thirty years, and birth rates have been dropping, pregnancy and reproductive rights remain linked to ideologies about gender roles, even if these ideologies do not necessarily reflect public opinion. Moreover, although the discourse around abortion and foetal personhood in relation to reproductive rights is well documented in the northern Americas, the debate on personhood takes on an increased complexity when thinking about regional and cultural specificity. Lynn Morgan (1997) suggests that the notion of foetal personhood in the Ecuadorean Andes, for example, is complicated when the *feto* (foetus) is more likely to be thought of as *criatura* (creature) or *venidero* (the one to come) rather than 'a culturally specific conceptual entity' (324). Morgan also notes that the term *auca* – to describe a liminal being – is not only used for the unbaptized newborn but also used to describe other peoples or tribes who are considered less than human. Ethnographic research conducted by Andrew Canessa (2012) and Tristan Platt (2001) in the Bolivian highlands, meanwhile, emphasizes the complexity of personhood when it is understood as something that does not begin in pregnancy, with the foetus or even with the infant. This reflects an ambiguity or uncertainty not only about foetal personhood but also with the notion of existence itself. The cultural specificity of Morgan, Canessa and Platt's discussion is beyond the scope of this book, but I suggest that my analytical discussion would be of critical importance here. Their findings suggest to me that there needs to be more discussion that engages with the complexities of foetal personhood and pregnancy as a lived body experience, and as part of the communal human existence.

It is important to recognize that experiences of gender and sexual difference do not mean the same thing to all people, and that this is not a nation-specific debate. Philosopher Ochy Curiel (2016) explains that feminist methodologies, whether Eurocentric or Latin American, can make assumptions about the universality of female experience and female subjectivity, and she calls for a decolonizing approach to gender and sexualities. According to Cecelia Belej and Ana Lía Rey (2013), gender has an additional dimension when translating the Anglophone word into Spanish as *género* or 'genre'. This offers a more nuanced understanding of gender. It is an important semantic difference because gender, as a category or type, often replaces the notion of the woman (*la mujer*) not only in the Latin American context but also in global feminist discourses. Philosophically, this is complex. There are, suggests Nancy Fraser, 'multiple intersecting differences' (1996, cited in Claudia de Lima Costa 2007: 172) that are pertinent to the multiplicity of any lived body experiences. We should also be mindful, María Lugones (2007) suggests, of how gender roles have been imposed in Latin America by colonization. She argues for a move away from notions of patriarchy to understand the coloniality of gender as more akin to Aníbal Quijano's (2000) notion of the coloniality of power. Although de Lima Costa argues that 'the male or female gender designates an inhabitable ontological place' (2007: 173), I would not suggest that gender is an impossible, or unwieldy, mode of being. I do, however, think it is crucial to complicate notions of gender in order to consider what else is controlling narratives of reproduction, like the abortion narrative, for example. The aim of this book, however, is not to provide answers to the philosophical question of what constitutes a 'woman', nor do I seek to provoke arguments about what is or what is not female subjectivity.[10] This is not a negation of the female experience, nor does it ignore what it means to live and die in a gendered body. The much-needed conversation about gender identity and identification in relation to women's rights and female subjectivity is of crucial importance. The political discourse around essentialism of the body, the social construction of gender, female corporeality and gendered subjectivity underpins this book.[11] I acknowledge these discussions in Chapter 2, but I also want to note that it is beyond the scope of this book to do this justice. My analytical focus is to bear these discussions in mind as I develop a vocabulary about narrative space and ways of looking that can, in turn, be shared by other scholars of the body.

Corpus of films

Grouping the films as I do, from regions with common attitudes to pregnancy and reproductive rights rather than national and/or language groups, offers a departure for film studies in relation to pregnancy and to the study of the Americas. Bringing together a range of films from different national cinemas, however, is not unprecedented. As Dina Iordanova, David Martin-Jones and Belén Vidal (2010) suggest, cinema is not only centralized in countries or nations (as in Eurocentric or Hollywood-centric), but it also exists on the periphery. As small nation cinemas become increasingly visible and accessible, they argue, there needs to be increasingly complex discussions about nation and nationhood that question and reassess established national cinematic canons. Importantly, for the purposes of this book, I am suggesting that the region of the Americas is distinct and of interest because of its attitudes to pregnancy and the pregnant body rather than for questions of cultural, economic or ideological sameness. It is not only the themes of pregnancy and reproductive rights across the Americas that share commonalities, the co-production histories across the Americas (and Europe) of transnationally produced and/or funded films demands, as Luisela Alvaray (2012) suggests, a re-evaluation of regional and national identities in the light of globalization. This book contributes to this shifting focus by bringing together filmic texts that are not always defined by their national or cultural equivalence.

Importantly, challenging the grouping of films means that I introduce a corpus of films that would not be considered in other circumstances. As Michael Chanan (2006) suggests, there is already a 'cousinhood' that connects films from the north and the south of America (47), and he explains that there is huge interest – not only in the Americas – in creating new definitions and in looking more widely at how films are grouped for analysis. The term acknowledges the shared style, or aesthetic, common to populist postmodern cinema across the Americas.[12] Both Chanan and Laura Podalsky (2011) explain that Latin American cinema has come to increased prominence globally as a result of directors working not only in Latin America but also in Europe and North America.[13] Podalsky argues that cinema in Latin America has engaged with affect in a significant way that has brought individual directors to transnational prominence. This turn to (visceral) affect as an aesthetic, she suggests, has not always been welcomed by film critics who remain influenced by the political and social movements in Latin American Cinema in the 1960s and 1970s such as *Cinema Novo* and *Third Cinema*, movements that railed against the influence of dominant (First World) film production.[14] Podalsky argues that films which engage with affect are 'complex and call upon us to reconsider how aesthetics and politics intersect in today's cinema' (2011: 3). And, I would add that as films now circulate in more complex ways, there must be a process by which theorists can approach world cinemas that does not always refer to national political movements.

Of relevance to this book is to remember, as Chanan argues, that the essence of political cinema that came out of the Latin American region in the 1960s and 1970s embraced diversity or *différance*.[15] Although Eurocentric film movements such as the French New Wave were also politically influenced, the new Latin American Cinema of the 1960s and 1970s, according to Chanan, was not an aesthetic wave in the same way, but 'invoked an avant-garde spirit of iconoclasm [. . .] and was therefore, in aesthetic terms, radically pluralist' (40). This is something that has been forgotten in discussions of post-2000 cinema in Latin America, which largely concentrates on the influence rather than the connectedness of Hollywood. It is also crucially important to recognize that not every nation in Central and South America or the Caribbean has a viable film industry. Countries such as Costa Rica, El Salvador and Nicaragua did not produce feature films until the late twentieth century, and the Caribbean island Grenada not until 2006. This contrasts sharply with other nations such as Cuba, Chile, Peru and Argentina where industry infrastructures have produced rich cinematic heritages. The region of the Americas, I argue, cannot be thought of as homogenous and I do not consider it as such.

The more pressing question, I suggest, is how to engage with contemporary cinema transnationally. I understand the term 'transnational' to offer a language that describes how the historical perceptions of the national, the international and the global have changed and reflects that which operates without or beyond national borders. It is of crucial importance to acknowledge, as Martine Beugnet (2007) does, that in relation to a phenomenological reading of film, context is important. As Beugnet says, she understands the positioning against 'constructing yet another ahistorical or universalising method of appraisal', but she explains that the transnational is a response to the 'problematisation of nation as a label' (12). There is also, I suggest, not only a dissatisfaction but also a confusion about historical or cultural specificity in relation to film production. In effect, the global circulation of films now offers filmmakers a platform for their films that is unprecedented in recent times and this emphasizes what Nataša Ďurovičová (2010) and Steve Vertovec (2009) suggest is an ontological and epistemological repositioning of the global, the national and the international. I have found Vertovec's suggestion that we think of the transnational and the essence of its meaning as a post-national sensibility a useful way of thinking through my film corpus.[16]

Although I define the films in my corpus as personal dramas, this is not an obvious or self-explanatory category. I consider this corpus of films as ones that have a dramatic arc based on everyday life as part of a domestic narrative. Although some of the chosen films may cross genres, I have intentionally excluded films that I consider to be firmly within the horror genre. This is because the horror genre has been written about extensively in relation to the female body and pregnancy, as I have indicated earlier and discuss in Chapter 1. Chapter 1 challenges the existence of a pregnancy genre in film studies outside of a well-recognized list of Hollywood films. I situate my discussion and review of the literature not only in film studies but across other disciplines. The notion of abjection, for example, is often associated with analysis of pregnancy and maternity, and I take time to consider why this is important to a discussion on reproduction. There is often a tendency to include but not question the use of abjection in film studies, and I argue for more deliberation and analysis of the filmic text before attributing abjection. Chapter 1 also considers the importance of documentary filmmaking to emphasize that pregnancy can function beyond a narrative device or generic tropes seen in fiction films. Chapter 2 establishes the feminist and phenomenological discourses about pregnancy, the foetus and the pregnant body that underpin my analyses. In Chapter 3, I bring Sobchack's notion of the premises for perception (1992) and Roberts's notion of collaborative coding (2012a, b) into dialogue with each other to establish that the uterus is a narrative space where multiple narratives intersect in *Juno*, *Gestation* and *Stephanie Daley*. In Chapter 4, I discuss the importance of biotourism as a conceptual framework. Biotourism and the film analysis of the internal body by critical theorist Kim Sawchuck (2000) have already been used in discussions on the foetal scan, and I bring this cross-discipline scholarship together to establish how biotourist narratives are created in *The Milk of Sorrow*, *Ain't Them Bodies Saints* and *Apio verde*. In Chapter 5, I consider how the Marksian notion of the recollection-object can help to understand how narratives around the uterus cross the threshold of life and death to establish a bond, not only with the foetus but also with objects that are associated with pregnancy in *Up*, *The Bad Intentions* and *Birth*. In the final chapter, Chapter 6, I consider the importance of the *mise n'en scène*, a term that Eugenie Brinkema uses to describe narrative space that is beyond the frame but integral to the affective quality of the film, to read *Ixcanul* and *Arrival*. The importance of *mise n'en scène* is the way that it articulates absences and omissions in films that cannot be explained as on-screen or off-screen narrative space. I will then offer some concluding thoughts at the end of the book on how my analytical study of pregnancy and reproduction can be used to open up more avenues of discussion in film studies and feminist critical thinking.

I begin Chapter 1 with a discussion about the existence of a 'pregnancy genre'. This chapter considers where and how pregnancy appears in personal drama films to investigate how narrative conventions can lead to a lack of variety in filmic texts. The chapter will unravel how pregnancy and reproduction are often used to add depth to narrative without necessarily saying anything new about the subject of pregnancy or the lived body experience. This chapter will also consider how abjection has proved so compelling as a controlling idea in the analysis of pregnancy and reproduction, adding analytical weight to characters and themes that are often lightly drawn. This chapter will also look briefly at documentary approaches to the subject of pregnancy as these films often tackle pregnancy and reproduction as a lived experience in a more complex way than commercially driven films.

1

Challenging the pregnancy genre

As I explained in the Introduction, there needs to be a recalibration of how pregnancy, reproduction and the body are analysed in film, and this demands a rethinking of pregnancy in narrative and genre. This chapter, therefore, will first understand where pregnancy appears in personal drama films and discuss its narrative function, before moving on to consider the usefulness of abjection when thought of as connectivity. The chapter will also touch on the importance of non-fiction films that are not given a pregnancy genre label as such but are often the source of more complex narratives of pregnancy and reproduction. Although the films included in the first part of this chapter might appear to be merely part of a list, I want to illustrate the lack of variety in the way that these films – some of which might be classed as part of a pregnancy genre – use pregnancy and reproduction in their narratives. My point is that with little apparent narrative variation, some of these films about pregnancy can encourage a depth of analysis that is not always justified. There are some films that feature pregnancy, for example, where the pregnant or labouring body serves little or only a specific narrative function.

Although pregnancy sits comfortably in films about life, kinship and the fear of mortality, the way that it is so tied to narrative and generic analytical conventions challenges the existence of any well-defined pregnancy narrative or genre. Depth in analysis is often a result of a critical discussion that begins with representation. By that I mean representation of a woman, representation of the pregnant body or what pregnancy itself represents. The lack of variety and level of repetition in each narrative, however, is not always taken into consideration as something that might affect critical and textual analysis. This may be one of the reasons why tropes of horror and science fiction are welcomed into analysis of reproduction and the labouring body in all genres of film, almost by default. It might also explain why the notion of abjection has been so readily applied to analysis. This chapter will investigate how abjection has become an important element in narrative and genre analysis of pregnancy. The reason to include abjection in my discussion is to suggest its usefulness in narrative analysis in how it can articulate connectivity. The aim is not to ignore established ways of thinking about genre and narrative but to suggest that there are other ways to begin a close analysis of pregnancy and reproduction.

Clearly, the existence of pregnancy in a film serves a narrative purpose even when it is not a significant part of the overall plot development. The presence of pregnancy appears frequently on the screen when it is needed to form the basis of a subtext for the spectator. This subtext can be used as a shorthand in the character development of the pregnant protagonist or to signal the relationship of that character to other protagonists. As Currie K. Thompson (2014) explains, pregnancy and a woman's response to it is often used as a narrative shorthand for a woman's character development. Pregnancy alone, he adds, can be placed in a narrative to expressly signal a sense of mood in a film. Thompson, who writes on Argentinean cinema, explains that it is the concept of maternity that creates narrative, rather than pregnancy itself.[1] The construction of maternity, he explains, can be divided into three parts, 'witnessing a woman give birth, the discovery that a woman is pregnant, or the expectation that she will become pregnant' (73–4). This suggests to me how difficult it is to identify a pregnancy genre – is it a film that uses pregnancy to create a mood or one that conceptualizes maternity and pregnancy? Is it a film that uses pregnancy for dramatic irony? Or is it a film about waiting for pregnancy to happen or for pregnancy to finish? Of course, a film might be about any of these things, but should each film be included or justified as part of a pregnancy narrative or genre? Furthermore, if pregnancy can be used as part of a conceptual narrative to create mood, to aid character development or to guide the spectator's response, a logical conclusion is that a conceptual narrative can exist even if there is no pregnancy on screen. This is something that I address throughout the book, as I suggest that approaches to pregnancy and reproduction must bear in mind the non-pregnant, the un-pregnant and the post-pregnant. In Chapter 2, I develop methodological strategies for how this can be investigated in critical analysis, but in this chapter, I want to begin by looking at the different ways in which pregnancy is developed in film narratives. This is not an exhaustive list of films as the aim is to highlight the variety, or lack thereof, in films from the Americas that include pregnancy.

There is surprisingly little written about the lived body experience of pregnancy as a topic in the cinema, and what there is concentrates on mainstream – mainly Hollywood – cinema. Individual films can be given importance under the themes of sexual politics (Heather Latimer 2013), motherhood (Isabel Arredondo 2014; Asma Sayed 2016), women filmmakers in world cinema (Patricia White 2015) or regional cinemas (Stephen Hart 2015). These discussions are often rooted in crucial discussions about the sociopolitical implications of reproductive governance and the social and cultural representations of mothers. Some of this scholarship also tackles how cinema is funded globally, challenging what can be described as a regional film output. As I mention later in this chapter, pregnancy lends itself to the aesthetics and themes of bodily changes and alien takeovers in the horror genre. This has provided a rich scholarship on pregnancy and the maternal as they appear in the horror genre (Courtney Patrick-Weber 2020; Gustavo Subero 2016; Sarah Arnold 2013). Beyond horror, Parley Ann Boswell (2014) writes about pregnancy in cinema and literature to insist that mainstream Hollywood film always follows on from current trends, so that 'if Hollywood is doing it, then everybody else has already done it' (2). This is a bold claim, but I can find no clear evidence that cinema outside of Hollywood has tackled pregnancy in any significantly different way. Although pregnancy is certainly a recurrent theme or narrative device in horror and thriller films, and there are nation-specific cinemas that treat the topic of pregnancy and reproduction in socially specific ways, the term 'Hollywood' indicates that there is another cinema or cinemas to which we can refer when looking for evidence of a pregnancy narrative.[2] Whether Boswell considers this other cinema as independent, documentary, experimental or art house is not clear. As White (2015) suggests, funding bodies in the global North are often attracted to what interests them about perceived narratives of nations in the global South. White explains that funders are attracted to a film like *The Milk of Sorrow* and its director because 'the festival circuit frames [Claudia] Llosa as a national subject whose relation to human rights, feminism, and the exotic is appealing but difficult to decipher' (187). This is part of a much wider discussion on how Hollywood, or rather Anglo-European funders, outsources topics including narratives of pregnancy through their funding of other global cinema productions. Nevertheless, it is not clear who Boswell's (2014) 'everybody else' might be. I do agree with her, however, when she says that looking at canonical films (and literature) 'through a frame of pregnancy will change them for us, revealing aspects either that we have never thought about, or have never taken seriously' (2).[3] She argues that, through its reframing, pregnancy 'behaves like a Trojan horse, opening a narrative to reveal all sorts of human emotions and behaviours that have little to do with pregnancy itself' (5). Reframing and re-evaluating pregnancy inside and outside of what is understood as Hollywood or the mainstream is crucial, but identifying pregnancy and reproduction as only narrative or generic conventions means that the pregnancy genre, if it exists at all, is extremely limited.

The conflation of Hollywood and mainstream cinema, I have suggested, introduces a confusion between commercial cinema from Hollywood and the notion of the popular. Kelly Oliver (2012) in her important work on pregnancy in cinema, for example, does not explain how she defines her Hollywood corpus. While it is clear that she is talking about popular films that are intended for commercial cinemas, there is some difference between the box office figures of a film such as Judd Apatow's *Knocked Up* (opening weekend: $30, 690, 990) and Hilary Brougher's *Stephanie Daley* (opening weekend: $3, 401).[4] It is not my intention to argue that Hollywood or mainstream only means box office success, but my point is that Hollywood is often used as an explanatory term to describe an enormously diverse set of films. It is worth mentioning that Oliver draws on other films that are outside of Hollywood, such as *4 Months, 3 Weeks, 2 Days/4 luni, 3 saptamani si 2 zile* (2007, Cristian Mungui) from Romania, *Bella* (2006, Alejandro Gomez Monteverde) from the United States and Mexico, and *Moon* (2009, Duncan Jones) from the UK in order to widen her discussion. Boswell (2014) also widens her mainstream Hollywood discussion to other nations, notably to French New Wave filmmaker Jean-Luc Godard's *Breathless/À bout de souffle* (1960) to explain Godard's influence on a generation of North American filmmakers. She argues that *Breathless* contains a pregnancy narrative that is not developed, even though the 'silent pregnancy runs the show, in unconventional ways: without melodramatic fanfare, and through a rear-view mirror', to insist that the pregnancy is shared with the spectator through dramatic irony and 'informs everything in the film' (172; 173). Boswell makes an important observation when she says that the dramatic use of pregnancy, as an embodied state, is then not used to further any plot development. It is not necessary, however, to go all the way back to 1960s France to see evidence of the superficial narrative treatment of pregnancy.

Pregnancy is often only important when it highlights conflict between characters as maternity, under the guise of pregnancy, functions as narrative device or turning point. In Alicia Scherson's film *Tourists/Touristas* (2009, Chile), an aborted pregnancy underlines the fragmented relationship between husband and wife Carla (Aline Küppenheim) and Joel (Marcelo Alonso). The pregnancy functions as a narrative turning point. Importantly, the pregnancy, because of abortion, ceases to exist, which means that there is no pregnancy on screen. It is the memory of pregnancy and the way that it was ended that causes conflict in this film. In *Kept and Dreamless/Las mantenidas sin sueños* (2005) by Martín de Salvo and Vera Fogwill (Argentina/France/Netherlands/Spain), a young mother, Florencia (Vera Fogwill), with a backstory of being irresponsible in many ways, lies to her mother about being pregnant so that her mother will give her money. Again, there is no pregnancy on screen, only the financial implication that pregnancy will have to the main character. In *Maria Full of Grace/María llena eres de gracias* (2004, Joshua Marston, Colombia/Ecuador/USA), the ultrasound scan confirms María's (Catalina Sandino Moreno) pregnancy, and the photograph of the scan establishes her in a new geographical location, which has implications for the legal status of her and her child. The lived body experience of pregnancy, however, is not sustained within the narrative. In *Lion's Den/Leonera* (2008, Pablo Trapero, Argentina/South Korea/Brazil/Spain), a pregnant woman Julia (Martina

Gusman) is charged with killing her partner and must give birth in jail. The birth in jail is given little narrative time, which means that the birth is used as a narrative device to increase the level of threat or obstacles that the main character must overcome in the narrative. In *Junebug* (2005, Phil Morrison, USA), pregnancy creates a mood of suspense and unspoken familial guilt. Ashley's (Amy Adams) pregnancy is the narrative device through which to understand the conflict that exists in an extended, and fragmented, family. Ashley's pregnancy unites the family as they wait for the birth. Although the pregnancy in this film forces the family to spend time with each other, when the baby is stillborn the family fragments once again. The pregnancy loss is added to the familial group's memory, but essentially the pregnancy has been used as a narrative glue for the characters. In *Revolutionary Road* (2006, Sam Mendes, USA/UK), the discovery of pregnancy creates conflict for the main protagonists, as April (Kate Winslet) and Frank (Leonardo de Caprio) reveal their opposing views about their future lives. April wants to go and live abroad, but Frank has been promoted and wants to stay in the United States. The pregnancy, which will be their third child, emphasizes the conflict between the two characters. The pregnancy also offers each protagonist a narrative way out. Frank uses it as an excuse to take his promotion and stay in the United States while April dies after performing an abortion at home alone. In *Undertow/Contracorriente* (2009, Javier Fuentes-Léon, Peru/Colombia/France/Germany), pregnancy is used to emphasize the battle that the main character (who is having a sexual relationship with both his wife and his male lover) has with his sexuality. In this film, the pregnancy helps to develop the male character's narrative conflict and emphasizes what he might lose if he leaves his wife. What these films demonstrate is that pregnancy often underpins the emotional subtext of the narrative, but pregnancy often has a subsidiary, and therefore undeveloped, role as a narrative device.

By contrast, the centrality of pregnancy as a key narrative device in contemporary popular cinema has allowed extensive plot lines around the complexities of parenthood and new reproductive technologies. As Oliver (2012) notes, a new generation of films, particularly from the United States since 2000, has engaged with different ideas about family or kinship groups. Assisted reproductive technologies (ARTs), such as in vitro fertilization (IVF), have introduced different ways of seeing the family. Kinship groups in these films are drawn not only from biological connection but also by scientific means, and sometimes by subterfuge. In *Labor Pains* (2009, Lara Shapiro, USA) and *Preggoland* (2014, Jacob Tierney, Canada), for example, the false pregnant belly demonstrates how the status of being pregnant adds to the perceived positive personal qualities of the pregnant person, even though they are not actually pregnant and there is no pregnancy on screen. In *Baby Mama* (2008, Michael McCullers, USA), the faked pregnancy in the uterus (prosthetic belly) of the surrogate Angie (Amy Poehler) hides an actual pregnancy. The foetus in the surrogate's uterus belongs, biologically, to the surrogate's husband. The main protagonist Kate (Tina Fey), by contrast, has a 'hostile' uterus that supposedly cannot support a pregnancy. The comedy and pathos are finally resolved by the notion that Kate's uterus can hold a pregnancy but only through natural conception with the right male partner. Surrogacy, however, as a popular theme is not always about parents but occasionally about grandparents. In *The Brothers Solomon* (Bob Odenkirk, 2007, USA), the two brothers John (Will Arnett) and Dean (Will Forte) become increasingly close in their relationship when they try and create a grandchild for their father. They also become close to the surrogate Janine (Kristen Wiig) and her extended family and partner, creating an ever-expanding kinship group. In *Misconceptions* (2008, Ron Satlof, USA), surrogacy is positioned as a religious calling when an evangelic Christian woman Miranda (A. J. Cook) and a gay man Terry (Orlando Jones) form a close friendship when Terry moves in with Miranda to help with her pregnancy. In *Quinceañera* (2006, Dir. Richard Glatzer, Wash Westmoreland, USA), pregnancy has an effect on the wider community, and this is shown through the narrative of Magdalena whose pregnancy is controversial because she is not yet an adult (woman), and because she claims that she is a virgin and has not had sexual intercourse. In *Saved!* (2004, Brian Dannelly, USA/Canada), teenager Mary (Jena Malone) has sex with her boyfriend for procreation and to prove to *him* that he is not gay. Mary sees this as giving her virginity not as a gift to her boyfriend but to God. When Mary is then ostracized because of her pregnancy, she then finds kinship with her gay boyfriend and other solitary teenagers so that pregnancy is not only the main focus of the narrative but also a vehicle for bringing groups of characters together.

Pregnancy as a vehicle or device for characters with disparate personalities and lifestyles to form an alternative kinship group is a common filmic trope. *Unpregnant* (2020, Rachel Lee Goldenberg, USA) forces pregnant Veronica (Hayley Lu Richardson) into a friendship with Bailey (Barbie Ferreira) because she has a car and can drive her across the state lines to have an abortion. In *Who Says It's Easy/¿Quién dice que es fácil?* (2007, Juan Taratuto, Argentina), the main protagonists, Aldo (Diego Peretti) and his pregnant tenant Andrea (Carolina Peleritti), fall into a relationship which results in Aldo being present at the birth as Andrea's birth partner. In *Music on Hold/Música en espera* (2009, Hernán A. Golfrid, Argentina), musician Izequiel (Peretti again) pretends to be the father of Paula's (Natalia Oreiro) unborn baby in return for her helping him to find music for his latest composition. The supportive male friend in these films, I suggest, deflects the pregnancy narrative so that it shines a narrative light back onto the male character to explore questions of masculinity or fatherhood beyond paternity. Sperm trickery, where the sperm donation is not from the expected donor, in *The Back-Up Plan* (2010, Alan Poul, USA) and *The Switch* (2010, Josh Gordon and Will Speck, USA), succeeds in subverting biological kinship or sameness based on inherited characteristics. The rite of passage into fatherhood or the subject of young manhood, is not common. In the film *Too Young to Be a Dad* (Éva Gardos, 2002, USA/Canada), however, Matt (Paul Dano), a teenager and biological father, accepts his changed role and puts aside his planned career to support his girlfriend, Francesca (Katie Stewart). Matt goes further and supports his partner in the fight to prevent their child being adopted. In *L!fe Happens* (2011, Kat Coiro, USA; emphasis in original title), pregnancy provides the narrative complication rather than the main storyline as a young mother Kim (Krysten Ritter), who is trying to date, pretends that she is not a mother at all. The events that led up to her pregnancy are important, but the pregnancy itself is not the focus of the narrative. Even when the main focus of a film is pregnancy, as in the multi-protagonist film *What to Expect When You're Expecting* (2012, Kirk Jones, USA), for example, the main narrative is how the individual pregnancies of the couples interconnect. Each pregnancy is different, but the narrative remains focused on individual characters. Similarly, in *Casa de los babys* (2003, John Sayles, USA/Mexico), a disparate group of North American women are forced into close proximity with each other as they adopt babies from Mexico. The undercurrent of the film is of exploitation and poverty, but this is lightly drawn as the film concentrates on the disparate characters and how they cope with the same situation. Rarely, if ever, does a narrative film use the uterus itself as a subject or a plot point as it does in Isabel Croixet's film *My Life Without Me* (2003, Spain/Canada), which centres on the subject of uterine cancer. The uterus in this film represents the centrality of motherhood for the female character Ann (Sara Polley). The image of the uterus, and what it signifies for the main character, is highlighted in images of the diagnostic scan. The main focus, however, is how the concept of the uterus is a central marker for what it means to be a mother. This is reflected in the pivotal role of the uterus in relation to Ann's own body. The narrative here is less about the materiality of the uterus and more about the uterus as a palimpsest, or even a synecdoche, of the character's own reproductive life.

According to Oliver (2012), as I have mentioned, it is only recently that pregnancy itself has been at the centre of film narratives. This is reflected, she says, in the proliferation of mom-coms (mother comedies) functioning as rom-coms (romantic comedies), which place pregnancy rather than the woman in the centre of the frame.[5] The pregnant person and the pregnant body in this sub-genre of romantic comedy function as narrative devices for both male and female character progression, and this signals a shift from pregnancy signalling only motherhood or maternity. Comedy also allows the gendered male voice to enter the uterus as part of the foetal experience of being in the uterus. This is an established trope in fiction film marked by the trilogy of comedy films of the late 1980s and 1990s – *Look Who's Talking* (1989, Amy Heckerling, USA), *Look Who's Talking Too* (1990, Amy Heckerling, USA) and *Look Who's Talking Now* (1993, Tom Ropelowski, USA). These films gave voice to the sperm and foetus in utero. The intention of each of these films is comedy, however, and not an expression of foetal worth. The Christian evangelical film *October Baby* (2011, Jon Erwin, Andrew Erwin, USA), by contrast, gives the foetus a voice that allows it a subjective testimony of its experience of remaining alive when an abortion fails. In this film, a young woman Hannah (Rachel Hendrix) begins to display physical signs such as fainting and the feeling of not being able to breathe. This, she discovers, is a consequence of her experience as a foetus when she 'survives' the abortion. When Hannah collapses, and when she is recovering from her collapse, she describes the feeling of drowning, saying, 'I feel dead inside.' This film dramatizes and anthropomorphizes the unborn foetus to highlight the possible long-term effects of abortion. In *El colombian dream* (2005, Felipe Aljure, Colombia), the aborted foetus narrates the story of his family fourteen years after his death in utero. The film is not ostensibly pro-life, yet the film creates a narrator who has not forgiven those around him for his premature death. The more reflective pro-life drama *Bella* does not use the aborted foetus as a narrator. In this film, the foetus becomes part of the redemption process for the male protagonist José (Eduardo Verástegui) who is responsible for killing a child. By talking his colleague Nina (Tammy Blanchard) out of an abortion and offering to adopt and raise her unwanted baby, he makes the foetus the focus of *his* narrative. The role of the pregnancy, therefore, is to develop the narrative of the adoptive father rather than develop the narrative of the biological mother. In Eliza Hittman's 2020 film *Never, Rarely, Sometimes, Always* (UK/USA), abortion is treated as everyday and normal, if hard to procure. Although the film includes well-recognized tropes of the pregnancy test and the scan, the film is designed to allow a positive message about the importance of abortion. In *Unplanned* (2019, Cary Solomon, Chuck Konzelman, USA), however, Abbey (Ashley Bratcher) is conflicted about her job at Planned Parenthood because of her own history of having two abortions. The pro-life film suggests that abortion is a money-making industry rather than a horrific experience.

Although I do not specifically tackle horror film in my analyses, I do think that the focus on horror and pregnancy must be addressed. The horror of the offspring emerging from the pregnant body, for example, often relates to the unseen mother. This is compounded by the arrival of a child, by adoption or cloning, with unclear parentage into an established family as in *Godsend* (2004, Nick Hamm, USA/Canada) or *Orphan* (2009, Jaume Collet-Serra, USA/Spain/France/Italy). Sarah Arnold (2013), who charts the horror genre from *Rosemary's Baby* (1968, Roman Polanski, USA) through *Eraserhead* (1977, David Lynch, USA) to *Grace* (2009, Jeff Chan, USA/Canada), explains how the films 'all relate to the fear of monstrous, deformed or mutant offspring' (156). Arnold suggests that the monstrous, female reproductive body can be negated in the horror narrative by being coded as 'mother', and the monstrous offspring or foetus can be negated by being coded as 'baby'. In her discussion, Arnold argues that psychoanalytic theory is useful when looking at motherhood, suggesting that horror film is already predisposed to the myths and symbolism associated with a psychoanalytic reading of the maternal body (2013: 2). She explains that melodrama and the horror film have much in common, and that although 'there has been a wealth of research on the mother in melodrama [there is] relatively little on the mother in the horror film' and that 'there are enough similarities in terms of the construction of motherhood to warrant the use of psychoanalytic theory usually reserved for the melodrama' (4). As Arnold says, one of the major similarities between horror and melodrama is the 'disruption of the ordinary [and] its shift from the normal and its provocation of anxiety' (2). This may well be the case in terms of genre conventions in both horror and melodrama. This approach, however, highlights the inherent difficulties in analysing the mother, maternity and the reproductive body through psychoanalysis and linking this to a 'normative' shift. In order to recognize the shift from the normal, there needs to be a definition of what is normal. Arnold explains that she does not attempt to comment on the notion of the 'really lived' mother, but it would have been useful to know how the 'really lived' mother can be understood as normative and as a starting point for research (1). Of course, bringing together the two genres of horror and melodrama certainly widens the scope of research on the maternal. Taking a psychoanalytic approach and not defining the normative, however, inevitably narrows the scope of analysis and does not tackle the complex nature of pregnancy outside of gender-specific narratives and genres.

Maternity and the maternal are often compounded when generic categorizations are blurred. As Lucy Fischer (1996) suggests, gender entanglement has led to maternity being discussed within the melodrama genre as 'maternal melodrama', but that this genre classification complicates themes like maternity (10–12). Fischer encourages a shift from this discussion to investigate 'questions of maternity outside their assumed generic "home"' to explore other genres, but also to bring a different perspective to maternity as a gender-divided genre (8). Confining the subject of pregnancy to gender-identified genres ignores other ways of looking at pregnancy, such as pregnancy as part of the everyday. Patrick-Weber (2020) thinks of horror as a rhetorical genre that speaks to the real horror of pregnancy and childbirth and the unspoken traumas of miscarriage and stillbirth, while Erin Harrington (2018) talks about 'gynaehorror' as a way to describe the fascination with all stages of reproduction from the sexual organs to the post-menopause in the horror genre.[6] The fearful embodied experience of pregnancy is often read as horror, but this 'horror', nevertheless, is part of the everyday lived body experience. This is emphasized by Fischer when she reads the film *Rosemary's Baby* against the grain of a horror analysis to consider it as an 'utterance of women's private experience of pregnancy' (76).[7] Importantly, she notes that the embodied reality of pregnancy, a central motif in the film, reflects the real emotions of the pregnant person. By normalizing pregnancy as an experience, she moves the discussion of pregnant embodiment beyond pathological abnormality. This shift to the normal is crucial but little discussed, so it is worth thinking about why pregnancy has become so genre dependent. Horror, comedy and melodrama genres depend on their affective quality, so pregnancy in any of these genres is there for horrific, comedic or melodramatic effect. Brinkema (2015) suggests that the horror genre is identified by its relationship to negative affect and that this separates it from comedy. The 'circular impulse towards generification', she suggests, causes problems not least because the classification of horror includes films that do not horrify and excludes films identified as belonging to other genres, not horror, but still 'produce moments of disturbing affective intensity' (264). Caetlin Benson-Allott (2015) adds that the classification of horror is defined not by truly horrific historical events but by the feelings of disgust and fear that are generated because of the interiority of bodily function.

Creed (1993) argues that, in relation to the horror genre, it is the 'fertilisable' nature of the female body that singles it out when the horrific '*alterations* in the womb' which 'swells to monstrous proportions' or become a 'disgusting growth' can be transposed to another part of the body like a 'displaced tumour' (50, emphasis in original). The supposed inside of the womb, Creed explains, is an inspiration for a set design where labyrinthine paths lead to 'a central room, cellar or other symbolic place of birth' whereby 'the womb is depicted as grotesque' and is where the monster will give birth (53). Yet, it is not only how the womb lends itself to set design that fascinates. The womb as an imaginary location creates horror. Canonical films, therefore, depend on the spectator's ability to imagine the womb as a horrific place. In the 1976 thriller/horror/coming-of-age and arriving at puberty drama *Carrie* by Brian De Palma (USA), a teenage girl Carrie (Sissy Spacek) develops ever-increasing telekinetic powers as she enters puberty. Her powers, propelled by the natural function of her uterus, lead to her own death and her ability to threaten beyond the grave. In the *Demon Seed* (1977, Donald Cammell, USA), a woman is impregnated by a computer with artificial intelligence. The computer, presumably, can only replicate itself with human characteristics if its foetus develops inside a human uterus. In *The Brood* (1979, David Cronenberg, Canada), offspring are created by asexual reproduction triggered by a woman's psychological trauma and born through an external uterus. In *Alien* (1979, Ridley Scott, USA/UK), non-humans develop inside unsuspecting human body cavities, creating uterine spaces inside non-maternal bodies. The sequel to Scott's film, *Aliens* (1986, James Cameron, USA/UK), returns to the abandoned spaceship where alien eggs are found waiting to hatch, suggesting the power of the uterine space to wait for optimum conditions. In David Cronenberg's *The Fly* (1986, USA/UK/Canada) – a remake of Kurt Neumann's 1958 film – a man is reconstituted and reborn as a fly but wants his partner to carry their child so that his humanness can be replicated. In these films, the 'womb' is the location of horror but is understood as separate from the woman. Even when the films deal with real human fears where the body is a transformative site, their *raison d'être* is horror. These films speak to the fear of the unseen alien growing in the body, and the abject or disturbing nature of reproduction itself, which leads me to think about the importance of the theory of abjection.

Learning to love abjection

As I have said, pregnancy and maternity as subjects and themes lend themselves to a familiar set of narrative and generic conventions where they define conflict between characters, help to create kinship groups, bring disparate characters together and articulate the very real fears around human reproduction. The route into analysis of some films, however, is often Julia Kristeva's (1982) notion of abjection. Abjection is a useful theoretical tool, but analysis often conflates the pregnant body or pregnancy with the figure of the mother. This then lends itself to a negative analysis not only of the pregnant person but also of the interior body and maternity, and this needs to be challenged. Imogen Tyler (2009) argues that the abject is useful in feminist theory and study but cautions against its overuse in Anglophone discussions on the maternal. Her argument is twofold: first, she explains that Kristeva does not place herself within a feminist framework, so her discussion is not feminist; second, the maternal in Kristevan terms does not prioritize the woman and is therefore problematic when discussing maternal subjects and subjectivity. Kristeva's essay, however, is not one concept but an analytical conversation about self. Her essay emphasizes that what is considered by societal groups as abject is often linked to subjectivity or how humans see themselves in the world. She explains that one aspect of the abject is about bodily waste that must be expelled for the body to remain healthy or alive. In this way, the abject, she argues, is a necessary part of the living being.

Importantly, Kristeva talks about how the abject is an integral part of the lived body, and, while stressing the societal exclusion of women because of what their bodies do and despite thinking of abjection as 'what disturbs identity system and order', her essay also stresses the connectivity of the abject to the world that surrounds it (1982: 4). Kristeva does not ignore the importance of women in her essay but considers how they have been excluded by many societies because of their bodily function in menstruation and reproduction and this is conflated with being female. However, I do agree with Tyler (2009) that abjection – when thought of as only negative – should not be automatically associated with the female or the maternal. Tyler argues strongly against the notion of abjection in relation to the maternal, as she believes it does not 'address [. . .] the social consequences of living as a body that is identified as maternal and abject' (2009: 78). Her premise, with which I agree, is to encourage feminist theorists (following Iris Marion Young (2005) and Toril Moi (2001)) to re-centre the lived body experience as a response to the social and cultural value of the maternal body and as a way to address the critical differences between the female and the maternal body. In light of Tyler's discussion, it becomes increasingly problematic to conflate horror and the abject with the maternal. Yet, the notion of the abject is critical to Creed's theoretical positioning of the female reproductive body in the horror genre. Michael Grant (2004), however, argues that film theorists like Creed have drawn on Kristeva's notion of abjection without discussing the nuances of the theory itself. Grant posits that this is a fundamental flaw, with which I agree, and he suggests that, for example, when Creed discusses Scott's *Alien*, she concerns herself with mise en scène to the exclusion of narrative development. As Grant argues, the fact that the sets of *Alien* are blatantly uterine – and designed as such – weakens the richness of any further psychoanalytic discussion on meaning.[8] Grant explains that the sets of *Alien* have been created to reflect the idea of the monstrous-feminine and that to attribute any additional meaning based on Kristeva's theory of abjection is unnecessary and thus misguided. Grant says that the '*mise-en-scène* picture allows one to envisage the monstrous-feminine, the Other, as vaguely object-like. As a result, its relation to the film's action remains obscure' (181). Grant applauds the originality of Creed's analysis, but strongly argues that she does not bring any additional meaning to the film by applying any notion of the abject, as this is already reflected in the intention of the filmmaker.

In Creed's defence, her argument centres on the representation of the female as a monster that is defined by her gender and sexuality, and her argument is intended to move away from the idea of the female in horror as victim. She refers to Kristevan abjection in her analysis of the horror film to describe how the genre works by taking the idea of perverse pleasure and using the abject to create conflict in the narrative. Furthermore, Creed's work revolves around female embodiment and representation. Carol J. Clover (1992), by contrast, questions the dynamic of narrative and gender identification by addressing both plot and narrative space. She argues that the male audience, particularly the younger male, can identify with central victim–hero female figure in the horror/slasher movie.[9] A key factor in the representation of the victim, she explains, is spectator identification and that 'a figure does not cry and cower because she is a woman; she is a woman because she cries and cowers. And a figure is not a psychokiller because he is a man; he is a man because he is a psychokiller' (13). This suggests that the notion of abjection when applied to horror is not gender specific. This nuance must be remembered when attributing any significance of abjection to the pregnant body and to the maternal. Clover goes on to argue that 'film theory's conventional assumption that the cinematic apparatus is organised around the experience of a mastering voyeuristic gaze' is flawed (7–9). As Clover suggests, the idea of the male and female point of view as opposites is 'a relatively modern construction that sits, in fact, rather lightly on large sectors of the culture' (13) and this should not be forgotten when discussing the reproductive body.

Nevertheless, it is accurate to say that pregnancy and the reproductive body are compelling in the way that they are marked by the physiological process of producing fluids. These interior bodily fluids are understood as being affective, and their presence is often an integral part of understanding the abject. Kjetil Rødje (2015), however, makes a crucial point about the problems inherent in discussing the abject in relation to blood, particularly menstrual blood. He says that Kristevan approaches 'fall short of providing satisfactory explanations for the wildly differentiating effects and functions of various visual and cinematic images where blood plays a part' (93–4). He insists that imagery in the cinema is not only about the symbolic; it is also about affect and that Kristeva is not talking about the affective nature of cinema in her analysis.[10] Rødje goes on to say that incidences of blood increased in North American cinema in the 1960s (which Sobchack (2000) also notes), and is mainly associated with violence.[11] The affective quality of blood, he writes, is in its viscerality and ability to create an affective encounter with the spectator, and this applies to the ultra-violent action and the ultra-gory horror film. Rødje talks about the affective quality of the presence of blood that is 'out of place', explaining that this happens 'when the surface of the body is broken or when blood flows from body orifices (such as during menstruation)' (2015: 90). This reference to menstruation as 'out of place' appears to be an unthinking comment rather than a critique of the (ab)normal qualities of the female bodily function, but he raises this point to interrogate Kristeva's position in singling out menstrual blood. He argues that when she talks about menstrual blood, it is to demonstrate the centrality of its meaning and signification in relation to the 'universal female', where this universal female is conceptual.[12] This focus on bodily fluids, however, returns the discussion to what it is to be female, and this is more complex than Rødje suggests.

As Lauren Rosewarne (2012: 93–120) explains in reference to menstruation, and Christine Battersby (1998) reinforces in relation to the body, the female (and I would add male) reproductive body has only the potential for reproduction. Nevertheless, the markers or signals for menstruation – such as bleeding – are useful devices on-screen and are used as shorthand for bodily functions. Menstruation, for example, signals reproductive potential, yet it is often seen as a universal function of the female body.[13] The unused packet of sanitary towels, however, signals the missing period, and the pregnancy test confirms that the missing period is a pregnancy and not something else (such as menopause). Rosewarne (2012) suggests this is a synecdoche where the bodily function of menstruation is replaced by physical symptoms or commercial products and that this provides a more acceptable – or less uncomfortable – reference to menstruation.[14] I suggest that it is perhaps more useful to bring in Kristeva's essay 'Women's Time', written in 1981. In this, she explains that the biological and the conceptual are integrally linked. Kristeva argues that the foundations of female biology are found in repetition, cycles and eternity that form 'the fundamental, if not the sole, conceptions of time in numerous civilizations and experiences, particularly mystical ones' (1981: 17). Although 'Women's Time' was written with reference to the sociocultural and political history of the feminist movement in Europe, her discussion of time suggests that female subjectivity is bound by both cyclical (biological) temporality and monumental (infinite and imaginary) temporality. Her point is that female subjectivity and lived body experience connects distinct generations and civilizations in a way that is inherently different from notions of linear time.

I draw attention to Kristeva's discussion on time to stress this notion of connectivity in her work but also to point out that this understanding of the temporal cycles inherent in the female reproductive body is not one that is generally applied to the male reproductive body. The biological male body – like the female – only has the *potential* for reproduction. Sperm, however, is given a life of its own as reproductive fluid that is personified. As Lisa Jane Moore (2009) notes, the language used to describe the sperm and its journey reflects the 'endless fascination with the real or imagined capabilities of this [. . .] proliferating and endless resource' (45). Not only is its supply seemingly never ending, 'sperm "is spent", "reabsorbed", "swims", "spurts", "careens", and "crashes" through ducts, penises, vaginas, test tubes, labs, families, culture and politics' (49). She argues that this language is masculinized through speech to reflect the stereotypical male models of the 'fierce competitor, the benevolent father, the impotent wimp, the good catch, and the masculine threat' (47). This bodily reproductive function or product, as she sees it, does not share the same negative focus as the female secretions.[15] This highlights a flaw in attributing abjection to the maternal as this relies on gender specificity and a biological definition of male and female that can be confused with human attributes of masculinity and femininity. Understanding reproductive bodies needs re-evaluation, and I argue that there is still much analytical ground to cover before the notion of abjection can be reclaimed within the pregnancy narrative or genre. The notion of the abject, then, poses some problems regarding the understanding of the female reproductive body and the maternal. I am not arguing against its use, but I suggest that it should not be used as a shorthand that replaces a more complex analysis of pregnancy. There is positivity in Kristeva's analysis in the way that it discusses how the body functions as an expression of ourselves. This positivity, which I suggest should be understood as connectivity, helps to understand how analysis of pregnancy and reproduction becomes meaningful when thought of as lived body experiences that are shared.

Pregnancy as non-fiction

Although this book is about fictional drama, I cannot ignore the fact that the lived experience of pregnancy and reproduction is often given the complexity that it deserves in documentary filmmaking. Documentary filmmaking addresses narratives that are not fully always explored in contemporary commercial drama. The subjects of pregnancy and reproduction in the Americas throughout the 1990s, 2000s and 2010s in documentaries are often, but not always, made by women. These documentaries focus on the broader preoccupations of women's lives in the Americas such as sexuality, access to contraception and economic struggle, all of which are often linked to the female reproductive body.[16] The interest in women's reproductive lives has encouraged not only documentaries but short films made for social media. In recent years, the use of green handkerchiefs (*los pañuelos verdes*) to create a green wave (*la marea verde*) has symbolized the National Campaign for Legal, Safe and Free Abortion in Argentina. During the campaign and the street protests in 2019–20, the green handkerchiefs have been used on the body, as hairbands, as bras and as bracelets. The reproductive and sexual body, understood to be a critical site of contention, in this way becomes a body of people. Erika Teichert (2019) has written about the use of the green handkerchief as a symbol of the spirit of conviviality and an expression of intergenerational solidarity.[17] This use of the body (as the critical site of contention) in protest echoes the slut-walks in the United States (and the United Kingdom) in 2011 and 2012, where women took to the streets to wear what they wanted and to walk freely at night. More recently, this has also been seen in the campaign against rape and violence in Chile in 2019, where the feminist collective *Las Tesis* organized groups of women to dance in the streets and chant, 'the rapist is you'/'*el violador eres tu*', which went viral across global social media platforms.[18] The documentary film *Let It Be Law/Que sea ley* (2019, Argentina/France/Uruguay) by Juan Solanas demonstrates how individual reproductive and sexual bodies that take to the streets en masse become the aesthetic of the film and highlights how the body occupies the streets as a wall of sound as well as wall of bodies. But, as Deborah Martin and Deborah Shaw (2017) suggest, there is a tension in Latin American studies about the specificities of gender which can be absent in political discussions, but much needed when writing about women filmmakers.

Martin and Shaw's research complements the work of the Women Make Movies (WMM) collective in the United States, which promotes and catalogues films, mainly documentaries, made by women filmmakers globally. During my research, I found that documentary films about pregnancy and reproduction are not easy to find, and some of the films that I mention in this section are only available to view through WMM. The availability of both fiction and documentary films from South America and the Caribbean is a research hurdle. Although many filmmakers will be able to stream their films, access is still an issue. Nevertheless, it is possible to give some thoughts on the history of pregnancy and reproduction in the documentaries from across the Americas held at WMM. Abortion as a subject matter is highlighted in the documentary *Jane: An Abortion Service* (1995, Kate Kurtz and Nell Lundy, USA), which charts the rise of lay abortionists in the United States in the late 1960s and early 1970s who provided terminations for women who could not afford the procedure even when it became legal to do so. The film traces the 125 women workers who performed 12,000 abortions between 1968 and 1973. Without the aid of ultrasonography, the workers performed the terminations by touch, relying on their understanding of the physiological nature of the body from the vagina to the cervix and to the uterus. Pregnancy and antenatal care are explored in *The Motherhood Archives* (2013) by Irene Lusztig, which includes narratives of twentieth-century US public-information films about pregnancy, birth and motherhood where the (middle-class, white) expectant mother is described as a 'traveller in an unimaginable foreign country'. The film traces the embodied experience of pregnancy from antenatal exercise classes to the journey from their homes into hospital. Therese Shechter's *How to Lose Your Virginity* (2013) from the United States examines female virginity as a rite of sexual passage that, in the heteronormative-patriarchal definition, is understood as the penis crossing the vaginal threshold. In the film *Virgin Tales* (2012), director Mirjam von Arn explores the lives of Christian evangelicals in the United States. The film hears how interviewees describe how the male, through sexual intercourse, 'opens your womb', and how the existence of the womb is understood to identify the female as 'life giver'. Again, the subject of pregnancy and reproduction broaches many philosophical and conceptual notions of the gendered body. Importantly, these documentaries record a gendered notion of pregnancy and reproduction as well as testimonies of people who have dealt practically with the lived body experience of unwanted pregnancy.

There is a broader discussion here that I am not able to address in this book, about fertility as an embodied potential, which complicates notions of the gendered body. Fertility, the right to fertility and the consequences of fertility are important subjects. Documentary films reflect the complexities of reproductive rights when fertility is controlled. The film *Las Libres: The Story Continues* (2014, Gustavo Montaña, USA/Mexico/Argentina) documents the criminalization of women for having abortions, even when there is no technical pregnancy at all. Florence Jaugey, in her film *From Girl to Mother/De niña a madre* (2005) from Nicaragua, investigates untold narratives when she interviews pregnant girls about their childhood, their partners and reproductive responsibilities. In *Rosita* (2005) filmmakers Barbara Attie and Janet Goldwater document the legal procedures in Nicaragua and Costa Rica as authorities and parents deal with the pregnancy and human rights of a nine-year-old girl who is pregnant through rape. The documentary *Beautiful Sin* (2014) from Costa Rica/United States investigates the implications for prospective parents of a ban on in vitro fertilization (IVF). By contrast, the question of enforced sterilization in Brazil informs the work of filmmaker Ana Luiza Azevedo as women speak about their thoughts and feelings (negative and positive) in *Ventre Livre: Freeing the Womb* (1994). These documentaries, particularly the ones about very young women who become pregnant, reflect the constant paradox of the pregnant person's reproductive and human rights, and agency in their fertility, when placed alongside the opposing forces that prioritize foetal rights.

It is worth mentioning here that reproductive rights and rights to fertility are often confused by the concept of virginity, and this applies to fiction and non-fiction.[19] The notion of the virgin birth in Christianity, for example, has provoked not only theological but also anthropological discussion. As scientist and social anthropologist Edmund Leach suggested in 1966, the myth of the virgin birth is part of the 'metaphysical topography of the relationship between gods and men' (39) and that this is separate from what people believe as actually happening to the body. Isabel Arredondo (2014), writing on motherhood and Mexican cinema, draws attention to the Virgin as a construct and argues (agreeing with Marina Warner (1976)) that 'the Virgin tells us about people who created the myth. [. . .] [It] is not imposed by an outside force but is made by the society who believes in it; its origin is within society' (36). The concepts of *marianism* or Mariology – the worship, devotion and reverence of the Virgin Mary, mother of Jesus Christ – are often used to promote the ephemeral cultural qualities that women are expected to have in Latin American society. To differentiate between Christian worship and gender roles, Evelyn P. Stevens (1973: 90–101) coined the word *marianismo* as a counterpart to *machismo*. While femaleness and maleness in this context are not entirely comparable, Stevens initiates an important discussion that revolves around the perceived superior moral and spiritual qualities of the (idealized) woman capable of reproduction. Stevens's work concentrates on Mexico, and as such is culturally and regionally specific, but it highlights the complexity of gender roles and the genealogy of such roles. As she insists, social class bears heavily on the development of many of these concepts. There is disagreement about whether these notions of masculinity and femininity result from colonial cultural imperialism, but as Stevens explains, the concept of the fertile female as a superior being (or goddess) is something that is shared globally. It is worth remembering that fertility, as a marker of having a uterus, is neither guaranteed nor desired.

Finally, I want to think about the specific subject of the ongoing trauma of separation when a baby or foetus is taken, disappeared or stolen from the pregnant or post-partum person where the uterus is one of the last locations of contact. In the documentary *A Girl Like Her* (2011) from the United States, Ann Fessler interviews women in the present day who gave up their babies for adoption throughout the 1960s and 1970s. The central narrative is how the women who were physically and unwillingly separated from their babies have suffered through their lives with ongoing trauma. *The Mothers of the Plaza de Mayo/Las madres de la Plaza de Mayo* (1985) directed by Susana Blaustein Muñoz and Lourdes Portillo also tells the story of loss when groups of mothers and grandmothers search for their lost children and grandchildren who disappeared under the military repression in the 1970s and 1980s Argentinean Dirty War. In Noemi Weis's documentary *Abuelas: Grandmothers on a Mission* (2012) Estela de Carlotta, one of the grandmothers of the *Plaza de Mayo*, describes the search for the remains of her daughter Laura, who was imprisoned when pregnant and killed soon after the birth of her son. De Carlotta's search led her to Laura's bodily remains which showed the presence of pregnancy in her pelvic bones. Although a concrete sign that a pregnancy existed, there was no evidence of where the baby might be, if it was in fact still alive.[20] The uterus, in these cases, is a physical location of biological contact. This creates an embodied and conceptual link not only between the pregnant person and the child but also between the remaining relatives and the child as part of kinship. Gaston Biraben's fictional drama *Captive/Cautiva* (2003) from Argentina, based on actual testimonies, dramatizes a schoolgirl's traumatic experience of having her (illegal) adoptive parents taken into custody and then being re-introduced to her biological family. The trauma of identity is also depicted in a dramatic reconstruction in *The Blonds/Los Rubios* (2003) from Argentina and the United States. The film depicts the abduction of director Albertina Carri's parents and describes her emotional and conceptual journey to find out where they were and who knew their story. In all these films, the narratives of pregnancy as a lived experience include the loss to other generations. I suggest that this book can offer a useful route into analysis of the uterus as the last place of contact.

To summarize, this chapter has argued that there are many critical elements that surround pregnancy when it appears in a fictional narrative – its use as a narrative device, the conflation of pregnancy with maternity, the theme of pregnancy (real or not) to comment on reproductive technologies and pregnancy as critical to a sociopolitical understanding of abortion – that to group these films into a pregnancy narrative or genre is really quite difficult. As this chapter has suggested, cultural notions or beliefs can lead to confused notions of maternity, virginity, abortion, which are then often conflated with femaleness, fertility, the feminine or the ideal woman. Moreover, if pregnancy as a theme or a bodily state is only present in a film as a vehicle for cohesion, more consideration should be given to its narrative importance before assigning a film to a pregnancy genre. To go back to Arnold's comment about not wanting to write about the maternal as part of a 'real' lived experience, perhaps it is worth doing just that to recalibrate analysis of pregnancy and reproduction in film. Although my research suggests that there is not a critical mass of filmic texts on this subject, this chapter has highlighted an important area for future research – the last location of contact of stolen or disappeared babies or foetuses. This area of research, I suggest, will benefit from my film readings. This chapter has also called for a rethink in the use of abjection to move beyond some of its negative connotations about pregnancy or the reproductive body. One of the ways to do this, as I have mentioned, is to stress its importance to connectivity. This would then offer an opportunity to think differently about the way that pregnancy is categorized within genres. Overall, this chapter has argued that genre and narrative can be misleading places to start a discussion about pregnancy and reproduction. Chapter 2, therefore, will offer some suggestions about methodology. Principally, Chapter 2 will engage with phenomenology as a methodology and will investigate ways of looking that include the foetal ultrasound scan to establish how the uterus can be understood as a frame for narratives.

2

Phenomenologies and pregnancy

The importance of phenomenology to this book is in its ability to articulate spectatorship *and* narrativity which, when applied to pregnancy, means that the lived body and the lived body experience can be understood as part of a spectatorial encounter. I argue that if the uterus is thought of as a frame for narrative, it is possible to understand how pregnancy can be understood not only as a lived body subjectivity but also as a conceptual encounter. Of relevance to the book's overarching discussion is the Sobchackian notion of the frame as a '*premises* for perception' (Sobchack 1992: 134, emphasis in original). Sobchackian phenomenology in film studies has emphasized the differences between the structure of vision and the embodied experience of seeing. Critical discussions on the foetal ultrasound have also explored how narrative is created through ways of looking. Roberts's (2012a: 99; 2012b: 305–9) notion of 'collaborative coding', for example, explains how bonding narratives of kinship are created around the technological image of the foetus on screen rather than just a response to the pregnant body. This (in)attention to the screen explains to me how the pregnant body can be very visible but not crucial to the act of seeing. The discussion in this chapter, therefore, is about searching for an appropriate methodology that can engage across other disciplinary critical discourses on the pregnant body, as well as phenomenology and spectatorship in film studies. This is not a straightforward task, but I suggest that anchoring the discussion in the analytic threads that come out of Sobchackian phenomenology allows me to think of narratives in ways that stress their connectivity.

Phenomenological enquiries have often been built on a frustration with established theories in film studies. Sobchack (1992), for example, rails against the view that phenomenology is 'mushy' or subjective, or that its use in film studies is merely 'sloppy liberal humanism' that then negates its academic rigour as a methodology or as a theoretical enquiry (xiv). Her point, which she argues strongly, is that well-established psychoanalysis and

Marxist analyses (often the basis of critical discussions of reproduction) have 'not exhausted her own experience but [have] exhausted her patience' and have 'grounded and circumscribed' film theory to a discussion of spectatorship that is limited to representation and apparatus (Sobchack 1992: xv). Although there are some limitations with representation, and notions of apparatus theory can be overly mechanical, the importance of Sobchack's frustration is that visual (and linguistic) based theories can ignore the process of looking that is embodied and involves more than sight. The broader argument that Sobchack, as a linguistic expert, emphasizes is that although structures of meaning can be explained, they are always limited by language. Semiotics and the ideological study of the gaze, she explains, do not deal with the specificity of the lived body experience. When spectatorship is thought of as an embodied experience, it challenges, as Marks suggests, 'the critique of ocularcentrism [that] has a considerable legacy among feminist theorists, who link vision to the distanciation from the body and to the objectification and control of sense and others' (2000: 133). As Marks argues, prioritizing distanciation and objectification takes away the importance of interconnectivity and the haptic and what Sobchack calls the 'meaningful relation between cinema and our sensate bodies' (2004: 54). Even when structurally limited by the frame, Sobchack says, the spectator, through perception and experience, sees beyond the frame to make sense of what the film is presenting to them. Images presented on screen or within the frame, as such, are not bound by the geometry of the frame and do not just disappear when they are out of frame or off-screen. Sobchack suggests that although images are framed, they do not disappear when the frame changes; they disappear gently. In Chapter 3, I explore this notion of gentleness in the way that images move gradually out of the spectator's attention to explain how the pregnant body can be present on screen, yet absent for the spectator. Sobchack (1992) explains how the frame, as the orientational point of film, can be understood as like the field of the body – as the orientational point for the lived body experience. This is worth remembering in a search for analytical clarity when, on the one hand, narratives of pregnancy are constructed as external to the pregnant body, and on the other hand, narratives are focused on the internal workings of the pregnant body. This is where I think that the scholarship on the foetal scan can add depth to a discussion on off-screen space.

Of course, the foetal ultrasound is not universally accessible, and the technology comes with its own set of contradictions, but my enquiry echoes that of Roberts when she laments the lack of scholarship on the foetal ultrasound as a 'multi-sensory process' (2012a: 81). Roberts describes the connectivity of spectatorship and narrative in bonding scans as 'collaborative coding' which, she explains, articulates the shared narrative concern around the screen in the scan (2012a: 99; 2012b: 305–9). The visual image (of the foetus) and the narrative device of the scan provoke a suturing whereby the spectator attributes identification – recognizing the image of the foetus as something familiar to them – as an integral part of the process of establishing kinship. Roberts, looking at the discursive exchanges between sonographers and clients in the scan room, explains that 'the sonographer can translate the image on the screen into a signifier of a baby' (2012b: 310) but that 'imaginative interpretations [. . .] made by one observer are picked up and repeated, moderated or expanded by another' to create multiple narratives that form a 'mutually acceptable interpretation of the images on screen' as part of developing kinship (2012b: 307). I suggest, therefore, that collaborative coding stresses identification *and* intersubjectivity whereby spectators interpret the image (of the foetus) in relation to how they see themselves and how they position themselves as part of a kinship group with the foetus. This is a wider discussion that goes beyond interpretation and incorporates active visualization (of the foetus) and active storytelling around the frame of the uterus. Thinking of the uterus as a frame for narrative allows for a discussion that moves beyond personal subjectivity to a spectatorial encounter of something that is communal or shared. Thinking of the shareability of the pregnant experience is subtly different if thought of in Sobchackian terms. As she suggests, a theoretical approach to spectatorship in film should pay attention to 'the film experience [as] a system of communication based on bodily perception [and] as a vehicle for conscious expression' whereby 'the viewer, therefore, shares cinematic space with the film but must also negotiate it' (Sobchack 1992: 9–10). These negotiated structures of vision, Sobchack suggests, are both empirical and philosophical. By this she means that structures of vision are measurable when thought of as sight, but interpretative when thought of as the lived body experience of looking. The vision of the spectator and the projected vision of the film meet, she suggests, at the cinema screen so that the film experience should be considered as a form of communication and a doubling of spectatorship, and this is useful for how I analyse images of pregnancy and the pregnant body.

Iris Marion Young (2005) suggests that the foetal ultrasound offers a route into the shareability of the pregnant experience through vision. Yet when Young offers a phenomenology of pregnancy, it is only from the point of view of the pregnant subject. Her philosophical analysis does not elaborate on spectatorship beyond objectification of the body and subjectivity of the pregnant person. Shareability in Young's enquiry, therefore, means subjectivity. The act of looking, however, is not always looking from the same point of view, nor is it divorced from the embodied moment of the encounter as a self-reflective experience. Whether it is the scan or the film, self-reflexivity depends on the spectator's ability to empathize or sympathize with the subject of the narrative (pregnancy) and/or the protagonists (pregnant person, foetus) where the encounter is part of the lived body experience. I discuss this in more detail in Chapter 4 when

I talk about how the uterus, when thought of as a bioscape, becomes a point of contact for overlapping narratives. As Charlotte Kroløkke (2011) explains when talking of the foetal scan, the (expectant parent) spectator's response to the visual image on the scan (whether or not it can be understood as a real or actual image) is part of a performance that is coupled with a conventional narrative around the scan as part of a shared subjectivity.[1] A shared subjectivity suggests a communal viewpoint that in the scan is often read as bonding. In Chapter 5, however, I discuss how recollection-objects can help to understand narratives that move into and outside of the uterus as a more complex notion of bonding that is not limited to the image on the screen or to the subjectivity of the protagonist.

Notwithstanding the tension in film scholarship that exists in competing philosophical analyses of vision and the frame, I believe there are important crossovers that are crucial to how I read pregnancy and the space of the uterus. For example, the Sobchackian idea of the frame as a premises for perception intersects with Deleuzian notions of off-screen space or out-of-field (*hors-champ*) as an 'Elsewhere' (1986: 18).[2] Gilles Deleuze does not write about the embodied spectator and is not identified as a phenomenologist; he does acknowledge the power of off-screen space.[3] What I find useful about Deleuze's discussion is the way that he, like Sobchack, investigates what the frame does and understands that the spectator is an active part of the viewing process. The frame, Deleuze explains, gives information in two ways: as saturation – where the frame contains a great deal of visual and sonic data; and rarefaction – where the frame is stripped of extraneous detail through the use of a single object, sparse sets or the blank, black or white frame (1986: 13–14). The frame, he suggests, can also be an essential part of the spatial composition in a film when, for example, the iris is used to open up or close down an image to enhance or support the information within the frame. But when Deleuze talks about the frame as geometric or physical, he is not just talking about the shape of the frame. As he says,

> [t]he screen as the frame of frames, gives a common standard of measurement to things which do not have one – long shots of countryside and close-ups of the face, an astronomical system and a single drop of water – parts which do not have the same denominator of distance, relief or light. In all these senses the frame ensures a deterritorialization of the image. (Deleuze 1986: 16)

Perhaps it goes without saying but is worth remembering that the very nature of film's corporeality is that it frames that which is not framed in life. In doing so, film has already created a distinct way of looking at things.

Importantly, when Deleuze explains that out-of-field always connects what is in the frame to what constitutes the whole outside of the frame, he suggests that this is the fourth dimension of time, or the relationship of the virtual to the whole. I find his discussion on the crystals of time is helpful here when understanding this notion of the actual and the virtual as two sides of an image but also as a relationship with time. He explains that 'the cinema does not just present images, it surrounds them with a world' and that the crystal image suggests how imagery is not static, but constantly shifting between what has gone before (the present that has moved into the past), and what is now in the present (that had been in the future) and so on (Deleuze 1989: 66–8). The crystal articulates the shards of time that resonate in this circuital process of the actual and the virtual image. But it is Deleuze's notion of an Elsewhere that adds something extra to how Sobchack describes the process of looking and to the way that narratives around the scan are understood by Roberts and Kroløkke. This something extra is in acknowledging that the properties of the frame involve what is understood to be actual (as an image and in the world of the film, including that which is understood as being just out of view) and virtual (images that resonate in the world of the viewer and the viewed film). Although Deleuze speaks specifically about the formal qualities of the frame and not bodily space, he highlights how off-screen narrative space is an interpretative space based on spectator perception where the gaps in visual information are filled with a sense of what the images mean to them or what they think might be happening off-screen. To be clear, Deleuze is very specific about how he understands off-screen space: on the one hand as part of a 'homogenous continuity' (1986: 18); on the other hand, as part of the virtual.

As David Deamer (2016) explains, this Elsewhere *is* the virtual as '[t]he frame subsists, not spreading out to create a world, but to turn in upon itself. The actual images are overrun by its virtual connections: the spectator must read the image, but the connections are so weak it is the spectator's own thought that is important here, not a pre-determined response' (2016: 164). As Deamer explains, 'the power of the shot is elsewhere other than its place in the film. This elsewhere is not its actual cinematic materiality, but what the image engenders in the brain of the spectator, its virtual coordinate' (2016: 165). What Deleuze suggests is that film does not only exist as a closed system of framing and angles but that it has properties that cannot be explained only by technical considerations. Importantly, Deleuze explains this as a circuit: a mirror image, for example, that becomes an actual image that pushes the actual image into the out-of-field so that it becomes virtual. He explains that this 'constitutes an objective illusion' that is not 'in someone's head' (1989: 67). This describes the way that the scan is read, not just as one image but is constructed as many images, actual and virtual. This, I argue, links closely with the gentleness of the frame described by Sobchack.

While it could be argued that multiple narratives around the uterus are in fact extra diegetic rather than off-screen, this does not address the profundity of these narratives or images, as Deleuze and Sobchack suggest.

Extra diegesis suggests something that is obviously part of the world of the film but positioned outside of the main diegesis so that, in other words, the spectator is aware of its presence. When the cinematic frame, according to Sobchack, provides the 'orientation point' for the spectator, 'it functions as "that by means of which" the film has access to its world and the world exists for it (and for us)', and narrative space is created around a frame which is 'both invisible to the film's seeing of its world and yet visible to us [and] provides the *synoptic center* of the film's experience of the world it sees' (Sobchack 1992: 134, emphasis in original).[4] One of the most compelling arguments that Sobchack makes about the cinematic frame, as I have said, is that its properties include gentleness where the spectator is not always aware of the geometric limits of the frame. Gentleness, in this context, describes how action that takes place on-screen moves into off-screen space. The perception of visual information, she suggests, remains for the embodied spectator so that it is interpreted and perceived as part of an off-screen narrative space. Although it is impossible to visualize or effectively describe what this off-screen narrative space actually *is*, it is possible to analyse how it functions in relation to the spectator. I discuss in more detail the specifics of cinematic off-screen space later in the chapter, but first, I discuss the mode of address of the foetal ultrasound, where the screen and the image of the foetus are not the only elements necessary in the process of interpretation.

Collaborative coding as 'perceptual glue'

Narrative space around the uterus in relation to the ultrasound scan is much wider than the scan, the scan room or the foetus, and collaborative coding provides the perceptual glue that links and makes sense of the narratives around the uterus. The notion of perceptual glue comes from visual perception studies and refers to how the spectator makes sense of images that, in themselves, are hard to understand.[5] These narratives may be initiated by visual imagery, as I have indicated earlier, but – importantly – the narratives may not be directly concerned with the foetus or the pregnant person. Collaborative coding, according to Roberts, allows the image of the foetus to be interpreted and understood by the spectator as both visual (through the ultrasound scan) and conceptual (through multiple narratives in the scan room).[6] The main features of these narrative processes, Roberts suggests, are family resemblance, foetal personality, voicing the foetus and mapping seeing and feeling (2012b: 304). Roberts's research concerns ultrasonic images of the foetus and non-diagnostic bonding scans, but I suggest her findings relate directly to the importance of off-screen space and how the broader narratives around the uterus interpret and contextualize the visual experience for the spectator.[7] Narratives, in this context, are constructed according to the spectator's perceptual ideas about what the foetus (and pregnancy) means to them, irrespective of the ultrasound scan. Collaborative coding places the image in a narrative context for the spectator, where narratives may not always be directly concerned with the foetus, and often not with the pregnant body, but certainly depend on the centrality of the uterus.

The foetal scan is understood as a technology whose focus is the foetus, and although the scan creates an image of the foetus which can be interpreted as a baby, this is not its main purpose.[8] The main aim of the diagnostic ultrasound scan is to investigate any abnormalities in the foetus, to check its position in the uterus and to check the location of the placenta.[9] Any additional outcome, such as bonding and emotional connection, is based on a 'kind of common sense appeal – based on a longer history of thinking about attachment and bonding and on faith in the visual', according to Roberts, who suggests that this does not bear up to closer critical scrutiny (2012a: 85). I discuss more fully the notion of bonding in Chapter 5, but it is worth remembering that any question of attachment or bonding through the ultrasound scan (whether diagnostic or bonding) is highly subjective and depends on creating the image of a baby, rather than of a foetus. In fact, any claims to realism, Roberts suggests, 'rely on a comparison of the technofoetus with imagined generic models or specimens, or the imagined infant-to-be' (2012a: 85).[10] Collaborative coding, therefore, does not describe how the image of the foetus becomes a baby; it explains how this process of perception and interpretation might work in the ultrasound scan where the notion of a 'baby' is an integral part of that perception. Collaborative coding, according to Roberts, is, on the one hand, a visual process where images of the foetus are deciphered according to physical likeness to the familial spectator (shape of nose, length of limbs), and similar familial mannerisms (sleepy, active); on the other hand, a conceptual process in which narratives of kinship and family histories are established and strengthened by being told and retold. This formulation of conceptual narratives suggests that part of the interpretative process, although initiated by images of the foetus, is not dependent on the foetus itself.

The conceptual narrative that is constructed around the ultrasonic image, where the uterus is a frame or premises for narratives, exists outside of the frame, outside of the scan room and independent of the foetus. This construction of a conceptual narrative is an integral part of non-diagnostic bonding and highlights some of the difficulties and contradictions that surround the different uses of foetal ultrasound technology.[11] Far from being a straightforward technology, the scan creates ethical dilemmas not only in its use as a diagnostic tool but also in the way it is used to interpret images of the foetus which are, in effect, highly technical snapshots of foetal development. The foetal ultrasound has been called a 'Janus-faced technology' by José van Dijck (2005) who questions whether the ultrasound can be restored to function as a purely medical tool separated from its sociocultural connotations (2005: 102–6). The ambiguity that the ultrasound attracts is not, van Dijck says, as a result of how it is used but because it is already 'inscribed in the technology itself' (106). Ultrasound technology shows information that is ambiguous because its interpretation is dependent on the quality of resolution of the image and the operating skills of the practitioner. This creates a conflict based on the information that is relevant to diagnosis and the information that is relevant to – or dependent on – the notion of a 'baby'. Moreover, the increased resolution of the foetal ultrasound does not mean that the image can be easily deciphered.

Although the ultrasound relies on visualizing, its 'benefits and limitations [need] to be interpreted in the light of other sensory information' which is often forgotten, according to Roberts, when the ultrasound scan is 'held up as a natural and unmediated view of the womb' (2012a: 9–10). The ultrasound is not natural and unmediated. Interpreting the scan is a complex process, one that involves translation and interpretation of mathematical data into images, which depend on the presence, Roberts suggests, of a guide (the sonographer) who contextualizes the scan images. The meanings of images produced by the high definition scan '[lend themselves] to elaborate narratives of fetal personality' (2012b: 310). These elaborate narratives of foetal personality overlap with elaborate narratives of kinship and bonding that operate more broadly at a conceptual level around the foetus while it is contained in the uterus. The foetal image is interpreted as a continuing narrative of the foetus in utero to birth. New visual information in the modern scan, due to increased resolution and a more realistic dimensional perception of the human shape, makes the foetus appear more lifelike. For that reason, it is interpreted as interacting with its audience. The ultrasound, in relation to bonding, according to Roberts, remains a 'one-way process and not an interaction' (2012a: 82), and this is often forgotten. The foetus may react to the pressure of the transducer and react physically to the technology, thus making it appear to be responding.

Rather than thinking about interaction, the process of communication or perception is closer to Karen Barad's (1998, 2007) concept of agential realism where she suggests the term '*"intra-action"* to signify *the inseparability of "objects"* and *"agencies of observation"*' (1998: 96, emphasis in original).[12] This inseparability suggests a fluid intra-action where the screen image is an integral part of the dynamic between protagonist and spectator, and I will refer to intra-action rather than interaction throughout the book. Importantly, Barad suggests that '[b]odies do not simply take their places in the world. They are not simply situated in, or located in, particular environments. Rather, "environments" and "bodies" are intra-actively co-constituted. Bodies ("human", "environmental", or otherwise) are integral "parts" of, or dynamic reconfigurings of, what is' (Barad 2007: 170). The image produced on the ultrasound screen, the body of the foetus, is therefore a product of visually deciphered mathematical information that has, nevertheless, come to be understood as a cultural object. This may be, in part, because of the cognitive dissonance created by the unreadability of the foetal image and the sonic presence of the heartbeat as a marker of life. The ultrasound detects a heartbeat most usually before the bone mass can be seen and before eight weeks of pregnancy which, van Dijck explains, is seen (as movement) and heard (2005: 103). It is not, however, until bone mass can be seen as limbs, spine and skull, which occurs in the second trimester (thirteen to twenty-eight weeks of gestation), that the foetus begins to make visual sense to the spectator. The foetus may make perceptual sense in that the 'cloudlike pattern' in shades of grey, as Barbara Duden (1993: 31) describes it, is someone's child. Nevertheless, the scan remains an 'act of translation' achieved by the sonographer, and the spectator of the scan, creating narratives that return to 'family resemblance, fetal personality, voicing the fetus, and mapping seeing and feeling' (Roberts 2012b: 304).[13] A mapping of seeing and feeling describes the way the image on the scan invokes emotion and resonance by engaging memory, shared history and knowledge. Importantly, this process is intermittent or incomplete during the scan but is the source of continuity outside of it. This suggests that family resemblance, foetal personality and voicing the foetus are intrinsically linked to the clarity or resolution of the ultrasonic foetal image. Mapping seeing and feeling, by contrast, describes the conceptual intra-action with the technological image. This is where narratives intersect.

Of importance to this book is the way that this notion of collaborative coding on the one hand describes the actions of the foetus as meaning something to the spectator, but, on the other hand, articulates how much the spectator adds to the perception of the image and to the narrative. This is a helpful way to explain how off-screen space works. The short-lived, episodic nature of the ultrasound implies that the narrative in the scan room is transient. This narrative, however, resonates in the increasingly complex narratives around the uterus that continue to exist inside and outside of the scan room. This process of collaborative coding, I argue, adds more complexity to any discussion of pregnancy and specifically to the discussion of narrative space in this book. The frame of the uterus in the foetal scan, if thought of as a point of intra-action, has similar properties to how Sobchack understands the gentleness of the frame and to how Deleuze understands an Elsewhere. Bringing these three ways of understanding the frame together helps to articulate the way that narrative is created outside of the pregnant body, and aside from the pregnant person. Mapping seeing and feeling (with regard to the foetus) takes place in the space around the frame of the uterus: in off-screen space.

Recognizing absence on screen

In the ultrasound scan, the spectatorial dynamic, as I have said, can be described as collaborative coding, whereas in cinema, the dynamic can be described as a process of identification – or suture. Suture recognizes the existence of absence on the screen. In other words, integral to the understanding of suture is the understanding that off-screen space exists. In off-screen space, there is narrative space that is on the one hand understood spatially, and on the other hand understood as perceptual. As I have mentioned, Deleuze theorizes off-screen space as 'out-of-field' (*hors-champ*) which he argues 'refers to what is neither seen nor understood, but is nevertheless perfectly present' (1986: 16).[14] Off-screen space, as part of narrative progression, suggests spatial continuity and is threaded throughout a film. In this way, the spectator understands that what is happening off-screen is part of a continuation of the action. This off-screen space is conceptual and relates to the relationship of the spectator to the frame. Off-screen space also has a temporal quality – which relates to its existence rather than a movement through time. This relies on perception and is related to Sobchack's ideas of the gentleness of the frame. The viewing dynamic is affected by the way the 'visual freedom [of the frame] in the activity of seeing gently comes to an end' (1992: 131). Sobchack takes her notion of gentleness from the work of Maurice Merleau-Ponty (1968) who says that the spectator is 'not shut up in one sector of the visible world', and that vision exists beyond the frame to create other narrative possibilities (100).[15] These possibilities are not only of the spectator's making, but they are also an integral part of how cinematic narrative functions. As Merleau-Ponty suggests, the 'contours of [vision] are not lines, and [vision] is not cut out against an expanse of blackness' and, despite the physical boundary of any frame, vision constantly looks towards the horizon (100). Sobchack also argues that the limits of the frame do not limit vision, rather that vision and the frame are entwined with each other, and she says that 'the frame is a limit but like that of our own vision it is inexhaustibly mobile and free to displace itself' (1992: 131). In other words, the film presents a world that exists beyond the frame, where neither the function of the frame nor the vision of the spectator could strictly be described as 'a geometric act' (134). Rather this 'act of viewing' articulates the way that the spectator perceives the world of the film as on-screen and off-screen where the spectator, according to Merleau-Ponty, 'is of it and is in it' (1968: 100).

As I have said, it is Deleuze who suggests that all framing, however closed, or self-contained, creates an out-of-field that is 'a more radical Elsewhere, outside homogenous space and time' (1986: 18).[16] The Elsewhere that Deleuze mentions depends on the affective nature of each film and the frame. Recognizing the affective qualities of the frame as part of a sensorial, corporeal space – or an embodied narrative space – means refocusing traditional narrative analysis that only prioritizes the image on the screen. For example, as David Bordwell et al. (2002) assert, 'centering, balancing, frontality, and depth-all these narrational strategies-encourage us to read filmic space as story space' (2002: 54) and, as Christian Metz (1974) says, 'narrative has *a beginning and an ending*' and 'is, among other things, a system of temporal transformations' made up of images, filmic descriptions of images, and a series or sequence of shots which create narrative (1974: 17, 19, emphasis in original). This understanding of narrative space relies on prioritizing positionality within the frame: the mise en scène. Noël Burch (1973) recognizes that both on-screen and off-screen space constitute narrative space and lists six segments of off-screen space, four of which relate to the edges of the frame and exist as entrance and exit points (1973: 17). These entrance and exit points, Burch insists, have 'only an intermittent or, rather, *fluctuating* existence during any film' (1973: 21, emphasis in original). This sense of narrative continuity is an essential component of off-screen space. My method of analysis takes into consideration the way that off-screen space contributes to narrative continuity. It is important, however, to re-evaluate traditional narrative analysis to acknowledge embodiment or the lived body experience as it applies to ways of looking at the reproductive body.

Uterine frame: Ways of looking

By prioritizing the image of the foetus, the ultrasound screen displaces the uterus as the frame. The presence of the uterus does, nevertheless, influence the imaginative and conceptual act of seeing. The uterus becomes spatialized, Rebecca Kukla (2005) suggests, as a place of performance – a theatre – and that Roberts describes as 'a metaphorical space' (2012a: 94). I discuss the spatiality of the interior and this quality of a metaphorical space throughout the book and in more detail in Chapter 4, but it is worth noting that during the scan the uterus is already a frame that has been replaced by the frame of the ultrasound screen. The ultrasound also displaces the embodied experience of the pregnant person by fragmenting the reception of the (foetal) image. This results in a blurring between embodied subjectivity – in relation to the pregnant person – and objectivity in relation to the technological image of the foetus. This blurring emphasizes the shift in perception that is crucial to visualizing technologies of the body. Nevertheless, as Rosi Braidotti (2013), like Roberts and Barad, emphasizes, these technologies 'are not endowed with intrinsic humanistic agency' (45).[17] It is more accurate to say that the viewing process has become more managed through imagined intra-action and, as Sobchack says of the cinema screen, that the viewing process in the scan 'ascrib[es] value to its objects' (1992: 130). The act of viewing engages the imagination and constructs meaning, which explains how meaning can be ascribed to the foetus as an object to be looked at in the ultrasound. This can be done without ascribing either meaning or importance to foetal location in the body.

The meaning that is ascribed to the foetus in utero is a result of what Catherine Mills (2011) calls 'sympathetic imagination', which allows the spectator of the ultrasound to identify with the foetus. This identification relies on the 'affective dimensions' of a relationship built on sympathy and to a certain extent on the belief that the foetus can feel pain (2011: 103–6).[18] This sympathetic imagination is a forceful factor in the interpretation of the foetal image as a vulnerable being, and sidelines the biological working of the uterus and the pregnant body in order to prioritize the foetus.[19] The strength of the imaginative viewing depends on the foetus remaining inside the uterus, which then becomes a frame for imagined interactions. The heartbeat, amplified by the scan, not only confirms the existence of the foetus but also confirms the baby as belonging to the pregnant person. In the films in this book, the foetus becomes 'my' baby or 'your' baby or even 'always hers'.[20] In this way, kinship groups can then be created around the image on the scan, or the sound of the heartbeat, or the portable scan photograph. A conceptual narrative highlights the separation between the pregnant body and the personhood/body of the foetus. This enables the personhood of the foetus to be acknowledged through interconnecting narratives. This suggests that the imaginative image of the foetus is as forceful as the actual scan image.[21] Mills argues that 'foetal images operate most effectively at the level of emotion or affect', and the forcefulness of the imagery relies on understanding the subtleties between sympathy and empathy (2011: 105). Importantly, as the foetus becomes corporeally visible through the scan, the affective dimension of sympathetic imagination is essentially disengaged from the frame of the uterus and – to a certain extent – the pregnant body.

Yet the technological image is not always an accurate representation of what the ultrasound transducer, or probe, can 'see'. The transducer, in contact with the pregnant body, records all information even if that information is not clear, understandable or describable. There is a distinction, therefore, between the technological image and the information produced by the technology itself. While it is clear that the technology of the scan is part of an embodied interaction as the technician moves the screen and the transducer, and the pregnant person prepares and moves their body for the scan to be successful, the technology itself, the machine or the screen, as I have already said, does not interact with the spectator.[22] It is the perception of the spectator and their emotional connection at the moment of the scan as part of intra-action that creates meaning. The scan photograph, as a technological snapshot, contributes to the separation of bodies and is understood to be part of a continuing narrative about the foetus as it circulates between people, but the uterus, nevertheless, remains part of this communal looking. This separation of bodies and transfer of narratives calls to mind the matrixial gaze, introduced by Bracha L. Ettinger (1995) in relation to painting, which re-emphasizes the importance of the uterus as a communal bodily space. The commonality in this case is that all humans share the experience of being in the uterus. Ettinger says, 'in choosing to infuse the term matrix' to the notion of the gaze, she 'restore[s] to it its ancient feminine/maternal source – as the word means uterus, womb (Latin)'

(1995: 22). She explains that this is to acknowledge the specificity of the uterus as having two sides: an inside and outside. This acknowledges the materiality of the uterus, but she also challenges the notion of the uterus as passive by considering it 'a dynamic borderspace of active/passive co-emergence *with-in* and *with*-out' (1995: 22–3, emphasis in original). I introduce this idea of interconnectivity as it refocuses the discussion of the body to a discussion of interconnectedness between the individual and the larger community as a '*sharable dimension of subjectivity*' (1995: 23; emphasis in original). Although the matrixial gaze is not linked to scholarship of the scan, it is, according to Griselda Pollock (2006), a fundamentally important way of understanding human relationships by concentrating on the interconnectedness of the self to others through the commonality of the uterus.

When thought of in terms of Marksian haptic visuality, the image of the foetus is something that the spectator 'brush[es] up against' (2000: xii). When Marks makes a distinction between the optical and the haptic, she says, 'optical visuality depends on a separation between the viewing subject and the object' and 'haptic looking tends to move over the surface of its object' and embraces the 'familiarity with the world that the viewer knows through more senses than vision alone' (2000: 162, 187). She describes the way the camera can present the spectator with partial images such as textures and colours that invoke sense memories and that the cinematic experience is something tactile that spectators 'brush up against', and this influences the way the materiality of the film is understood and analysed. Jennifer M. Barker (2009) also suggests that the cinematic experience is one of 'inspiration' whereby the process of experiencing a film begins on the surface of the skin, moving through the muscles into the viscera of the body, and 'animates [the spectator] with sensations and attitudes' that are then brought back to the surface as part of the embodied experience (146; 147). Roberts et al.'s (2015, 2017) work on commercial ultrasounds stresses the importance of imagination in the process of 'doing family' during the foetal ultrasound where resemblances can be real and imagined. Resemblance, Roberts et al. suggest, is only one part of a more complex process of recognition and identification, which helps to understand how the foetus is incorporated into the new family. Resemblance, they suggest, is not the only way to establish kinship around the scan, that the choice of scan partner and who gets copies of scan pictures are all part of rehearsing familial or kinship roles so that kinship is developed through the perception of foetal images and at a distance from the pregnant body.

The continual separation created by visualizing technologies creates, as Rosalind Petchesky (1987) argues, on the one hand a fetish foetal image, and on the other hand renders the pregnant person invisible (277). Petchesky explains how static ultrasound images in the US anti-abortion film *The Silent Scream* are used to produce a moving image which creates 'overlapping boundaries between media spectacle and clinical experience [as] pregnancy becomes a moving picture' (1987: 264–5).[23] By introducing movement to static images, she explains, pregnancy becomes not only an embodied experience but also a screened experience. The point of contact between the scan equipment and the surface of the body, the transducer (which contains the piezoelectric crystals necessary for the transmission of sound waves) becomes, as Barad suggests, the 'machine interface to the body' dependent on an intra-action between the technology, the body and the foetus, wherein the foetus becomes the phenomenon rather than the pregnant person (1998: 101). But the foetus and the foetal image have, nevertheless, come to be understood as culturally specific objects. The scanned and photographed foetus is commonly understood as the 'baby's first picture' (Lisa M. Mitchell 2001, who also talks about coding the scan) where the technological image – the freeze-framed foetus – ultimately becomes part of a kinship group.

Roberts stresses that contemporary high-resolution scans appear to present increasingly lifelike visual images, but that they 'rel[y] just as heavily on social interaction and discourse [as the 2D scan] to be meaningful' (2012b: 299). Crucially, one area that Roberts feels has been opened up by new reproductive visualizing technologies is the visibility of other parts of the body. She explains that '[i]t is not only the foetus that is rendered in new detail, the umbilical cord, the uterus wall and the placenta too are newly visible. These structures are the markers of the foetus' location in the body and might [. . .] be used to stress the *interconnection* of the foetus and the pregnant subject' (2012a: 135, emphasis in original).[24] Looking into these structures, according to Roberts, is where 'the human eye is mobilised and its visual capacities extended' (2012a: 92, 99). This 'eye' can move wherever the technology takes it.[25] In the ultrasound scan, the sound waves pass through the body into the uterus and bounce back from hard matter such as bone, so that a 'picture' can be created from data. This data can be reproduced on screen. The 'eye' then passes through various stages in order to be able to 'see'. Its visual capacities are extended when the 'eye' is mobilized to search in places that the human eye cannot see so that the visual capabilities that Roberts talks about are, in reality, a construction, which depends on the uterus being opened up to 'see' the foetus.

Prioritizing spectatorship of the foetus, over the pregnant body and the uterus, encourages the spectatorship of a disembodied being, separated from its place of growth, and it is this disembodied foetus that exists as a focal point. Importantly for my discussion, the separation of the pregnant body and the foetus, documented extensively in feminist discourse, involves, as Duden suggests, an 'un-skinning' of the woman (1993: 77–8). Referring to the critical shift from the pregnant body to the foetus, Duden asks, 'how did the unborn turn into a billboard image and how did that isolated goblin get into the limelight?' (7). She argues that pregnancy turns the woman into 'an ecosystem for the fetus' and laments the time when it 'could be featured only in the kinds of books that also showed labia majora and pubic hair' rather than the present day of being 'overwhelmed by fetuses' (7). Perhaps this overwhelming image of the foetus is not quite as ubiquitous as in the early 1990s when Duden was writing, but her point is that 'body history [. . .] is to a large extent a history of the unseen [where] until recently, the unborn, by definition, was one of these' (1993: 8). I suggest she is arguing for the symbiotic nature of the foetus and the pregnant body living together.[26] The unseen – which includes foetal movements and quickening, as discussed later – is part of the embodied experience but has been forgotten. Duden puts it very eloquently when she says, 'step by step, the physician's fingers, then his stethoscope, later X-rays, tests, and sonar have invaded women's gendered interior and opened it up to a nongendered public gaze' (81, note her emphasis on the *male* physician).

Duden's argument about shifting gaze from the pregnant body to the foetus and losing connection with the unseen is crucial to my discussion. Her careful analysis of foetal images and the lost emphasis on embodied sensation is where film theory on the senses can reclaim the essence of the (pregnant) body in analysis. Duden argues that Lennart Nilsson's well-known 1965 images of the foetus 'generate a persuasive illusion [that] result[s] in a misplaced concreteness [where] graphics convincingly create the illusion that abstract notions have a tangible reality [and] give the foetus an aura of bodily presence' (1993: 25).[27] Although I am not convinced that the foetal objects in Nilsson's photographs are 'abstract notions' in themselves, the photographs are certainly dishonest in their representation of life as they represent an interiority and an unseenness that only exists as an illusion.[28] The foetuses in the photographs are all dead but constructed aesthetically to represent the illusion of life. The foetal ultrasound also presents an illusion of materiality whereby the picture on the screen is of the foetus who does not exist outside of the body but is represented as the baby's first picture. This depends on the socially constructed interior. As Nathan Stormer (2000) suggests, 'biomedical discourse transforms the womb into a *social space*' (109, emphasis in original). He argues that the uterus – which he only refers to as 'womb' – is not analysed as a material object in itself. He says that 'to assume that [the womb as incubator] is simply wherever a woman's body exists is to undercut analysis of the womb as a discursive object' (109). Although he does not tackle this discursive space in great detail, he establishes that the uterus is not only 'a site of discourse about life, rights, and the essence of "woman"' but also a space that warrants separate discussion (109).[29] Importantly, these discussions emphasize that the ways of looking and the social and aesthetic quality of the uterine space depend on subjectivity and emotion.

Emotion and aesthetics

Aesthetic qualities mean little without the emotional engagement of the spectator. Tarja Laine (2013) argues that in order to introduce a critical methodological approach to emotion in the cinema, a critical response is 'to shift from questions of representation (what the film is) or signification (what the film means) to matters of agential practices, actions, and intensities (what the film *does*)' (2013: 4, emphasis in original). In this way, the intimate relationship between the spectator and the screen can be thought of in relation to film as an aesthetic form *and* as an experience. Within this discussion, there are fundamental questions to be answered about whether this turn towards the affective qualities of film should be regarded as part of reception (audience) studies, and thought of as representation only, or a return to film form and close analysis. Daniel Frampton (2006) suggests that 'both para-narrational "showing" and *mise-en-scène* aesthetics' or 'filmosophy' allows for new realities that are constantly created on screen, and he argues against formal close textual analysis – which he describes as 'technist' (2006: 39, 171, 172, emphasis in original). It is crucial, however, that we put representation to one side and understand that irrespective of how technical a close analysis might be, it should not be considered as mechanical or lacking in meaning. Laine maintains that the turn to affect in film studies has moved the reading of film as a text from something that can be done objectively to an understanding of cinema and the film itself as an 'emotional event' that is experiential (2013: 10–11). She explores what she calls the '*emotional core*' of the film which, she explains, includes the intrinsic emotions that any particular film has in relation to its structure that is intentional, as well as the emotions engendered in any single spectator (3, emphasis in original). Steven Shaviro (1993) also suggests that the spectator can be 'captivated', distracted' and 'touched' by cinema and that identifying with the film is actually 'sympathetic participation' or 'complicitous communication' as part of an affective encounter (1993: 53). The circumstances in which there is the potential for an effect, whether this effect is felt as a bodily (physical) or psychological (emotional) reaction, relies on empathy and sympathy which Sobchack calls '*interobjectivity*' (2004: 311, emphasis in original). Sobchack suggests that interobjectivity is a necessary counterpart to intersubjectivity, whereby both are complimentary, complementary and contrary.

Sobchack thinks of interobjectivity as a way to express what embodiment is, as the lived body is 'at once, both an objective *subject* and a subjective *object*: a sentient, sensual, and sensible ensemble of materialised capacities and agency that literally and figuratively makes sense of, and to, both ourselves and others' (1992: 2, emphasis in original). This circulation of affect is central to the ultrasound scan and is part of embodied spectatorship that allows my discussion to move between the spectator of the film, the protagonists and the corporeality of the film, which can be helpful when recognizing what Tyler suggests is the 'elasticity of pregnant subjectivity' that is not bound to the subjectivity of the pregnant person (2001: 71). Brian Massumi explains that the 'affective is marked by the gap between *content* and *effect*' (2002: 24, emphasis in original). This is a helpful way to think about the two sides of the affective encounter that Gregory J. Seigworth and Melissa Gregg suggest is an 'in-between-ness' of a potential resonance that results from an affective encounter (2010: 3). As Massumi argues, emotion is only one potential resulting affect in this encounter and that the two, emotion and affect, should not be conflated. Importantly, Massumi establishes the two-sidedness of the affective encounter to suggest that the emergence of affect is in its intensity or resonance. The turn to affect in film studies is part of the discussion that embraces the embodied spectator and the corporeality of the film form. As Eugenie Brinkema (2014) suggests, a return to the analysis of film form is a way to understand the 'forgotten dimension' of affect. Brinkema argues, however, for a closer inspection of form and insists that her own analyses are not about spectatorship (in fact, she argues that it is a de-contribution to spectatorship studies (36)) but about aesthetics and '*reading affects as having forms*' (37, emphasis in original) to produce 'new readings and new questions' (39). I find her use of the term *mise n'en scène* useful to my discussion of off-screen narrative space for the 'possibilities it sets loose' (46). As she says, '*mise n'en scène* suggests that in addition to reading for what is put into the scene, one must also read for all of its permutations: what is *not* put into the scene; what is put into the *non-scene*; and what is *not enough* put into the scene' (46, emphasis in original). Her call for new methodologies of reading for form does not ignore corporeality and physicality but presses for greater depth of close reading to discover 'what forms and bodies might mean to each other, [and] what form might cause us to rethink about bodies' (40). My method of reading the films brings into focus these ideas to look closely at each film to provide a textual reassessment of the way in which pregnancy and the uterus can be understood by engaging with form and the turn to affect.

Within this reassessment, however, I am mindful of what Imogen Tyler, Rebecca Coleman and Debra Ferreday (2008) refer to as methodological fatigue in feminist media studies. The methodological fatigue is understood by Tyler et al. as when theoretical debate is richly articulated, but the focus of that debate is less well defined. This lack of definition speaks to how I understand there to be something fundamentally missing from the subject of pregnancy in film studies. This something, I argue, is an understanding of embodiment as the experience of pregnancy, but also of the embodied experience of pregnancy that is separated from the pregnant person and the foetus and concerns other narratives. There is a rich history of feminist critical analysis on the body, and this book builds on this scholarship, but there is less work on the nuanced affective quality of the reproductive body on screen. I agree with Sobchack when she argues for an analytical framework that acknowledges the embodied experience of the spectator and maintains that the distinction of the lived body must include more than just gender or race. She argues that the lived body can also be 'diseased, impaired, or deprived' (1992: 160), and that this quality, of normativity, is not taken into enough consideration. Identification and subjectivity of the female body have a long and complicated history in film, as I have already suggested.

Christine Battersby (1998) suggests that, by normalizing the female reproductive body as one 'that births', it can be repositioned as a norm for analysis. The body 'that births' is not always seen within a normative context, and its definition is more accurately a definition of corporeal potentiality rather than an actuality. Margrit Shildrick suggests that the body should 'be addressed in its concrete specificity, not as some immaterial abstraction' (1997: 30), and she rails against the fragmentation of the female body, as does Elizabeth Grosz (1994), who encourages a turn to corporeal feminism. Grosz argues that she does not consider the non-biological act of reproduction as neutral, but rather male-centric and argues against binary approaches to subjectivity (and sexuality) by 'shifting frameworks and models of understanding' (1994: xiv). The tension between neutrality and gender-centricity goes some way to explain why, despite its centrality as a frame in pregnancy, the uterus has been sidelined or marginalized by being understood only as a marker for the female reproductive body. My own approach is interpretative, and my work crosses disciplines – a hallmark of feminist research – and my approach through phenomenology allows me to draw together scholarship from cultural, historical, geographical and anthropological studies to engage with memory, landscape and space, trauma, and embodied narratives. This scholarship allows me to think through what Patricia Clough calls 'the foraging of a new body [. . .] the biomediated body' (2010: 207). Clough suggests that the notion of the biomediated body is a much wider discussion on affect and bodies, and signals the recognition that bodies are not only organisms but constructed by the conflation of biomedia and new media, which changes the notion of not only what the body is but also what the body can be made to do. Rosi Braidotti suggests in her notion of the 'posthuman', that posthuman theory is 'about coming to terms with unprecedented changes and transformations of the basic unit of reference for what counts as human' (2013: 104).

Carolyn Pedwell and Anne Whitehead (2012), however, like Tyler et al., express concern about how feminist theory can engage with the affective turn without losing some of the principles that inform feminism. Tyler (2008) explains that any reflection on (feminist) politics and (media) analysis should return to ideological positioning to understand what kind of questions feminist critique should address. Moreover, Pedwell and Whitehead argue that affect is not a new concept and that 'feminist scholars have been at the heart of [. . .] engagements with affect', clarifying that 'feminist analyses are of most critical value when they attend reflexively *both* to what might be gained *and lost* through claiming a "new" conceptual paradigm' (2012:

115, 118, emphasis in original). Pedwell and Whitehead do acknowledge that feminist study of affect examines how 'affect travels within and across cultures, situating feminist debates [. . .] within international, transnational, cross-cultural, and cross racial contexts' (2012: 124). Pedwell and Whitehead's concern is that the 'turn to affect' can remove ideological questions. While I understand the concern from other feminist scholars, I do not believe that the turn to affect is anti-ideological. On the contrary, it can offer ways to reposition feminist critique in relation to pregnancy and the uterus. The turn to affect in film, I argue, is not a turn away from something, nor is it a turn towards something else. It is a (re)turn to film form and close reading of the film text which explores the in-between-ness that exists in the spectatorial encounter with the body. As Gaylyn Studlar (1990) argues, 'like feminism, phenomenology cannot be considered to be a unified theoretical stance', but its usefulness is in providing 'new conceptual models for understanding film within the framework of feminist response' (1990: 70, 71). Helen Marshall (1996) argues that not enough attention is paid to empirical research when discussing the body and that theories of the body are most useful when they are brought into dialogue with empirical research into real experiences.

This chapter has argued, therefore, for a different way of approaching analysis of pregnancy and reproduction by paying attention to empirical research on visualizing technologies to examine other ways of looking into the uterus. The importance of this research for the purposes of this book is the way it adds to the already complex notion of off-screen space in film studies. Off-screen space, as this chapter has explained, describes the processes of spectatorial negotiation and collaboration, which for Sobchack involves the body in the process of seeing, and for Deleuze is an appreciation of what cannot be explained by the mechanisms of filmmaking. Off-screen space also articulates the shareability of spectatorship that explains how the pregnant person can become involved with narrative progression of pregnancy that begins with, but is not always focused on, their own body. This suggests a shared or collaborative spectatorship that emphasizes the connectivity of pregnancy and reproduction rather than a separation caused by the presence of and attention to the foetus. This chapter brings new perspectives to feminist critique that progresses, not limits, feminist film theory and feminist enquiry of pregnancy, reproduction and the pregnant body. The following chapter examines how this connectivity of technologies, of the body and of the uterus, as negotiated narratives, is constructed in off-screen space.

3

Narrative negotiations in *Juno, Gestation/Gestación* and *Stephanie Daley*

This chapter will focus on the construction of narratives that are collaborative and negotiated around the space of the uterus. As I explained in Chapter 2, critical discussions around visualizing technologies such as the foetal scan can add to what we already know about off-screen space in film. The separation of the foetus from the pregnant body during pregnancy, I have suggested, creates an off-screen narrative space that is framed by the uterus, and this emphasizes connectivity in both spectatorship and narrative. I have argued that the Sobchackian notion of embodied viewing can be aligned with a Deleuzian Elsewhere to articulate the shareability of spectatorship. The foetal scan offers a way to understand this shareability. In this chapter, therefore, I bring Roberts's notion of collaborative coding, which expresses the way that spectators construct narratives from imagery and embodied histories around the ultrasound scan (2012a, b), into dialogue with how Sobchack expresses the screen and the body as premises for perception and organ[s] of perception (1992: 134). In both cases, narrative information does not end with the image, the shot or the sequence but is interpreted constantly by the spectator. The Sobchackian gentleness of the frame, I suggest, is a useful way to understand how intersecting narratives are negotiated through off-screen space in *Juno* (2007), *Gestation/Gestación* (2009) and *Stephanie Daley* (2006). As Sobchack suggests, 'our vision ends gently rather than geometrically' and that active seeing is not limited by the frame of the screen but 'gently comes to an end'. As she explains, in the act of seeing 'the frame is *invisible* to the seeing that is the film' (131, emphasis in original). The broader point that she is making, like Deleuze, is that the frame does not necessarily limit the spectator's perception of images.

This chapter demonstrates how the uterus functions as a frame, and it could be argued that it is a virtual frame, when it is thought of as an orientation point and a premises for perception to articulate the gentleness of spectatorship. The frame of the uterus can then be understood as 'that by means of which' foetal images, both actual and virtual, are negotiated and interpreted collaboratively by the spectator. The usefulness of collaborative coding to the way I read each film in this chapter is in its application to the scan process and beyond the scan room. The static scan photograph, for example, is not an image of the foetus in utero. In reality, the foetus moves and constantly changes as it grows, and this cannot be reflected in the static or once-viewed scan. Nevertheless, interpretative narratives around the scan screen continue to be created around the frame of the photograph, which can be understood as taking the place of the scan screen that has, in turn, replaced the frame of the uterus. Collaborative coding (which Roberts applies to bonding scans rather than diagnostic scans) is a way to understand how the pregnant person, family members and medical practitioners narrate the foetal image by looking at it, then recognizing it and interpreting what it is doing. This negotiated spectatorship allows the foetus to be given familiar characteristics or behaviours that are understood as meaningful to the spectator. This complex process of assembling technical images alongside the lived body experience speaks to the world of film viewing and the world of the film spectator. Moreover, the embodied experience of pregnancy becomes separated in the process of mapping seeing with mapping feeling. This explains how what is happening inside the body such as the foetus moving or the transducer touching the belly is separated from what can be seen on the screen. Collaborative coding, therefore, suggests that the lived experience of pregnancy is a factor but not essential to negotiated narratives.

As I discussed in Chapter 2, the construction of narratives around the pregnant body depends on not only how off-screen space is negotiated as homogenous continuity but also where 'the actual images are overrun by [their] virtual connections' in a constant process of interpretation and negotiation (Deamer 2016: 164). This describes how the foetus that is in utero, where it is unseen by the naked eye, can also exist outside of the uterus in the scan or the scan photograph. The uterus is predominantly an unseen space in the diegesis of each film, and one of the ways that the interior of the uterus is visualized is through the medium of the foetal ultrasound. Conceptualizing the image on the scan, however, demands an ability to 'see' the foetus as a 'baby', as I have already explained. When narratives of kinship are told and retold as part of the familial recognition of the foetus, it can provide a contrast to the way the pregnant person maps what they 'see' and feel onto their embodied experience of pregnancy. And so, how a person feels when they are scanned may be at odds with what they can see on the scan screen (Roberts 2012b: 308). This demonstrates how spectatorship is not dependent on imagery alone. As Sobchack suggests, one does not need to put images to one side in order to see the next. The process of seeing and developing narrative is interpretative as well as collaborative. Moreover, the spectator (as viewer or character) does not always follow the focal cues given on screen. The adoptive parent's narrative in *Juno*, for example, must be read not only for how each character engages with the technological image of the foetus as their unborn child but also for how they engage with the presence of the pregnant body and the foetus in the uterus.

When Roberts thinks of the uterus as a metaphorical space, as I mentioned in the Introduction, she says that the foetal ultrasound should be considered as multi-sensory and dependent on interpretation. Moreover, she explains that the two-dimensional photograph as a technical image of the foetus is hugely significant but only a part of the way that the foetus is negotiated in the scan (2012a: 81). When thinking of the still photograph, it is worth returning to how Sobchack describes it as 'a presence without past, present, future' that offers 'the *possibility* of meaning' (1992: 59, 60, emphasis in original). When the foetus is identified as a baby, therefore, it takes on a conceptual quality that is both open to interpretation and to other possibilities of meaning. To go back to my point about the uterus as a frame, when a conceptual narrative is constructed beyond the scanned image of the foetus and beyond the pregnant body, the uterus is the point of connection rather than the pregnant body or the foetus. It is the uterus that becomes a narrative space where multiple narratives intersect. Importantly, as I have indicated, these negotiated narratives are not necessarily dependent on understanding what the pregnant body represents to each character. The complex questions of kinship in *Juno* sometimes centre around the foetal image on the scan or the scan photograph, for example, rather than Juno. In *Gestation*, the pregnant body provokes a narrative of putrification and sin that has more to do with another character's belief system than the pregnant person themself. In *Stephanie Daley*, pregnancy, pregnant bodies and foetuses are narratively entwined to suggest equivalent pregnancy loss for each character. The scan, in this case, confirms the weekly stage of gestation for one pregnant character so that it can be compared to the stage of pregnancy of the character who is accused of killing their baby at birth. The stages of pregnancy highlighted by the scan in this film also initiate a narrative of foetal viability outside of the uterus.

In each film in this chapter, the pregnant body can be (un)read as an integral part of narrative negotiations when the focus is on understanding the foetus as 'baby'. Roberts suggests that in the scan a visual cue (hands raised) or a theme (sleepiness) can describe the character of the not yet born 'baby' when it is interpreted as something that is socially or personally meaningful (2012a; 2012b: 306). In the scan, according to Roberts, it is the 'classic profile shot' of the foetus where the head, nose and mouth become recognizable that helps it to be easily identified as 'baby' (2012a: 126). The technical image and how it is constructed, however, establishes a dynamic between the protagonists and the internal body that involves more than just visual information. This explains why the static ultrasound photograph has an affective power when it has captured a moment that has already passed and where future narrative possibilities are created around a frozen moment in time. As André Bazin (1960) suggests, the 'objective nature of photography confers on it [. . .] credibility' where the object in the photograph is '*re*-presented, set before us, that is to say, in time and space', and he suggests that the purpose of the photograph is not to 'create eternity [but] to embalm [. . .] time' (7–8, emphasis in original). While it is accurate to say that the scan photograph embalms the image of the foetus, its strength, I argue, is in its power as an orientation point, a frame through which to conceptualize narrative possibilities. When looking at the foetus, the focus is on the narrative of being a baby. This suggests that being a baby, rather than being a foetus, is what appears in off-screen space. The gentleness of the frame articulates this shift, and dissonance, between what is being viewed (the foetus) and the narrative that it provokes (of a baby) on the screen. The quality of gentleness, which suggests an Elsewhere, depends on the foetus remaining in the space of the uterus. This is why the notion of collaborative coding is a useful addition when understanding virtual and actual images as narrative. Thinking of the uterus as a Sobchackian premises for perception and a frame that has the properties of gentleness makes sense of how virtual and actual images are integral to collaborative narratives and to narrative analysis.

Importantly, it is not the viewpoint of the pregnant person or even the presence of the foetus that drives the narrative around the uterus. Although the films in this chapter tell the stories of young, pregnant women, and their narratives reflect the themes of underage sex, single parenthood, and the lack of social status, the pregnant person is sidelined by the conceptual narratives of the 'baby'. The continual shifting focus between on-screen and off-screen space explains how the protagonists in each film 'read' the body and the foetus (via the uterus) according to their own conceptual narrative of a baby. To a certain extent, this relies on Mills's (2011) notion of sympathetic imagination, discussed in Chapter 2, where the foetus is given agency based on sympathy and by understanding that the foetus feels pain. This again creates an identification with the foetus while it is in utero. The frame of the uterus is therefore critical to an imagined interaction. In this whole process, the pregnant body can become separated from the foetus and then separated again from the perception of a baby.

The scan and the scanned photograph of the foetus appear at different narrative moments in each film. In *Juno*, the scan becomes a moment of bonding for Juno, her best friend and stepmother. The photograph reproduced from the scan then becomes an integral part of how Juno transfers the image of the foetus away from her own uterus to the adopters' narrative. In *Gestation*, the scan appears at the end of the film to establish the aliveness of the foetus and to emphasize the familial connection with the grandparent. In *Stephanie Daley*, the scan appears frequently to create a narrative link between the pregnancies of the two main protagonists. The scan also acts as a conceptual punctuation to allow the foetus to be constantly reimagined. In each film, the scan becomes part of the different narrative possibilities. The still photograph also becomes something else or something more once it is viewed by others. Importantly, the uterus remains the frame and 'that by means of which' the foetal image can be viewed outside of the pregnant body, as a scan image or photograph. As I explained in Chapter 2, thinking of the uterus as a frame emphasizes the connectivity of narratives and the intra-actions that are not only subjective but also communal or shared.

Juno

The main protagonist of *Juno* (Ellen Page) is a teenage girl still at high school when she discovers that she is pregnant after having sex for the first time with her boyfriend Bleeker (Michael Cera). She visits an abortion clinic and meets a fellow student protesting against terminations who tells her that her foetus already has fingernails. Juno decides, nevertheless, that she will give birth to the baby and have it adopted. Juno chooses a middle-class couple, Vanessa (Jennifer Garner) and Mark (Jason Bateman), and signs a contract with them for a closed adoption. This means that she will not have any contact with them or the child in the future. Mark eventually leaves Vanessa, but Juno decides to continue with the agreement that she has made with Vanessa, allowing her to adopt the baby when it is born. Bleeker is in close contact with Juno throughout her pregnancy but does not see the baby when it is born. When he joins Juno in hospital after the birth, the baby is already with Vanessa. Juno's pregnancy drives the main narrative but the multiple narratives around the uterus, although integral to the narrative arc of the film, are less concerned with Juno herself.[1] These narratives reflect the main themes in the film of adoption, intergenerational relationships and parenting. The theme of adoption establishes a parallel narrative linking the narrative space of the uterus that carries the foetus to the narrative of the adoptive parents.

The future child will not, however, be part of the everyday kinship or familial group for Juno, her father Mac (J. K. Simmons), her stepmother Bren (Allison Janney) or Bleeker who is the biological father. This means that Juno must transfer the focus of the pregnancy – the foetus – from her own body and her own narrative to construct a narrative for Vanessa and Mark. Juno does this by narrating, or translating, the scan photograph for each of them in turn. In doing so, she displaces the frame of her own body and her uterus and encourages Vanessa and Mark to imagine the foetus that is growing in her uterus as their own child. Juno narrates the image of the foetus, but to do that successfully, and for this narration to provide a perceptual glue, the foetus must be understood as a 'baby' by Vanessa and Mark. This act of translation depends on shifting the scan image of a moving foetus to the static technological photograph of the stilled foetus. Juno can then make sense of, and contextualize, the foetal image for the adoptive parents through a process of collaborative coding.

The movement of narrative from on-screen to off-screen space can be understood when Juno presents the portable foetal photograph to Mark as an image of his future child. Despite the short-lived nature of the ultrasound event, the ultrasound scan has captured an image which is frozen in time. Juno, nevertheless, uses this image to begin a process of collaborative coding, which began with the scan, and starts to transform the narrative around the foetus. The frame of the photograph takes the place of the ultrasound screen, which in turn has taken the place of the frame of the uterus. The edges of the photograph have taken the place of the edges of the uterus. The photograph becomes an orientation point as 'that by means of which' Juno and Mark can begin a process of identification and attachment to the idea of a 'baby'. Importantly, when Juno begins to transpose the narrative space of her uterus onto the photograph, she is noticeably pregnant. The foetus, therefore, is with them in the room, but it is the technological image, the snapshot, with which Juno and Mark engage.

When Juno holds the image up for Mark, her face is hidden by the edges of the photograph. Only her hands and the (out of focus) top of her head can be seen from his point of view (Figure 3.1). The photograph, then, almost

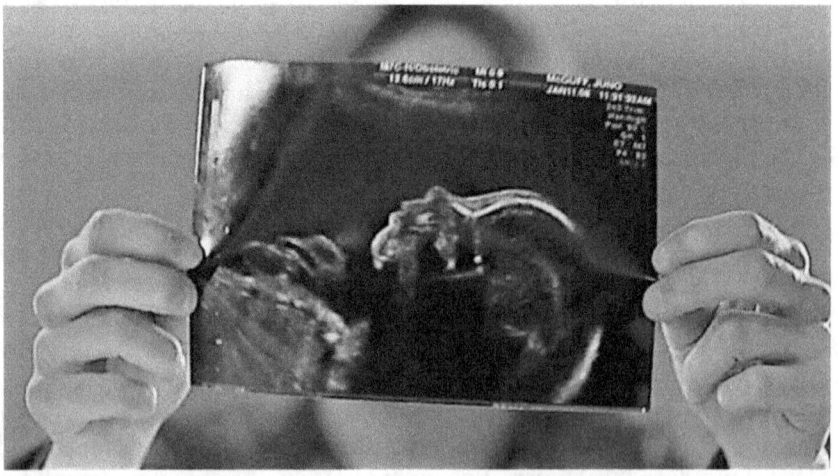

FIGURE 3.1 *Mark's point of view focuses on the photograph, not Juno, in* Juno.

fills the screen and prioritizes the profile of the foetus's head, shoulders and arm. The photograph obscures the pregnant body. Juno then presents the foetal photograph as an authentic representation of a 'baby', which she has been told (by the sonographer) is hers. The reality for Juno is that the foetus in her uterus is not going to be her baby. Therefore, when Juno introduces the foetal photograph to Mark, she begins coding it, telling him 'behold, good sir, your future child'. She transfers the narrative assigned to her and to her foetus so that she can initiate a narrative for Mark about his future child, changing the conceptual focus. In the reverse, close-up shot, Mark's eyeline shows that he is looking closely at the scan photograph rather than at Juno (Figure 3.2). Again, this juxtaposition of shots emphasizes the gentleness not only of the cinematic frame but of each frame: the screen, the uterus and the scan photograph. In effect, Juno forcibly creates a narrative space around her uterus that displaces the image inside her body in order to communicate with Mark. This means that although the uterus remains the premises for perception and remains the narrative space, Juno uses collaborative coding to place the technological image of the foetus (that is actually inside her body) into a narrative context for Mark. Juno distances herself from the foetus that will not be her future child and Mark is presented with a vision of his future as a father. When Mark takes the photograph from Juno, he stares at it and turns it round in his hands to look at it from different angles asking Juno if she knows whether it is a boy or a girl. In response, Juno narrates the scan photograph, by describing and ascribing likeness to the foetus, saying, 'I think it looks like my friend, Paulie' referring to the biological father Bleeker. In order for Mark to bond successfully with the

FIGURE 3.2 *Mark's eyeline confirms he is looking at the scan photograph, not Juno, in* Juno.

foetus – and Juno's narration of his future life with the foetus – he must also come to terms with his biological disconnect with the foetus and understand the foetal photograph as 'his baby'.

It is significant at this point that Mark's focus of attention moves from the scan photograph of the foetus to concentrate on Juno. Juno becomes *his* frame of reference in the narrative that *she* is developing for him. Although Mark tells Juno he is going to make some CDs for her to play 'while my kid's in there', Mark's orientational point is Juno. She is the frame, not the foetus in her uterus or the scan photograph. In this way, Mark looks beyond the frame that is presented to him to see the whole picture as he understands it. Collaborative coding, it should be noted, is also about un-recognizing the foetus to reject likeness, or to be relieved that the foetus is not familiar (Roberts 2012b: 306). Despite Juno's insistence that he looks at the foetal image, Mark spends the time getting to know Juno, finding out what music and films she likes. He gives her movies and music to take home with her. It is not clear whether Mark has ambivalent feelings towards the object that is the foetus or to the narration that Juno has created, but it does indicate that an emotional intra-action has been established through the exchange of the scan photograph. This emotional intra-action is significant for Mark as it does not revolve around the foetus, but Juno. The perceptual glue that Juno hopes to achieve with her translation of the photograph of the scanned foetus produces a negative reaction from Mark. He does not respond to the visual cues presented to him and does not allow his process of seeing to be guided by Juno, the foetal image or the framed photograph.

Of course, the foetal photograph serves a different purpose to the scan itself: it is portable, and the foetus can be viewed repeatedly away from the pregnant person. The ultrasound, however, presents a more immediate frame that is technologically connected to the pregnant body. Nevertheless, in the ultrasound sequence of the film, collaborative coding means that the actual image on the screen is less important, or not as important, as the narratives developed by the protagonists. The scan is the moment in the film when Juno's best friend Leah (Olivia Thirlby) and stepmother Bren see the foetus for the first time. Bren and Leah, who have both provided emotional support to Juno throughout the pregnancy and the birth, continue their imagined intra-action with the foetus through the scan. It is the sonographer, however, who begins to create a narrative, by interpreting the image in the scan screen. Juno's hands can be seen at the edge of the frame, with her pregnant belly in centre frame, holding her shirt up. The sonographer dips and moves the ultrasound transducer through the gel that she has squeezed onto the belly – and this is the only sound that is heard apart from the ambient sound in the room. The camera moves from the belly to a mid-close-up of Juno's face looking out of the frame towards the scan screen and then cuts to the scan screen. The screen and the foetus are now in focus as the narrow depth of field blurs the detail around the frame. This means that the screen appears to float in the centre of the frame rather like the foetus is floating in Juno's uterus.

There are only a couple of seconds before the foetus becomes recognizable in the screen and the sonographer says, 'there's your baby', which prompts Juno, Leah and Bren to take a sharp intake of breath in unison as if they are waiting for confirmation of what they can already see. Notably, this reaction only starts when there is a clear picture on the screen of what the sonographer calls a baby rather than a foetus. The sonographer describes the parts of the body that can be seen – the hand, an arm and the feet. This identification, or coding, of the foetal body parts establishes the presence of a 'baby' and provokes an emotional reaction from all three women, which for Leah is shock and for Bren is tears. The image of the 'baby' for Leah, however, is partly grotesque as she says, 'check out the baby big-head – dude that thing is freaky looking' when they view the skull. The shocked reaction from Leah subverts the sonographer's narrative of the scan as a baby, as Leah thinks of it as a foetus growing in a body. This is a continuation of her horrified reaction in an earlier scene where Leah imagines the foetus 'who has fingernails' scratching its way out of Juno's vagina. Importantly, the foetus is not identified as resembling anyone, nor is it described as having any particular characteristics that mark it as part of their familial group. Nevertheless, the sonographer continues her narrative coding of the foetal body, but she goes beyond the scan to the teenage pregnant body and by association to the familial kinship group, which she considers to be unsuitable environment for a baby. Imposing her moral view onto the pregnant body and the kinship group, her reaction suggests that she is narrating the foetal scan but as she also believes that the foetus is a baby, she is concerned for its safekeeping once it is born. She demonstrates how, for her, seeing the ultrasound image of the foetus has been overtaken by the frame of the pregnant body. She shifts her orientation point from the frame of the scanned foetal image to the frame of the pregnant body. This suggests that the sonographer understands the foetal scan image and the foetus in the uterus as a baby. In this way, the sonographer moves between the frame of the pregnant body and the frame of the scanned image to construct a narrative that is not based on the life or health of the pregnant person and that exists in the future, out of the scan room and off-screen.

Vanessa, in contrast to the sonographer and in contrast to Mark, engages with the narrative space around the uterus by focusing on the foetus and the pregnant body in turn. For Vanessa, the uterus is a conceptual space where her future child grows, and she transposes her own narrative onto the space of Juno's uterus. This narrative could be transposed onto any uterus. The scan photograph plays a significant part in the way she views the space of the uterus, but collaborative coding for Vanessa forms a much wider interpretation of the space of the uterus. It does not matter to Vanessa whether it is Juno's uterus or someone else's. What matters to Vanessa is that she has been able to build a relationship, through an imaginative intra-action, with any foetus. This is strengthened when Juno shows Vanessa the photograph of the scan and narrates it for her, coding the foetal image by telling her, 'it's your baby'. Juno tells Vanessa the foetus in the photograph looks like it is waving and then voices the foetus saying, 'Hi Vanessa, will you be my mom?' Vanessa nods in agreement as if she is replying to the 'baby'. This suggests that Vanessa is receptive to this translation of the scanned image and indicates that the process of collaborative coding around the foetus, for her, creates a positive emotional bond. When Vanessa holds the photograph, she stares at it intently and turns it round in her hands. She continues to stare, touching the photograph with her fingers as if to feel the foetus itself. Vanessa is framed holding the photograph with Juno beside her, in contrast to how Mark is placed in the frame (Figure 3.3). This framing again emphasizes the disconnect between the actual foetus growing inside Juno and the foetus – 'baby' – that is created conceptually in both Juno and Vanessa's imagination. It is Vanessa who maps 'seeing' and feeling onto the scanned photograph rather than the pregnant person. The frame of the uterus is replaced by the scanned image which in turn has been replaced by the frame of the scan photograph. The static photograph then provides the 'by means of which' Vanessa can understand the foetus as hers. She looks beyond the frame of Juno's body and uterus, beyond the frame edge of the scan photograph of the foetal image, to create a narrative about the foetus that is meaningful to her. In other words, Vanessa accepts Juno's interpretative narrative which builds an image of the foetus that is visual (the photograph) and conceptual (foetal movements as a personal

FIGURE 3.3 *Vanessa stares at the scan photograph rather than Juno's pregnant body in* Juno.

greeting) moving between what is on-screen (what she can see) and what is off-screen (her own future) in a Deleuzian 'Elsewhere, outside homogenous space and time' (1986: 18). The scan photograph (framed by Juno's uterus) represents a foetus, but it also represents kinship for Vanessa. This kinship is not dependent on this foetus, but it is dependent on any foetus framed by any uterus.

Vanessa maps 'seeing' and feeling of the foetus through Juno's body which allows her to use the orientational point of Juno's uterus as a way to 'talk' to the foetus. Yet, Vanessa does not touch Juno's body until they meet accidently in a shopping mall and Vanessa is invited to feel the foetus through Juno's skin. A close three-shot holds Leah, Juno's best friend, in centre frame. During the increasing close framing on the shot-reverse-shot of their conversation, Leah appears and then disappears from the frame but continues to hold her gaze on Vanessa. This provides an eyeline focus to Vanessa's reactions. Vanessa becomes concerned when Juno winces. Juno explains that nothing is wrong but that it (the foetus) is 'kicking . . . kicking away'. This creates an image of an active baby rather than involuntary moments of the foetus. When Vanessa asks if she can touch Juno's belly to feel the foetus, Juno agrees and yanks her hand to her belly. The framing then brings Vanessa in a much closer two-shot with Juno. Juno tells Vanessa that everyone at school is always grabbing her and calling her 'the cautionary whale'. After a few moments of holding her hands on Juno's belly, Vanessa looks visibly disappointed and tells Juno, 'I can't feel anything . . . it's not moving for me.' Juno tells her to talk to it because 'supposedly they can hear you even though it's like ten thousand leagues under the sea'. This conceptual image of the foetus under deep water, not able to hear her properly, encourages Vanessa to move closer to Juno. The camera moves down with Vanessa as she kneels on the ground with both palms of her hand spread across Juno's belly. Vanessa, now in a mid-close-up shot, talks directly to the foetus through Juno's skin (Figure 3.4). Vanessa is centrally placed in the frame alongside Juno's belly. The rest of Juno's body is outside of the frame and outside of Vanessa's field of vision. Only Juno's hand remains visible, as she holds up her shirt. The central focus is the pregnant belly and the foetus. The pregnant body moves into off-screen space, but it is still understood to be on the outside of the frame.

The pregnant belly, formed by the uterus growing, becomes the narrative space, a premises for perception so that Vanessa can understand the 'it' of the foetus as 'baby'. Vanessa says, 'Hi baby, it's me . . . it's Vanessa . . . I can't wait to meet you . . . can you hear me baby?' Vanessa is in the centre frame, and in a slow zoom, the background visual environment of the shopping mall gradually blurs. The pregnant body is gently replaced as frame so that Vanessa can speak directly to the foetus. When Vanessa feels the foetus move, the rest of Juno's body is off-screen, but as Vanessa looks up at Juno, the camera angle changes to Juno's perspective looking

FIGURE 3.4 *Vanessa talks to the foetus through Juno's body in* Juno.

down staring directly at Vanessa, watching her reaction. Aesthetically, the pregnant person is separated from her pregnant belly and from the actual foetus so that Vanessa can read the foetus conceptually as her baby. The sequence demonstrates how collaborative coding shifts the narrative from the pregnant person to the adoptive parent and back to the uterus. The frame also shifts from the uterus to the scanned foetal image, to the scan photograph, to the pregnant person and back to the uterus. A continuous narrative is constructed that begins with the technological snapshot of the foetus as something that can be held and transferred between people. The narrative then moves through a conceptual imagined intra-action as the pregnant belly is separated from the pregnant body enabling the foetus to change from being Juno's 'baby' to being Vanessa's.

It is significant that Vanessa can even transpose the conceptual image of a baby to an imagined family photo on the wall of the nursery, explaining to Mark that it will be 'our first family photo right in the middle'. During this sequence, both characters are equally placed in the centre of the frame. The wall of the nursery, which is prepared but unpainted, creates another frame around them. When they turn to look at the wall behind them, the camera remains static. Vanessa lifts her hand towards the wall with her fingers spread so that her outstretched palm is framed between them as if showing exactly where their family picture should be. Mark does not join in with Vanessa's preparation, or 'nesting' as she describes it. When she explains to Mark that this readying for the baby is an important way to prepare for adoption, Mark makes fun of her asking whether she will be making a crib 'out of sticks and spit'. When she points to the space in which their family pictures should hang and says to Mark, 'can you see it?', he does not answer. This suggests that either Mark cannot 'see' the 'baby' or he cannot see himself in that family group. This is poignantly prescient given that Mark will eventually leave Vanessa. But Vanessa's nesting is not limited to painting and decorating as preparation for the arrival of the imagined 'baby' is also signalled in the rest of the house, which is filled with baby clothes and equipment. This practical preparation is also part of the narrative around the uterus that Vanessa has created which is based on becoming a caregiver.

This role, for Vanessa, revolves around the concept of 'being a mother', and 'being maternal', yet although there is no reason to doubt Vanessa's strength of feeling about becoming a mother, there is nothing in the film that suggests that Vanessa will be an effective caregiver or will be a better parent than Juno. Nevertheless, this conceptual narrative is how Vanessa understands her notion of a 'baby' while the 'baby' is in Juno's uterus. Narrating the foetus by coding it as 'baby' allows the transfer of the 'baby' from Juno to Vanessa. In this way, kinship moves from the pregnant person to the adoptive parent before and after the birth. The scan and the scan photograph become 'that by means of which' this kinship can be narrated. This depends on the pregnant body being displaced so that the uterus can then be a frame for Vanessa's narrative. Crucially, when the family picture is eventually framed and hung in the space identified by Vanessa on the nursery wall, it is not Vanessa, Mark and the baby; it is the note from Juno saying to Vanessa, 'If you're still in, I'm still in.' This continues their negotiated narrative of kinship.

Although Juno narrates the foetus and shifts her body as frame to position Vanessa and Mark as parents of a 'baby', she has a more profound embodied connection to Bleeker, the biological father. While the foetus is in Juno's uterus, the lived body experience of Juno and Bleeker foregrounds its presence. Juno frequently meets Bleeker at school, where she is noticeably pregnant to everyone around her. When she visits Bleeker at home, her expanding belly means that she sits down uncomfortably and with effort on a beanbag on the floor of his bedroom. This increasing heaviness contrasts with their experience when the baby is born when their lived body experience includes the empty uterus. This loss is physical in that the baby has been removed from Juno's body, but the loss is also conceptual. Bleeker experiences the pregnancy by looking at Juno's pregnant body and by feeling the foetus move in Juno's belly when she leans against him and presses her belly against his body. The uterus, as an orientation point, therefore, becomes a frame for the foetus in utero, but also frames its physical absence. The embodied experience for the two young protagonists is part of their character development in the narrative, and although this embodiment is subtly sidelined, particularly for Bleeker, their lived body experience anchors the film with a strong emotional subtext. After the birth, for example, Juno's body ceases to be the frame for the foetus. Her uterus, however, is still the site of the foetus and is now physically marked by the loss. This can be seen when Juno and Bleeker embrace in the hospital bed where Juno's body is post-partum – post birth. A blanket covers Juno's belly but she faces the camera so that the spectator can see the difference between the growing uterus – which has been a feature of the film throughout – and the post-partum body as the uterus returns to its original size.[2] Although Bleeker has not been part of the birthing process – and he does not want to see the baby – the physical, tactile connection between him and Juno is a significant part of their relationship. The uterus, now changed by the presence of the foetus, functions as an embodied palimpsest.

The presence of the growing uterus, seen throughout the film and highlighted by the tactility between Juno and Bleeker, becomes part of their narrative of loss. This can be seen aesthetically in two sequences: when Vanessa holds the baby for the first time (Figure 3.5); and while Juno and Bleeker embrace on the hospital bed (Figure 3.6). The two sequences are linked visually in a dissolve that emphasizes the presence of the baby for Vanessa and the physical loss for Juno and Bleeker. The camera moves from a mid-close-up on Vanessa holding the baby for the first time to a slow, brief tracking close-up on Juno and Bleeker's feet. The dissolve linking the two shots moves from Vanessa looking at the baby in her arms, to Juno's stripy, child-like socks and Bleeker's trainers still covered in mud from his run at school. Moving from the mid-shot of Vanessa holding the baby, as Bren watches, to Juno and Bleeker's teenage feet emphasizes the reason for the adoption – their youth. The slow transition from one frame to another and from one mise en scène to the other establishes the kinship connection between the main protagonists: the adoptive mother, the stepmother

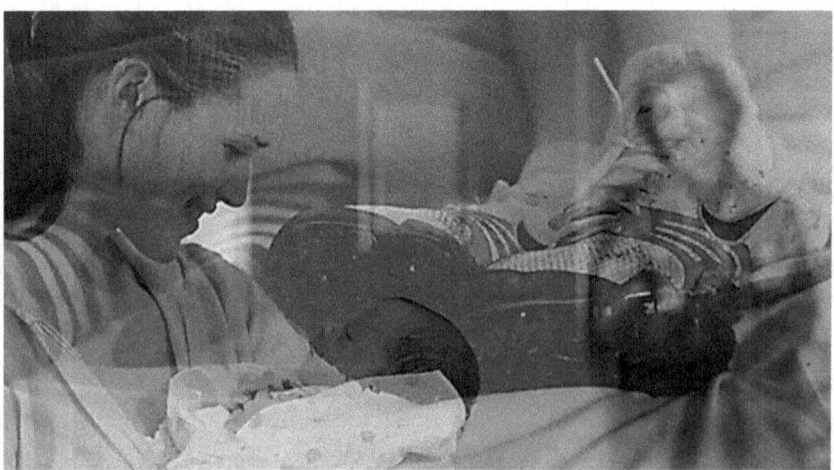

FIGURE 3.5 *The dissolve links kinship groups with a move from Vanessa to Bren in* Juno.

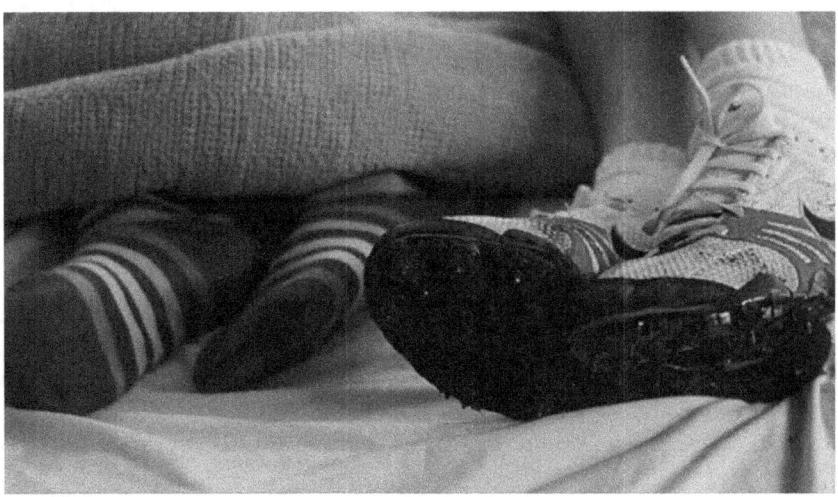

FIGURE 3.6 *Close-up showing Juno and Bleeker's feet emphasizing their age in* Juno.

(grandmother), the biological parents and the baby. It demonstrates the gentleness of the frame whereby the spectator is encouraged to make a perceptual link between the two sets of mise en scène on screen. The two scenes in juxtaposition emphasize how experientially different the presence of the foetus has been for each protagonist. The dissolve also hints to the way that the now shrinking uterus frames a narrative where Juno's foetus does not become her 'baby' but signals a successful narrative transposition where Vanessa is introduced to her new baby.

The successful transfer of narrative from Juno to Vanessa begins when the foetus is in utero, and this is confirmed after the birth when Juno says in a voice-over that 'he [the baby] didn't feel like ours, I think he was always hers'. Although Juno narrates the foetus for Vanessa and Mark to encourage them to identify as adoptive parents, she also narrates her embodied experience of carrying the foetus to Bleeker. There is an interconnection between Juno, the foetus and Bleeker that is biological and physical. Juno's emotional connection with Bleeker has a direct physical effect on the foetus as she can feel the difference in her body and from the foetus when Bleeker is present. When Juno decides that she is in love with Bleeker, she tells him, 'you don't stare at my stomach, you look at my face, and every time I see you the baby starts kicking super hard.' Significantly, she understands the foetus as 'baby' and attributes the 'baby's' characteristics as an emotional reaction to Bleeker. She places Bleeker's hand on her growing uterus and says, 'I think it's because my heart starts pounding every time I see you.' In this way, Juno describes the actions of the foetus as part of her own body, attributing the foetal movements to the 'baby's' personality. This physical connection is reinforced when Juno gives birth and Bleeker has a feeling that the birth has happened – as Juno's voice-over suggests, 'I didn't tell him, he just knew.' Although Juno does not tell Bleeker she is going into labour because he has a big race, his reaction to knowing the birth is imminent is physical. Seen in a wide shot, as he finishes his race, Bleeker stops and turns anti-clockwise while the camera tracks clockwise creating a disorientating effect, establishing visually that this is a moment of narrative change for him. Bleeker's embodied reaction is significant, as he never sees the baby, and he has only felt the movements of the foetus through Juno's body. When the foetus is no longer inside Juno's uterus, however, its absence is marked by Bleeker's first disorientated embodied reaction and his second, which is to wrap his arms around Juno's now un-pregnant body. Juno's uterus remains the narrative space and frame for the now physically absent pregnancy and foetus.

Gestation

There are some similarities between *Juno* and *Gestation* in that the growing uterus and the pregnant body of the teenager are narrative focal points. In *Gestation*, however, there is an increasingly complex reaction to the presence of the pregnant body, or rather what is happening in the uterus, more than the foetus. The main protagonist of *Gestation*, Jessie (Adriana Álvarez), is a teenage girl who becomes pregnant the first time she has sex with her boyfriend Teo (Edgar Roman). Jessie, who has a scholarship to attend a private girls-only Catholic school, lives in a less affluent part of the city than Teo. Jessie's pregnancy has substantial financial and practical consequences for her family. Costa Rica, where the film is set, has one of the most restrictive abortion laws in South America which means that any decision to have a termination places the protagonists in danger of losing their civil liberty.[3] The initial concern of Jessie's mother Patricia (Marla Bermúdez) is how they will afford another person in the house. A horrified Teo, by contrast, begins to sell some of his possessions so that he can buy abortion pills. Teo's mother and friends, meanwhile, encourage him to query paternity. Already, each narrative around the uterus begins from a different focal point. When Jessie decides to carry on with the pregnancy, however, she runs into difficulties with the head teacher at her school Sister María (María Bonilla). When Sister María finds out about the pregnancy, she allows Jessie to stay in school but segregates her from the other girls. A subsequent protest, supported by her classmates and a lawyer, eventually forces Sister María to allow Jessie back into the classroom.

On a conceptual level, the uterus provokes a visceral reaction from Sister María who creates her own narrative around the uterus, which functions as an orientation point that is personal to her. Although Sister María says, 'we'll make sure we do everything we can to make sure you have a safe pregnancy,' she is overwhelmed by the effort to control her feelings when Jessie is in front of her. The uterus becomes 'that by means of which' Sister María connects with, what she understands as, the undesired pregnancy. The growing uterus is a frame that is Sister María's orientation point and her premises for perception when she narrates Jessie's body as *una manzana podrida* – a rotten apple – that will contaminate the other girls at school.[4] In this way, she is creating a world around the pregnant body and the uterus by giving it the conceptual qualities of sin, as she understands it, as infectious and putrefying. It is not the pregnancy as such and not the foetus in particular that propels her interpretation of uterine space at first. It appears to be thinking of what will happen in the future when Jessie's pregnant body becomes visible which presents an ethical and moral dilemma. Sister María does not appear to be conceptualizing the foetus as a baby, although this cannot be ruled out given that the sin is both the conception and the future maternity out of marriage. The notion of sin is what encourages Sister María to intra-act with the frame of the uterus, as the location for the sin, the frame of Jessie's pregnant body, as a rotten and putrid apple. She is coding the pregnant body, including the uterus, rather than the foetus.

Sister María also begins to create a metaphorical and physical distance between herself and Jessie, almost as if her vivid interpretation has more power if Jessie is distant, outside her line of vision. She looks beyond the frame of the uterus and the frame of the pregnant body to create her own off-screen narrative space, her own Elsewhere. It is the function of the growing uterus, however, that inspires Sister María's interpretative imaginings. There is no real evidence that her interpretative imaginings are based on how she sees Jessie. Nevertheless, Sister María creates a distance between the two of them when Jessie comes to her office. Sister María asks Jessie directly if she is pregnant, speaking to her in formal language using *usted* rather than the familiar *tú* to address her. This choice of language creates a formal distance between the two.[5] Although Sister María remains calm and speaks quietly (Figure 3.7), her facial expression and gestures change markedly when Jessie confirms – by lowering her head – that she is pregnant. Sister María is filmed in close-up, and this framing remains the same as her changing emotional response is reflected in her facial expressions. Her speech becomes more rapid, she begins to use hand movements, her brows furrow and her lips purse (Figure 3.8). In the close-up, the frame is divided by the corner of the wall and by the string of wooden rosary beads that hang behind her. This mise en scène emphasizes the importance of the iconography of the Catholic Church to Sister María. The habit and the veil that she wears mark her celibate role in the church, and the rosary beads are there to structure prayers that are said as penance for sin.[6] She is enveloped visually by markers of her religious beliefs.

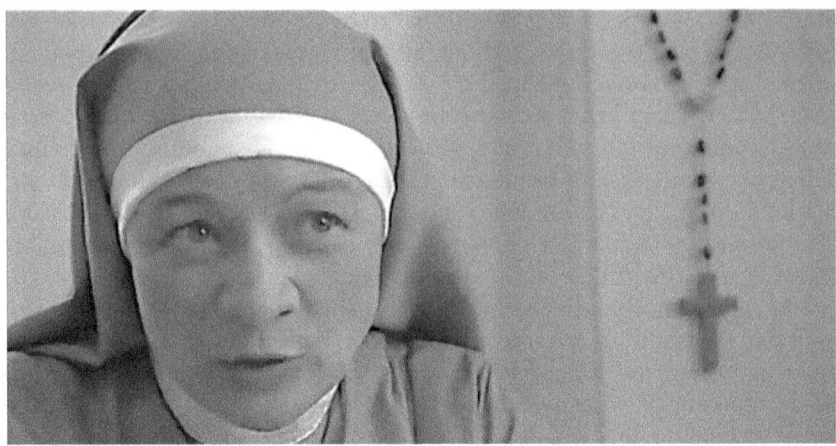

FIGURE 3.7 *Sister María speaks calmly and quietly to Jessie in* Gestation.

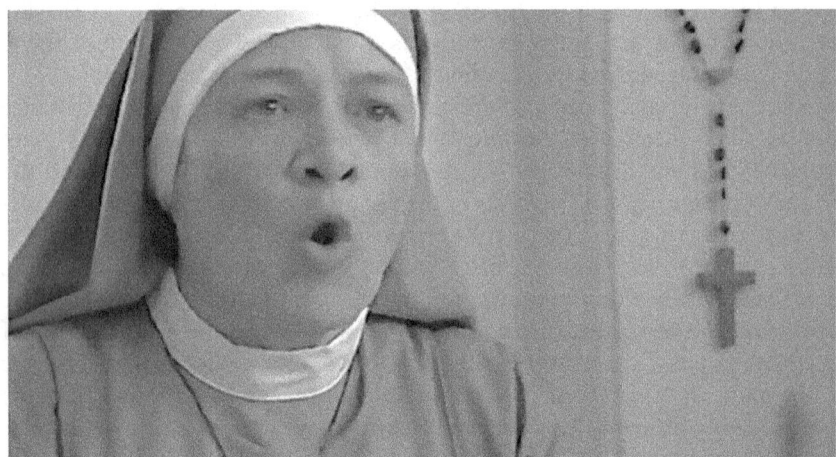

FIGURE 3.8 *Matching close-up as Sister María's facial expression changes in* Gestation.

But although her visceral response to Jessie's pregnancy might originate in her Catholicism, there is no evidence in the film that Sister María's vivid narrative around the uterus is shared by others who hold or are encouraged to hold similar beliefs. The male staff who work at the entrance to the school, for example, apologize to Jessie who is segregated and made to use a side entrance. The other schoolgirls, including Jessie's best friend Alba, challenge the narrative around the pregnant body. The measures taken to hide Jessie's growing uterus from the rest of the pupils are, Sister María insists, for Jessie's safety, but she has also told them that Jessie's body could contaminate them. The schoolgirls support Jessie by forming a protective circle around her using their own bodies. They link hands around Jessie in the schoolyard as if they understand that the pregnant body is an extension of Jessie and an extension of themselves. By their actions, they increase the frame of the pregnant body to include themselves. This makes it difficult for the head teacher to see past the frame that now includes all of their bodies. This subverts the image of contamination created by the head teacher. Included in this subversion of narrative are the other nuns who facilitate Jessie's segregation but try to persuade the head teacher to allow Jessie's presence in school.

When Alba shields Jessie from segregation, she includes the foetus. When the girls are alone, Alba talks to the foetus through Jessie's body. They chat on a dimly lit stairwell in school away from other people. It is a location that is private. This means that Alba can express her close physical relationship with Jessie and is also free to create her own narrative around Jessie's pregnant body. The uterus, therefore, becomes a premises for perception for Alba which includes the foetus. The intimate sequence is emphasized by the camera being placed at a lower point on the stairs, so that the spectator becomes a witness from a distance. At this point, the pregnancy has not been disclosed to the school and the two young women talk in general terms about their everyday life, talking about food they crunch green apples (visually foreshadowing the metaphor used by Sister María). As Alba places her hands on Jessie's belly, the camera angle changes to an overhead shot, which emphasizes the privacy of the moment but also captures the point of view of two other schoolgirls who are watching and listening surreptitiously. This means that the frame shifts between the spectator's point of view and the view of the two girls listening. Alba places both her hands over Jessie's belly to feel the movement of the foetus, then tips her head sideways and places her ear over Jessie's belly to listen. Despite the distance of the camera, the turn in the banister creates an arrow pointing to the two girls (Figure 3.9). Alba tells Jessie that the baby is giving little kicks – *patadas* – for her, coding the foetal movements as meaningful and creating a narrative in which the foetus actively directs its kicks towards her hands. She talks to the foetus and voices the foetus saying 'ay, little thing . . . it's trying to say something to me. . . . Hi, Auntie Alba, how are you? I want to see you.' She emphasizes the kinship she has with Jessie and the foetus inside her by creating narrative and voicing the foetus. In this way Alba demonstrates the way sympathetic imagination allows her to identify with the foetus, as a baby, as part of an imagined intra-action. Alba becomes the guide interpreting and explaining how the foetus gives not only kicks but 'little kicks'. This extremely specific physical movement of the 'little thing', she suggests, is in response to her voice. She then kisses Jessie's belly through her clothes as if she is kissing the foetus. In this way, Alba interprets the movements of the foetus through collaborative coding, forming a kinship with the foetus

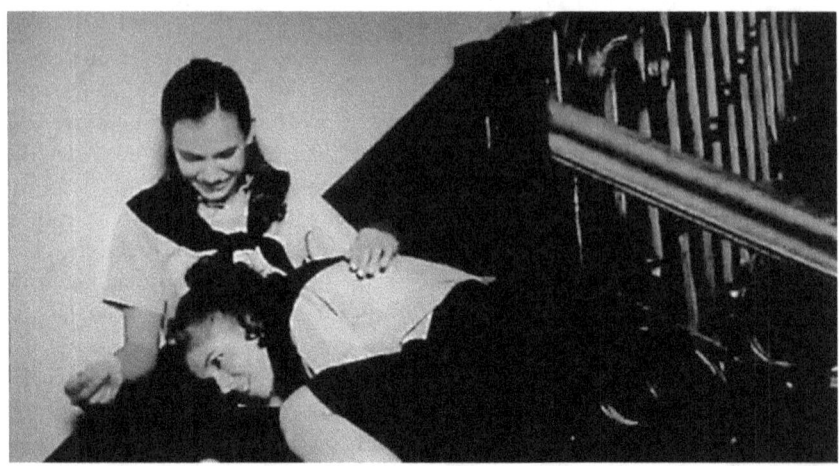

FIGURE 3.9 *Alba puts her ear to Jessie's belly to hear the foetus's response in* Gestation.

who is a 'baby' that can recognize her. Alba creates a conceptual narrative that is corporeal in that she engages with the foetus physically in her contact with the pregnant body. For Alba, the foetus exists in the frame of the uterus but remains part of Jessie's body.

Alba talks to and voices the foetus, but Jessie does not. She does, however, connect physically with her pregnant body in the privacy of her bedroom when she is shown stroking her growing belly (Figure 3.10). Although Sister María tells her that she does not have a 'normal' life anymore, the mise en scène emphasizes the normality of the pregnant teenager. A mid-shot reveals that the bedhead is covered in child's writing and stickers. A toy bear sits beside her pillow. Her growing belly subverts the image of childhood as it takes up the centre of the frame. As well as subverting the head teacher's narrative, the frame also speaks to the real experience of the pregnant person, who also lives a teenage life. Jessie touches her belly lightly with her fingertips and stares out of the frame. Until this point, her pregnancy and her pregnant body have been the focus of many narratives. Some narratives have separated her from her growing uterus, and some have included her and her pregnant body. Others, like Alba's, have included the foetus. In this frame, the pregnant body could be understood as separated from Jessie, but the way that she touches her belly emphasizes the embodied connection that she has to the foetus. The uterus is now an orientation point for Jessie. There is no evidence that Jessie is visualizing the foetus. The way that she touches her belly while looking into off-screen space echoes the experience of the scan, but in this case there is no technological image to interpret and no other presence to create a narrative around the space of the uterus. Rather than her belly being in her

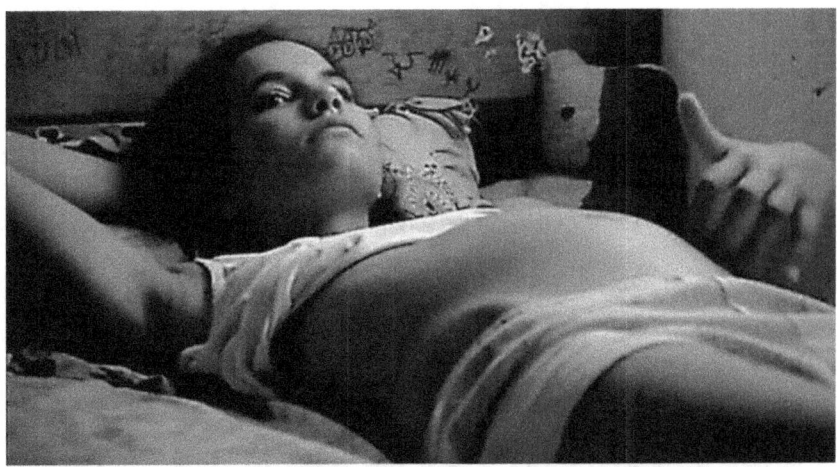

FIGURE 3.10 *Jessie, alone in her room, stroking her belly* in Gestation.

line of vision or voicing the foetus or talking to it, touching it through her body signals an embodied awareness of its presence. This moment of tactility, touching the foetus in the uterus through the belly, emphasizes the dissonance that exists between the conceptual narrative of the teenage pregnant body as a rotten apple and the embodied reality of a young woman who is pregnant.

The embodied reality of Jessie's situation, including the impact it has on her family, is clear in the scan room with her mother Patricia. The physical and emotional closeness between the two women emphasizes the kinship bonds that already exist between mother, daughter and the foetus. Importantly, this closeness has already been established before the foetus is visualized through the ultrasound scan. Patricia is aware of the physiology of Jessie's body so that pregnancy is signalled to her not by the visual presence of the foetus but by the absence of menstruation. Patricia recognizes the unused sanitary towel as a sign of pregnancy. She places the unused packet sharply on the kitchen table in front of Jessie so that it becomes an outward marker of what is happening inside the uterus. In the frame is the unused sanitary towel, off-screen is the absence of menstruation. The uterus, then, operates as premises for perception for Patricia who understands the regular, everyday working of Jessie's body. The packet of sanitary towels highlights how the unused towel signifies pregnancy.[7] The ultrasound scan, therefore, confirms what Jessie and Patricia already know, that Jessie is pregnant. This means that the scan is not the beginning of a narrative but the continuation of their kinship narrative.

When the sonographer runs the transducer over Jessie's belly, the sound of the ultrasound monitor is loud and distorted until she stops when the heartbeat is heard, signalling the presence of the foetus. Notably, although the transducer can be seen, the figure of the ultrasound technician is only identified by the arm and the white coat. It is as if the technology is an extension of the sonographer's body. The sonographer explains that the heartbeat 'is strong, it's really strong ... this is your baby'. At this point, the camera cuts to a close-up of Jessie's face as she smiles and looks up at her mother (Figure 3.11). The camera then cuts to a close-up of Patricia's face smiling (Figure 3.12). Their eyelines show that they are smiling at each other

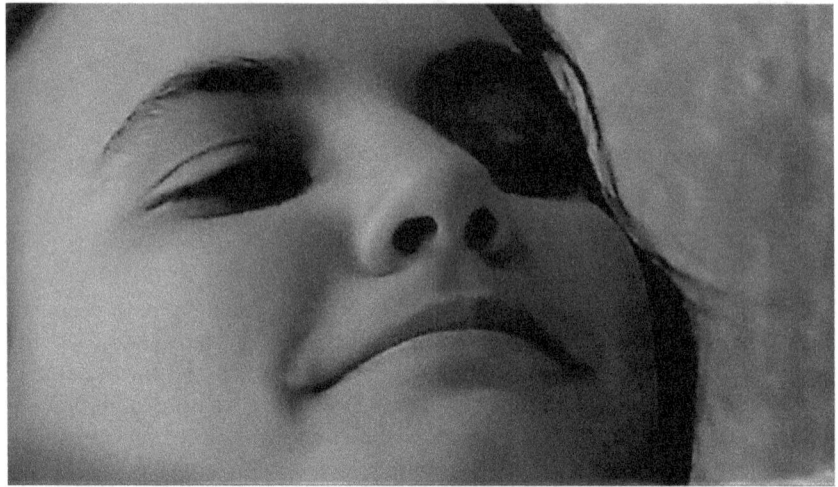

FIGURE 3.11 *Jessie's eyeline shows she is watching her mother in* Gestation.

FIGURE 3.12 *Jessie's mother's eyeline shows she is watching her daughter in* Gestation.

as the sonographer tells Patricia 'this is your grandchild, grandma'. The scan confirms pregnancy but the importance of its function in this sequence is to confirm the intergenerational kinship between the two women in relation to the foetus. Although they already know this, it is the sonographer who voices this narrative of the alive foetus and their relationship. The uterus is the orientation point and becomes the 'by means of which' their narrative is interpreted. The sonic heartbeat establishes an aliveness in the foetus, but the gentleness of the frame means that on-screen action (the scan) moves into off-screen space to provide a confirmation of aliveness that then reinforces Jessie and Patricia's ongoing kinship.

For the biological father, establishing kinship is complex and Teo is not concerned with developing a kinship with the foetus, nor is he able to narrate his own family history around the foetus. He rejects this narrative, as does his mother, and rejects any mapping of seeing and feeling to the foetus. His own conceptual narrative around the uterus does not include having a child or understanding that the foetus is a 'baby'. Jessie's subsequent refusal to take abortion pills marks a turning point in the narrative and a change of pace in her relationship with Teo. This is marked by how they are framed in the landscape of the city. When they meet to discuss the abortion, it is in the same gardens where they had previously been running. The earlier sequence, shot in daylight, uses high angle wide shots to observe their journey through the city. This means that the camera observes from a distance. Teo has leaflets for college courses and both characters are excited about their futures. As they run around the fountain (Figure 3.13), the wide shot illustrates the openness of the wider

FIGURE 3.13 *Jessie and Teo run around the fountain in the city centre in* Gestation.

FIGURE 3.14 *Jessie and Teo meet at the fountain to discuss the abortion in* Gestation.

location but also the enclosed nature of the area around the fountain, the curved shape of the seats (which suggests a uterine shape with fountain in the centre) drawing the two characters together as they run in circles around it. By contrast, when they meet to discuss the abortion, the scene is filmed at night and they are both seated (Figure 3.14). The integrity of the location has fundamentally changed. Rather than a landscape to run through, it becomes a visceral location that has drawn them in and is now imbued with embodied memories. Uplights around the fountain illuminate the scene and the pace of action slows as the fountain, although centre frame, becomes a visual and audio backdrop to their conversation. The musical soundtrack is low and unobtrusive. The scene, therefore, becomes intimate. The camera is placed at their head height, but behind them, as if to eavesdrop on the moment when Jessie says, 'we're not two anymore.' The changed location emphasizes how each character has now changed their perception of what is happening in the uterus. Still an orientation point, the uterus is 'that by means of which' the foetus becomes a 'baby' for both of them. This moment is significant as it is the moment when Teo is forced to think of the foetus in relation to the two of them. The 'baby' is already third person in the off-screen space of the uterus before it is born.

The off-screen narrative space propels Teo towards kinship as he makes decisions that are proactive rather then reactive and stops trying to secure an abortion. Importantly, the pregnant body in this scene is understood not as a site of contamination or infection but familiarity and kinship. Each character in the film, therefore, engages with the narrative around the uterus in distinct ways. The head teacher creates her own imagined intra-action with the uterus by trying to remove the pregnant body from any communal space. Alba codes the foetus as meaningful to her by voicing the foetus and creating a relationship with it that involves the foetus recognizing her as 'auntie'. Teo initially responds to the pregnancy by rejecting his part in the conception and this is reflected in his questioning paternity. Significantly, he does not reject the uterus as a premises for perception and is not rejecting the foetus in the frame of the uterus; he rejects his physical contribution to the pregnancy. Moreover, the sequences between Jessie and Patricia illustrate how the unspoken and unseen uterine physiological process of menstruation, that exists in off-screen space, underscores the revelation of the scan that the foetus is alive and has a heartbeat. The presence of the foetus is already part of the lived body experience, as the two characters already know.

Stephanie Daley

In the previous two films, the scan provides a once-only narrative punctuation that allows for character and plot development. In *Stephanie Daley*, the scan is used repeatedly to emphasize the disconnect between an unwelcome pregnancy and a much wanted one. The repeated scan in this film is there to give reassurance that the foetus is still alive to one character but understanding the uterus as a premises for perception makes sense of the narrative implications for both main characters. Set in the present day, the main protagonist of *Stephanie Daley*, sixteen-year-old Stephanie (Amber Tamblyn), gives birth unattended in the toilets while on a school ski trip. Stephanie is subsequently arrested and allocated to a forensic psychologist Lydie (Tilda Swinton). Lydie must make an independent assessment of Stephanie for the State prosecution in case she has to go to court and stand trial for killing her baby at birth – neonaticide.[8] Lydie herself is twenty-nine weeks pregnant. A previous pregnancy ended in a stillbirth and Lydie constantly seeks reassurance in this pregnancy from her husband Paul (Timothy Hutton) and her obstetrician Dr Peterson (Novella Wilson). Paul does not share Lydie's anxiety which provokes tension in their relationship. Stephanie discloses to Lydie that she has been coerced into having unprotected sex at a party and that she was a virgin at the time. She had visited the house of her assailant Cory (Kel O'Neill) after the attack but had not confronted him and had not told anyone that she was pregnant. The pregnancies of the two main protagonists Stephanie and Lydie are connected visually from the opening scenes, and this establishes the importance of their embodied experience of pregnancy and birth to the narrative of the film.

There is a direct comparison between the gestational stage of Lydie's current pregnancy, twenty-nine weeks, and the age of Stephanie's stillborn infant which was twenty-six weeks gestation at birth.[9] This gestational age is significant as it places each foetus in the territory of viability at birth where a foetus can survive outside the uterus, but equally, it may die if it is outside of the uterus. This is important subtextual information that provides character development for Stephanie and Lydie. Stephanie's pregnancy is told mostly in flashback, and these lengthy flashbacks are intercut with sequences of Lydie's current pregnancy. This means that the uterus frames each narrative. For Stephanie, it is whether or not she knew she was pregnant. This is something quite different from understanding that her changing embodiment is pregnancy. Within the frame of her body, Stephanie may not associate how her body feels with being a pregnant person, and this is one of the main plot points of the narrative. The fragility of the foetus in utero emphasizes the ambivalent – strong positive and negative – feelings towards pregnancy and the foetus that is central to both main characters. Importantly, a comparison is established between the death of the newborn in Stephanie's case and the constant monitoring of Lydie's (alive) unborn foetus. Despite Lydie's need for repeated antenatal care, for each woman the experience of being pregnant comes with negative perceptions: that 'something is wrong like last time' (Lydie), or that the pregnancy is a punishment from God (Stephanie). The uterus functions as a premises for perception for both women and for the spectator. Each narrative is stitched together by collaborative coding that surrounds both uteri as orientation points; Stephanie's narrative is unravelled in retrospect and Lydie's in the present. The implication is that the fate of each foetus might be influenced by the viewpoint of each woman to her own pregnancy. It also suggests that understanding their own pregnancy depends to some extent on each character's ability to sympathize or empathize with the foetus.

The subtext of emotional bonding with the foetus gives strength to the main narrative, but equally suggests the importance of how each character confronts the death of the foetus. When Lydie admits that she threw the ashes of her previously stillborn baby out of the car window, it is clear that this physical part of the baby (who was a foetus at death) signifies something emotional for her husband, Paul.[10] When he is confronted by Lydie who asks him, 'what happened to us?' Paul replies, 'last spring happened to us . . . we should have given her a name . . . had a service, but we pretended like nothing happened.' There is no indication in the film that Paul had seen the foetal scan before the stillbirth, but his involvement in Lydie's current pregnancy, attending the scan and discussion with the obstetrician, suggests that he felt very involved at all stages previously. If this is the case, and he understood the foetus as part of his kinship group, it existed not only as a 'baby', but as his 'baby' or their 'baby' in his own perception. This suggests that even the ashes of the foetus, who died in utero, that existed outside of the frame of the post-pregnant body and outside of the frame of the post-pregnant uterus signify a 'baby'. The ashes, therefore, exist as part of the off-screen narrative of a 'baby'. In order for Paul to accept this current pregnancy, he has to come to terms with the lack of closure on the death of his 'baby'. His successful collaborative coding from the previous pregnancy becomes his perceptual glue for this second pregnancy. Yet, Paul's identification with the dead baby is at odds with Lydie's. For Lydie, the memory of the baby affects her everyday life, as she tells him, 'I think about her every day.' This shows that the stillbirth affects Lydie's everyday life, but not in the same way as Paul. This disconnect with Paul is heightened by Lydie's interaction with Stephanie.

The death of Lydie's foetus in utero and the death of Stephanie's baby at birth fundamentally change the way the two female protagonists interact with each other. Although the lived body experience of each woman is crucial to the narrative around pregnancy, it is only Lydie who is currently pregnant. The conceptual narrative that she constructs around her foetus includes the possibility that the foetus will die. The scan of Lydie's uterus, therefore, functions on many levels. The scan demonstrates to Lydie that her pregnancy is healthy and establishes that the foetus is coded as 'baby'. This explains why she feels the need to return to the scan as a marker of her foetus being alive. The scan, however, is closely linked in the film to the birth and death of Stephanie's baby. Lydie's scan appears immediately after the opening sequence to the film, which shows the aftermath of Stephanie giving birth. In the opening sequence, Stephanie's post-partum collapse, journey to hospital and return home is followed by the non-diegetic audio of a heartbeat over an intertitle on a black screen. The intertitle moves the narrative forward five months, but the sound of the heartbeat has already formed an audio bridge to the close-up of the scan image of Lydie's healthy foetus (Figure 3.15). The outline of the foetus is shown and the shape of the head and eye sockets can be clearly seen as well as the heart beating. The foetal image takes up the full screen. When this is juxtaposed with Lydie's belly, the assumption is that the foetus takes up all of the space in the belly. There is no mention of Lydie's own body or of the content of the uterus. The scan is all about the foetal image. There is a brief close-up of Lydie's face reacting to the image. Her eyeline, however, shows that she is not looking at her own body but at the image of the foetus on the monitor. This demonstrates how her perception is constantly moving from the orientation point of her uterus to the screen.

The foetus is identified visually on the scan by the presence of the foetal skull and limbs, but there is no initial narration for the benefit of the spectator beyond the moving image of the foetus on the scan screen. When the camera cuts to the close-up of Lydie, it records her reaction to the movement of the foetus on screen. Notably, she does not appear to react to the movement of the foetus inside her body. Neither does Lydie register any reaction to the weight of the transducer that is being held against her pregnant belly. This suggests that her physical reactions are dependent on her

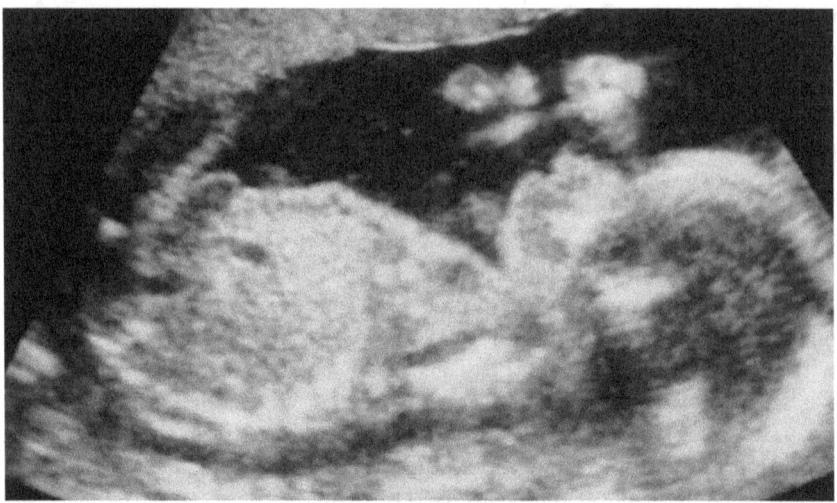

FIGURE 3.15 *The scan shows the foetus in profile in* Stephanie Daley.

seeing, rather than feeling, the foetus move. The camera cuts to an extreme close-up of Lydie's belly in profile as the transducer passes over it, which exaggerates the visceral nature of the scan (Figure 3.16). As the transducer passes over her belly, the soft squelch of the jelly and the light from the window reflecting in its congealed droplets on the surface of the skin around Lydie's umbilicus highlight the physical nature of the scan and the pregnant body. The pregnant-belly prosthesis as part of the aesthetic of the film makes the belly lifelike, but it also emphasizes the way the lived experience of the pregnant body has been marginalized in the scan process.[11] As Lydie watches the monitor, Dr Peterson says, 'three pounds, ten ounces, and twenty-nine weeks'. Lydie flinches and smiles in surprise when the image on screen moves, but she carries on looking at the monitor not her body. When Dr Peterson says, 'oh, there's a kicker', she is coding the foetal movements, calling the foetus 'a kicker' as if this is a description of its personality. Lydie replies and confirms this collaborative coding when she says, 'he's always kicking.' In this process, Lydie and Dr Peterson create a continuous narrative around the foetus where the foetus is identified visually through the scan, collaboratively coded according to foetal movements as a 'kicker' and conceptually understood as a 'baby'. The importance of this sequence is that it establishes the health of the foetus, which is important to Lydie's narrative, but it also codes the foetus giving it an identity (and a gender). It also builds narrative using the frame of the uterus, the frame of the pregnant body, the frame of the scan screen and the frame of the filmic screen. The characters and the viewer must understand that there is a gentleness to each frame as each set of images has to be understood and perceived together.

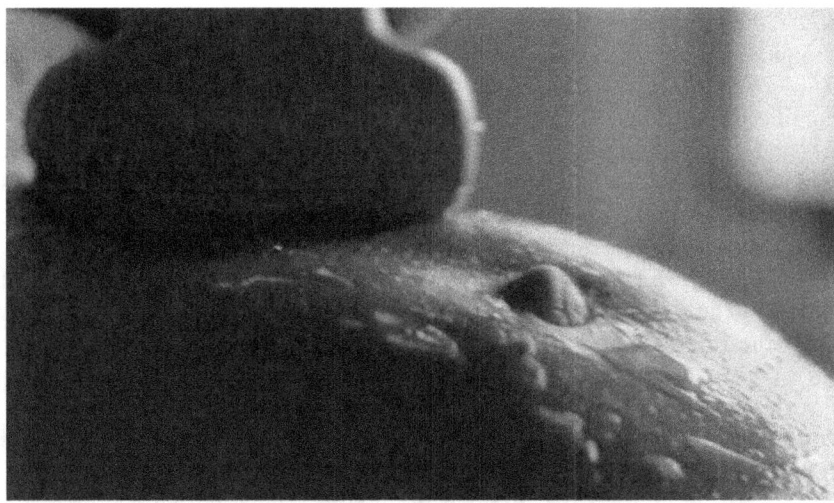

FIGURE 3.16 *The close-up shows the visceral nature of the foetal scan in* Stephanie Daley.

The narrative space begins in the frame of the uterus, and by juxtaposing the sequence of Stephanie's birth with Lydie's scan, Stephanie's foetus is also conceptualized, and coded, as a 'baby'. This encourages the spectator to make a narrative connection between the aliveness of Lydie's foetus and the death of Stephanie's 'baby'. The way that this ultrasound sequence is filmed suggests that by coding the foetal identity, its personality becomes more important than Lydie's actual embodied experience. This suggests that the lived body experience is secondary, or less forceful, than the perceived image of the foetus on the scan.

When Stephanie gives birth, by contrast, it is not clear whether she understands what is happening to her body, but the graphic representation of the birth suggests that Stephanie experiences a physically and emotionally profound embodied moment. Her pregnancy moves from the conceptual (where Stephanie is in control of what she thinks and believes; although, this may not include pregnancy) to the visual where she can see that there is a baby's head coming out of her body. The sequence emphasizes the dissonance between her understanding of her own pregnant embodiment (it is not clear at this point in the narrative if she understands that she is pregnant) and her embodied experience of the foetus leaving the uterus and her internal body. Although she can see what is happening in front of her, it is not clear if she fully understands the implications of what is happening to her body. The counter-narrative that she has created, where she does not acknowledge her pregnancy, is not subverted by the reality of the birth and this dissonance is reflected in the aesthetic of the film's mise en scène and sonic landscape. When Stephanie locks herself in a toilet cubicle, the moment of realization, that she is giving birth, is signalled by a sonic shift. The diegetic sound of washroom, the sound of loud music and people coming in and out of the toilets fade out just before she looks down into her underwear (Figure 3.17). She lifts the elastic of her underwear hesitantly with her fingers to peep inside, almost as if she is unveiling someone else's body, not sure what she will see. It is at this point that she registers the shock of seeing what is – presumably – the baby's head (Figure 3.18). In close-up, her face is almost frozen as the sequence continues with only the exaggerated sound of the toilet seat moving under her pressure as she bears down. This gives the impression that she has blocked everything out – including her own voice – apart from the discordant, mechanical sound of the toilet seat flexing under pressure. The sound design in this scene implies that Stephanie enters an altered state of consciousness for the duration of the birth, as the naturalistic diegetic sound returns as soon as she stops pushing. This soundscape, which creates an acoustic interval, suggests that she does not understand what is happening to her. It is almost as if the frame of her body remains an orientation point for Stephanie, but when the baby emerges, she is disorientated. The actual image of the baby becomes virtual for her – as if it has come out of nowhere. Although the birth occurs on-screen, it exists for Stephanie as an off-screen narrative.

It is only towards the end of the film when Stephanie tells Lydie 'I held her' that it is clear there became a point, not necessarily at the birth, when she understood that she had seen the infant as an actual image and identified it as female. Despite her refusal to give many details throughout their

FIGURE 3.17 *Stephanie looks down into her underwear to see the baby emerging in* Stephanie Daley.

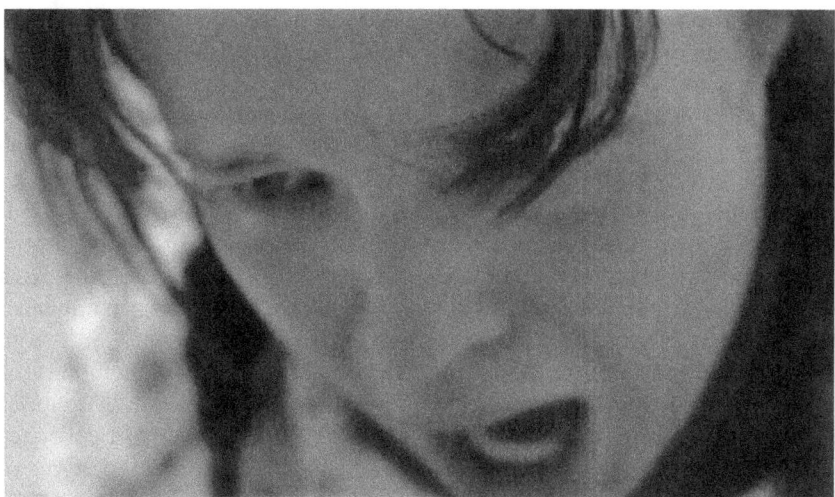

FIGURE 3.18 *The close-up shows Stephanie's shock at the physicality of giving birth in* Stephanie Daley.

discussion, Stephanie has a strong conceptual idea of the infant's identity. She tells Lydie, 'I knew that she wanted to live, but I didn't want her to so I told her to die . . . and she did. I killed her with my mind.' This is a complex process of perception on the part of Stephanie. Her description of what happened is in counterpoint to the forensic evidence that Lydie receives: that the baby was found with toilet paper in its mouth and pressed into its face. Importantly, this revelation emphasizes the difficulty that Lydie has found when coming to terms with the death of her own foetus in utero. The intercutting of Stephanie's backstory with Lydie's present-day pregnancy suggests that there are similarities in how they understand their own culpability in the death of their 'babies', which relates to how they think about their foetuses. Later in the film, Lydie is directly challenged to think about how her own anxieties could be passed on to her foetus. At a drinks reception for Paul's work, Lydie is stopped by a woman she does not know. When Lydie explains, in answer to the woman's question, that they will be organizing the nursery after the birth, she is told that she must not 'think cautiously' and that she should have 'a ballsy vibe' in relation to the pregnancy. If not, she is told, 'you're going to pass on all sorts of anxieties to your child.' This exchange shows that the woman believes that the maternal imagination has a direct effect on the foetus. She bases this on her own negative relationship with her mother, but she also suggests that this is because of her memory of being in the uterus. The presence of the foetus is reinforced when the woman tells Lydie that she is in regression therapy.

In this therapy, the woman remembers being in the uterus and the 'waves of panic' she experiences when her mother said that '[she] was destroying her figure and she didn't want [her]'. She also remembers her mother's heart 'beating above [her] in the dark'. This scene, which only lasts a couple of minutes, highlights the woman's sympathetic imagination towards the foetus. In fact, her sympathetic imagination is related to her own experience as a foetus, and this sequence reflects the anxiety that Lydie feels about her own foetus. This scene is foreshadowed by a musical bridge where the diegetic sound of background music of light piano is mixed with the extra diegetic soundtrack of cellos and violins, which are themselves accompanied by a rapid beat which reaches a musical peak at the moment she is told about 'anxieties'. The importance of this musical bridge is how it emphasizes Lydie's preoccupation with the health of her foetus. The uterus, as a premises for perception, however, has been reappropriated as a metaphorical space and an embodied space in the sequence. The guest transforms the uterus of her own mother into a premises for perception in which she – as a foetus – has a central role. She remembers not only her experience of being a foetus but also her emotional response to her mother's anxiety. The uterus becomes 'that by means of which' she can recall being a witness to her mother's everyday life, but more significantly, recalls her own emotional, embodied response to her mother's everyday life. This sequence adds to Lydie's virtual image of her own possibly unviable foetus that is actually healthy. Lydie's experience of pregnancy is a narrative that exists elsewhere; it is not on-screen and not off-screen but part of her imagination.

Stephanie's (dis)connection with the foetus is positioned initially in the film's narrative as a denial of pregnancy, but after constant flashbacks to the events that led up to the birth, it becomes clear that Stephanie, like Lydie, has very specific fears about her pregnancy. These fears are conceptual and revolve around the moral values that are promoted at her church. She rationalizes her pregnancy as being punished by God for being weak. But even if Stephanie enters a clinical state of disassociation at the time of the birth, there are clues that she realizes something is different about her body. She begins to wear loose-fitting clothes to change the appearance of her body and waits outside the house of the boy who raped her. When Stephanie describes her feelings after the rape, Lydie voices the significance of the event telling her, 'something just happened to you'. This significant 'something' is the physical act of rape, but it is also the moment when her body will begin to change in pregnancy. A key question for Lydie in her investigation is whether Stephanie knew she was pregnant. This question implies that she understood she was carrying a foetus who was capable of life and that she had a duty of care. 'Did you know you were pregnant . . .did you think it might be?' The court case rests on whether Stephanie is guilty of murder; therefore, this conceptual understanding of the foetus forms part of the prosecution. A conscious decision to kill the foetus suggests an ambivalence where she might have known that the foetus was alive, but equally did not care if the baby died.

The ambivalence shown by each woman in the film suggests there is no innate way that a pregnant woman relates to her pregnant embodiment or foetus.[12] Lydie's anxieties are manifest in her dreams about giving birth that contain potential metaphorical allusions to nature. This can be read as a long-standing symbolic connection of the woman's body to nature, but I would read against this. Susan Ayres and Prema Manjunath (2016), for example, argue for the textual importance of the water and blood that connect the two main characters visually and narratively. Framing their discussion around Caroline Lundquist's 2008 essay on maternal ambivalence, Ayres and Manjunath explain that the differences between the two women and their two pregnancies are crucial to the main narrative. The importance of similarities, they suggest, must be shown in other ways. They liken the close-up on the boiling water for coffee, for example, to the ultrasound close-up of Lydie's belly and explain that the wipers on Lydie's car windscreen echo the rhythmic sound of the foetal heartbeat. Blood, they suggest, is indicative of each character's mental state and that blood is used as a symbol of biology whereby each woman, literally and metaphorically, has blood on their hands. While it is certainly true that water and blood provide textual and textural structure, there is insufficient evidence in the filmic text that this use of water and blood can signify how 'biology controls women during pregnancy' or reflect elements of 'the abject – of madness and death' (2016: 45). As Kelly Oliver (2012: 15) points out, the film also uses elements from horror such as the visual references to dead animals, a trope that aligns women stereotypically to animality. Read differently, the references to animals, dead or alive, should be expected in a film that is set in a location surrounded by wildlife.

The three visual elements in the film – water, animals and blood – which might lend themselves to metaphors of birth as part of nature, actually form punctuation points in the narrative and provide visual links between the two women. Running water provides visual continuity that links Lydie and Stephanie. Lydie gets up to drink in the night and chases the cat to the toilet, which suggests a daily practical occurrence for a pregnant person. When the camera focuses on Lydie running the tap for a glass of water and moves to a close-up on the pouring water, however, the cut on a matching close-up reveals Stephanie as the person running water from the tap into a glass. When Stephanie stands and watches Cory, her assailant, outside his house hidden from view in the shadow of the trees, she uses the excuse of an injured deer to explain why she is out at night. Lydie, in a dream sequence, walks into the forest in the middle of the night to give birth, then during the day she passes a dead deer by the side of the road when she is driving. There is a limit to how significant dreaming while pregnant and passing a dead animal in the countryside can be to any symbolic meaning in the film.

In terms of blood, for example, in the film's opening sequence, blood on the snow is a visual narrative marker to establish that something significant has happened, but Lydie cutting her hand with a knife at her sister's house shows that she is distracted. Other than providing stylistic narrative continuity, there is no textual evidence that any of these elements have a connection to the pregnant body, the uterus or the foetus. The strength of the film's narrative, I suggest, is in the way that it transposes one pregnancy over the other. The two pregnancies are linked visually where the uterus functions as a premises for perception and an orientation point for off-screen space as the frame shifts from one body to the other.

In each analysis in this chapter, the uterus becomes a frame for narrative when thought of as a Sobchackian premises for perception and an orientation point and a Deleuzian Elsewhere. As Sobchack suggests, '[t]he act of seeing is an incarnate activity. It presents a world (any possible world imaged or imagined) whose horizons exceed its immediate visibility' (1992: 133). This echoes how Deleuze explains that the frame does not only confine the action as part of a closed set (where detail and action can also be understood to be just outside of the frame, in off-screen space, if the camera was moved) but that there are endless sets, outside of the frame. But this is not enough to understand how the spectator reads the image inside the body. Adding collaborative coding to this critical discussion demonstrates how distinct narratives intersect, or intra-act with foetal imagery. By understanding the process by which the spectator, as protagonist or viewer, makes sense of the technological image, or the virtual image, it is possible to centre an analysis that prioritizes ways of looking that is not dependent on the representation of the pregnant person. In Chapter 4, therefore, I want to extend my investigation to the internal space of the uterus by thinking of the uterus as a bioscape. I add Kim Sawchuck's (2000) notion of biotourism in film to my analysis and engage with how Charlotte Kroløkke (2010, 2011) and Roberts have extended this to the foetal scan. Chapter 4 moves beyond the frame to consider the uterus as a bioscape, an internal landscape and point of contact for biotourist narratives.

4

Internal landscapes and biotourist narratives in *The Milk of Sorrow/La teta asustada*, *Ain't Them Bodies Saints* and *Apio verde*

As I have explained, understanding the frame as a premises for perception and an orientation point helps to prioritize ways of looking rather than representation, but there remains a question about how to analyse narratives that are driven from inside the uterus. This can be when the foetus does not exist, for example, or when foetal viability outside the uterus is contested. This chapter, therefore, will add the notion of biotourism to the analysis. Biotourism means many things across different disciplines, but the notion of biotourism that is most useful to this book originates in Kim Sawchuk's (2000) film analysis of the landscape of the interior body in Richard Fleischer's 1966 film *Fantastic Voyage*.[1] Sawchuk's analysis includes the whole body, but my focus will be on the body as bioscape. In this way, I engage with how Kroløkke (2010, 2011) and Roberts (2012a, b) have used the term for their research on narratives in foetal scanning so that I can offer a specific analysis of the uterus in film.

The notion of a bioscape is one of the most important crossovers between film analysis of the internal body and the ethnographic study of the foetal ultrasound. For that reason, I will discuss biotourism in some detail at the beginning of this chapter before going on to consider how important the concept is to a reading of each film. The three films in this chapter, *The Milk of Sorrow/La teta asustada* (2009), *Ain't Them Bodies Saints* (2013) and *Apio verde* (2013), are all personal domestic dramas but are positioned differently within film genres. *The Milk of Sorrow* is a coming-of-age film that engages with ethnographic studies of communities fragmented by civil war and deals with how the aftermath of rape affects future generations. *Ain't Them Bodies Saints* is a love story that follows many genre conventions of the Hollywood Western to tell the story of a fugitive father in hiding who finds ways to communicate with his partner and child. *Apio verde* is a thriller–horror campaigning film that describes the experience of a woman who is pregnant with a foetus that has anencephaly. This condition, where part of the brain is missing, is understood to be incompatible with life outside the uterus, but the foetus is protected in law and the main character is not legally allowed to have an abortion. Despite their generic differences, all four films are concerned with the dynamic between the internal and the external body. This is expressed in the changing points of view of each character and how they negotiate the foetal presence. In each film, the pregnant body and the uterus are premises for perception, but more specifically, the frame of the uterus functions as a bioscape for narrative.

Biotourism

According to Sawchuk, there are four essential qualities of biotourism: the transposition of scale from miniature to gigantic; transformation of anatomy into landscape; the metaphorical voyage from the dark to the light; and a rhetoric of the sublime (2000: 11). It is the first two qualities – the transposition of scale (foetus and uterus) and transforming anatomy (uterus) into landscape or bioscape – that I consider most relevant to narratives around the uterus.[2] For Sawchuk, biotourism creates a bioscape that 'enlarge[s] somatic space, rendering [the] most infinitesimal cells, molecules and genetic structures into images on a scale that [. . .] can more easily [be] comprehend[ed]' (9). This gives the impression that the inside of the body is a landscape, described by Sawchuk as 'glorious vistas that can be visited' (10). In the scan, the uterus according to Roberts is constructed, 'as an alternative, metaphorical space in which one might travel to "see" or even "meet" the foetus [through] personalised narratives [and] imagined interactions' (2012a: 94). Understanding the inside of the uterus as a metaphorical meeting space suggests that the experience of meeting the foetus, even if it is separated from the body in the scan, is dependent on conceptualizing and then transforming the uterus as bioscape. It is the transposition of scale from miniature to gigantic rather than the intricacies of narrative, according to Sawchuk, that causes the spectator and/or other characters to express wonder at the internal landscape (2000: 12). A fascination, for example, of seeing a fully grown human become the size of a blood cell or the heart larger than the human. This interplay with scale is a recognizable trope within the science fiction genre but is also taken up in comedy. The *Look Who's Talking* franchise (1989–93) from the United

States that I mentioned in Chapter 1 produced a trilogy of films about the talking foetus in utero.[3] The foetus becomes larger in the frame, and in doing so the uterus is transformed as its anatomy takes up the full frame.

A transposition of scale, however, is not only dependent on what can be seen, but it also depends on the ability of the spectator to conceptualize what this change in scale means. When Sawchuk suggests that the journey through internal space is part of the 'fantasy that one can voyage into the interior space of the body without intervening in its life process, with silent footsteps, without leaving a trace', she is not talking specifically about the importance of conceptualization (2000: 21). However, the fantasy of not leaving a trace is integral to visualizing technologies of the body in that spectatorship has to be managed or interpreted. The fantasy, therefore, is not in the journey but in the perception of a voyage. When applied to the foetal scan, the voyage into internal space is not merely looking without leaving a trace. As Roberts points out, it 'involves interpreting and it is the act of interpreting' that influences and changes the spectatorial relationship around the foetus (2012a: 99). The spectatorial dynamic of a biotourist journey as one of spatial change or transformation, therefore, relies on this interpretation. This is expressed through a variety of narratives in each film: the foetal experience in *The Milk of Sorrow*, talking to the foetus in *Ain't Them Bodies Saints*, and conceptualizing a healthy child from an unviable foetus in *Apio verde*.

A biotourist journey could be described as any journey through the lived body, yet when talking about the uterus it is important to acknowledge that this bodily space is invested with cultural meaning and emotion distinct from other major organs or space in the body such as the heart or abdomen.[4] Not only is the uterus a physiological location where another human being can grow, but it is understood as a heavily gendered space integrally linked to the female in a way that other parts of the body are not. Although the space is gendered or sexed physiologically, the meaning created by and attached to narratives around the uterus is not inherently gender specific. This does not negate the ways in which the female and male reproductive body are understood as distinct. It is important, nevertheless, to acknowledge how unbalanced this becomes when narratives of reproduction rely on gender codes. The male reproductive organs, for example, do not have the same identities as cultural and emotional spaces. Male bodily fluids do, however, have some cultural significance. Emily Martin (1991) says that gender stereotypes in medical texts describe the anthropomorphic way the egg and sperm are given male and female (performative) gender characteristics and describes the way sperm 'have a mission' to 'penetrate' the ovum with their 'whiplashlike motion and strong lurches' on a 'perilous quest' (489). She compares this to the 'large and passive' ovum which has been sitting 'on the shelf [from birth], slowly degenerating and ageing like overstocked inventory' (486–9). As Monica J. Casper and Lisa J. Moore (2009) explain, sperm is considered in terms of the individual (man) rather than the life and death of the human species. By contrast, the bodily fluids of the female reproductive body such as breast milk, they explain, are 'made to speak about broader collectives such as families, communities, nations, and even the planet' (128–9).[5] This explains why breast milk – which physiologically relies on the action of the uterus and the foetus – is positioned as capable of transmitting trauma within communities, as is the case, for example, in *The Milk of Sorrow*.

Transforming internal space by reconfiguring scale to create narratives is a form of storytelling. As Kroløkke suggests, feminist communication analyses help to articulate a way of demystifying and 'deconstruct[ing] scientific storytelling' (2010: 139). Her use of biotourism in relation to the scan is to recognize the 'interplay between pregnancy and visualization technology' (139). As Kroløkke says, biotourism positions the pregnant body and the uterus as 'baby's first home', as well as a 'transparent container that we hungrily gaze through' and beyond in order to consume the experience on the scan screen (149; 151). This suggests once more that the frame of the uterus can function as a location or screen without having to pay any attention to the pregnant body. This is exactly what is happening in *Apio verde*, where the pregnant body, the pregnant person and the actual foetus become irrelevant to the way in which other characters construct a conceptual, or virtual, 'baby'. The bioscape of the uterus emphasizes the fragmentation or the slippage between the reproductive body and the foetal image (forming its own crystal image, see Chapter 2), which suggests that negotiating the image is different depending on who is looking. This takes on additional meaning when applied to pregnancy and the pregnant body. Fragmentation as a concept also suggests a coming apart – a degradation – or even a distortion where, in the scan, 'the foetal-maternal environment is turned inside out, the private made semi-public and the foetus is brought alive' (Kroløkke 2011: 33). The uterus turned inside out is a visceral image that not only fragments the maternal body; it also fragments and distorts the imagery of the whole body, meaning that the landscape of the body is changed conceptually, making it a virtual location. Making the uterus – and the foetus – public allows the space of the uterus to be read as separate from the body and from a perspective that is placed outside of the body. In this process, where the foetus is turned out to public gaze, the actual foetus disappears as it 'comes alive' as a virtual foetus. Or another way of putting it is that the foetus becomes something else because of this negotiation of corporeal imagery.

This idea of a negotiated, conceptualized spectatorship around the reproductive body speaks to the debate around the pregnant body and the separation of the foetus from the pregnant body, but it also suggests how the concept of corporeality is crucial to understanding what this separation does. Corporeal sensibility can describe the relationship of the lived body to the environment, and it can also explain the way a film is constructed for effect. Giuliana Bruno, when comparing film to architecture, says that both are visual media that are experienced haptically as a 'spatial form of sensuous cognition' and that 'film is a modern cartography [whereby] its haptic way of site-seeing turns pictures into an architecture, transforming them into a geography of lived and living space' (2002: 6–9).[6] Bruno's detailed analysis of the relationship between art, architecture and film helps to contextualize the interconnectedness of narrative through lived space where corporeal sensibility is understood as an embodied relationship with space, and with time. Yet when Sawchuk addresses biotourism and the bioscape, she describes the internal landscape as involving the whole body which is mapped out in visually recognized landmarks – the heart, the lungs, the blood vessels and the brain – each bodily part represented by its physiological function. These individual physiological functions are then seen as an integral part of the whole person. In the foetal ultrasound scan, biotourism is fundamentally different. Recognition is mapped by visually identifying parts of the foetus's body (leg, head, toes, face) as separate from the mother's body (placenta, umbilical cord, uterine wall). This fragments the physiological process by changing the nature of the internal landscape, opening it up to interpretation and foregrounding the virtual image of the foetus.

This can encourage the anatomy of the uterus to be thought of as 'noise' (Krolønkke 2010: 146) even as the foetus becomes the central feature of the ultrasound and takes on a life or aliveness of its own. As Krolønkke suggests, 'by visually objectifying the foetus, it becomes "alive"' (2011: 21). This objectification echoes Petchesky's (1987) notion of the fetishized foetus in the scan where the image of the foetus, separated from the pregnant woman, is understood as a living being that is 'suspended in space' (277). Although understanding the foetus as a fetishistic image in this way addresses the cultural iconography of the scanned foetus, it does not fully address the way the foetus, or rather the technological image of the foetus, sparks a narrative response. By narrative response, I mean the engagement of the spectator and protagonist to narratives around the uterus. This is a self-reflective process in each of the films in this chapter: in *The Milk of Sorrow*, the adult woman narrates her own interpretation of what she could see in her mother's uterus; in *Ain't Them Bodies Saints*, the conversation with the foetus is a self-reflective narrative with no input from the foetus itself; and in *Apio verde*, the scan image of the unviable foetus in the uterus contrasts with what others understand as a healthy child. Attributing meaning beyond the physiology of pregnancy and the physicality of the foetus ultimately silences (or eliminates) both unless the uterus is thought of as a bioscape.

Although the narratives in each film suggest that there is a form of corporeal or physical communication taking place, it must be acknowledged that the uterus itself does not have inherent interactive qualities. In each of the films in this chapter, I argue that the protagonists (and the spectator) are negotiating internal space. Thinking of the uterus as a bioscape emphasizes that this negotiation is not a response as such but a more complicated system of attributing meaning where none is inherently present. The foetus can be present in the bioscape of the uterus, but it is not accurate to say that any responses to it could be called an interaction, nor is it accurate to say that the foetus interacts with protagonists or the spectator. As I have already explained, rather than thinking about interaction, the process of negotiation is more akin to Barad's concept of agential realism where intra-actions speak to the 'inseparability of "objects" and "agencies of observation"' (1998: 96, see Chapter 2). When I mentioned this Baradian notion in my discussion on methodologies, I emphasized that this notion of interconnectivity – intra-action – between technologies and the body is a recurring emphasis throughout the book. Going back to my discussion about the uterus as a premises for perception in Chapter 3, it is worth noting that Sobchack gives a suggestion for this kind of intra-active dynamic when she describes 'the *perception of expression* and the *expression of perception*' (1992: 5, emphasis in original). Barad insists that the object (and I include the foetus and the uterus) does not come before interpretation and that agency is not something that is assigned; there is always an interconnection. Barad's critical discussion is more complex, as I have already suggested, but I think that her insistence that any engagement with technologies involves a question about intention (of the technology) and interpretation (of the technology) is crucial to understanding the dynamic of the scan. For the purposes of this chapter and the critical discussion in this book, the narrative space of the uterus is thought of as a place that depends on intra-action.

To return to the tension between the notions of separateness and connectedness, inasmuch as the ultrasound creates a separation between the pregnant body and the foetus, there is a sense that the separation is, in part, owing to the unacknowledged importance of the embodied experience of pregnancy. Sonia Meyers (2010) argues that even though the ultrasound scan 'visually deletes pregnant bodies', there is an interconnectedness of the machine with the body and with embodied existence that she argues is essential to understand (198–201). Whether it is intra-action, or interconnectedness, there is certainly an importance to how visualizing technologies give information as a way of 'seeing'. I touched on this in the Introduction when I talked about how the technician and the medic might think differently about ultrasound technology: the technician understands the importance of the transducer's connection with the body and the medic is interested in what the technology can tell them about the internal body. Meyers's argument seeks to 'rearticulate the technical aspects of fetal image production' to investigate how the scan can be considered as part of an embodied experience (199). The embodied experience, she suggests, depends on interconnectivity, not only in the scan room but also in the social environment.⁷ The constant pulling away from physiology and physicality of pregnancy and the uterus can be explained in part by how metaphors of the female reproductive body refigure them as a bodily space. The machine metaphor, used by Emily Martin (1987), encourages reproduction to be read as production on a grand scale and for birth to be considered as work, but it also suggests a spatial reconfiguration of the uterus where it can be transformed from a 'home' (for the foetus) into a factory (54–67).⁸ The uterus also then becomes a machine, or even *the* machine, rather than the woman, in the birthing process.⁹ This movement between models of pregnancy and birth explains how pregnancy becomes a 'mediated experience' used as a way for the pregnant person and those around them to frame their experiences to transform their lives (KrolØkke 2010: 142). When pregnancy becomes mediated, the foetus is also mediated so that it exists as a separate entity whose personhood is not dependent on the pregnant person. This is a key discussion point in the abortion debate, but when the pregnant body becomes detached or separated from the uterus, it suggests that the emphasis on mediation results in neither the pregnancy nor the space of the uterus belonging to the individual: it becomes a communal space.

Whether a communal space or a socially constructed space (as Stormer (2000) says, see Chapter 2), negotiating the uterus could be described as a form of cartography whereby protagonists and spectator must map and chart their way through the architecture of the uterus to construct their own narrative. This may be based on what they can see or hear or what they imagine can be happening in the body. In *The Milk of Sorrow*, for example, the protagonist places herself in the uterus and her voiced memory is of her looking out through it, as if the uterus were a screen on which she sees her past. As Bruno suggests, 'film and architecture share a dimension of living [as] the space of one's lived experiences. In other words, they are about lived space and the narrative of space' (2002: 64). The foetus looking out or the pregnant person looking in suggests that pregnancy can be reassembled spatially and temporally. The pregnant person can be separated from their foetus, as KrolØkke suggests, and encouraged to travel through their own internal space where they 'temporarily leave their bodies and enter a new spatial experience [as] both host (the one toured on) and visitor' (KrolØkke 2010: 148). This suggests that not only does pregnancy transform many narratives but the pregnant person can also see and experience their own pregnancy as something that they are external to and can travel through. Biotourism, André Jansson (2002) suggests, is an 'analytical concept' where 'being a tourist means temporarily leaving one's home for a certain preselected destination [...] for the main sake of gaining new spatial experiences' (431).¹⁰ The concept of tourism, while problematic in itself, is particularly helpful here to understand how a pregnant person can engage with their own body as if they are outside of it and as if they are experiencing it as something new.

Although the notion of tourism is culturally and historically specific, it nonetheless explains how spatial experiences can be attributed to an internal landscape that is not accessible and to a destination to which one cannot travel. But still, the metaphors around the internal body, the uterus and the foetus can be created and styled in the rhetoric of journey and discovery, not only of external outdoor landscapes but also of inside spaces. The uterine landscape (in promotional material for the scan) becomes a 'home, a playground, or a room', and the uterine wall a 'blanket, a pillow or a window' (Kroløkke 2010: 149). These metaphors, Kroløkke explains, encourage people to 'experiment with new identities [as] social, collective events' (2011: 19).[11] This is what is happening when the biological father in *Ain't Them Bodies Saints* creates a whole life for his unborn foetus, and when spectators of the pregnant body do the same in *Apio verde*. The process of interpreting the space of the internal body as outdoor locations, interiors, comforting textures and a way of foreseeing or creating new kinship identities is incredibly complex. It suggests a conceptual and tactile relationship with the body that does not depend on the body being touched. In some ways, this is similar to the sensorial quality of film where watching the film becomes, as Barker suggests, an '*intimate* experience [and] *close* connection' rather than something that is only visual (2009: 2, emphasis in original). What is important here is how it is the extreme complexity of spectatorship and of intra-action that transforms the body into something meaningful. Thinking through narrative construction as biotourism can provide a critical framework to articulate how bodily space can be understood as a journey through a physical landscape. This also offers a way to understand how the uterus as an unseen space within the body can affect the other bodies that it 'touches'. By touch, I mean not only the physical in relation to the pregnant body and its embodiment but also conceptually in the sense of evoking an emotional journey.

Somatic talk: Touch and the belly

A recurrent motif in each film is how touch, as tactility and as voice, suggests presence on the screen and adds to the sense of a journey through, and emotional connection to, the pregnant body. The voice has a corporeal quality whereby it can 'speak to' that which is inside the body. In the case of *Ain't Them Bodies Saints*, this enables dialogue to be addressed to the foetus even if the foetus does not respond. In this film, the voice-over defines character, but it also takes the place of physical presence when the character's presence can be 'felt' as their voice is heard reading their own letter. As Davina Quinlivan (2012) points out, the very notion of breathing 'stimulates new ways in which to question the nature of seeing, perceiving and sensing things which are not always entirely visible in film [and so investigate the] interstices between visibility and invisibility [where] sound serves to stimulate our perception beyond what is visible on screen' (1). What I find useful about what Quinlivan says is the way that she pinpoints the sound of breath as a haptic quality, explaining that her work 'envisages this point of contact according to the ways in which breathing unsettles borders between the inside and the outside [where] breathing suggests a relationship with the image that involves the *mind* of the viewer as well as the body' (21, emphasis in original). This helps to understand the liminality of narratives that are voiced around the uterus where 'haptic hearing' from the point of view of the protagonists and spectator is as important as visuality (21).[12] An appreciation of haptic hearing helps to explain how narrative is constructed by the intra-actions between the protagonists who appear on-screen and intra-actions with the hidden protagonist, the foetus, that take place off-screen. When the dialogue is addressed directly to the foetus, it performs, as Sallie Han (2009) argues, an important embodied communication which she calls, 'belly talk' (307).[13] The foetal object is not necessarily included in this intra-action but as Han suggests, talking to the foetus 'accomplishes important cultural work [...] as kin and kinship become constructed through talk' (305). Although in *Apio verde*, the foetal narrative is constructed as having both a positive and negative presence, the foetus is not voiced. Its perceived corporeal presence, however, is discussed as a 'baby' with a healthy future and also paradoxically as being a foetus that is unable to survive in the present. In *The Milk of Sorrow* and *Ain't Them Bodies Saints*, the foetal narrative is constructed by the main protagonists where kinship takes the form of voicing the foetus's past and future life. Corporeality and the spatiality of the body, then, affect narrative progression.

Corporeality depends on the corporeality of the film, the corporeality of the protagonists and the corporeality of the spectator. The perception of a biotourist voyage through the uterus is dependent on all three. My analysis of each film in this chapter is dependent on understanding where the point of contact appears. As Quinlivan suggests, understanding the importance of sound and voice is a question of diegesis, narrative and mise en scène. Quinlivan suggests that sound is a point of contact, but in my reading of the films, I suggest that there are multiple points of contact that can be understood to meet at the uterus. The way the voice, dialogue and sound touch each protagonist adds an additional complexity to the corporeality of the films. A cartography of the uterus, as a way to understand narratives around the uterus, must address the wider context of what Martine Beugnet describes as 'the specificity of film's corporeality' including the effect of rhythm, tone and framing (2007: 6–10).[14] The point of contact may be when protagonists recall their own physical presence in the uterus as a location (*The Milk of Sorrow*), or to making their voice heard to the foetus who cannot hear them (*Ain't Them Bodies Saints*), and for other protagonists to read the pregnant body and foetus as different to how they are physically

(*Apio verde*). In my reading of each film, the uterus will be considered as a bioscape for narratives. I suggest that the bioscape – the uterus – should be thought of as a point of contact for narratives.

The Milk of Sorrow

In *The Milk of Sorrow*, a young woman, Fausta (Magaly Solier), lives a sheltered life in present-day Peru. She lives in the outskirts of the capital Lima with her mother Perpetua (Bárbara Lazón) and her uncle's family. They have all been displaced because of the civil war that occurred in Peru in the 1980s. The family believe that Fausta has been affected by *la teta asustada*, the frightened teat, a condition caused by her mother's traumatic experience of attack and torture in the civil war. This *teta asustada* began when Fausta was in the uterus and continued when she was a baby as she drank her mother's breast milk. The condition means that Fausta is anxious around unfamiliar people and is prone to frequent nosebleeds and fainting. After Fausta's mother dies, Fausta takes a job working in the house of a middle-class pianist Aida (Susi Sánchez). She does this so that she can pay to have her mother's body taken back to the place she was born. Fausta slowly gets accustomed to walking through the market to the house but remains shy and taciturn. One day she faints, and her uncle takes her to the doctor where she is found to have a potato growing in her vagina. The potato is now infecting her uterus. Fausta tells her uncle that she has not placed the potato there for contraception, but as a protection against violation. Fausta gains more confidence, but her employer steals the tune she sings every day saying she can earn the pearls in her necklace if she does so. Although Aida does not give her the pearls she promised, Fausta manages to take her mother's body on the journey north to her homeland. Fausta has a sophisticated knowledge of historical events that happened to her and her family while she was in her mother's uterus and she recounts this memory as a foetus. She tells this story through song to recollect the past and contextualize the present. Fausta retells her mother's testimony of violence, creating a biotourist narrative. She appears in this narrative as a foetal character. This foetal character is her and she explains what she saw and what happened to her family.

The dual narrative reflects the film's two main themes, the lived reality of a community displaced by civil war and a young woman who has led a sheltered life entering adulthood in the outside world after the death of her mother. The title of the film is taken from the notion of fright – *susto* – as an embodied reaction to trauma and can be translated literally into English as 'the frightened teat'. The film speaks to the reality of the lives of indigenous people resettled in the capital Lima after the 1980s civil war in Peru, and the context of the film is taken from Kimberley Theidon's (2013) ethnographic research which catalogues the testimonies of women who were systematically sexually assaulted and raped during the war.[15] The film has invited many interpretations that are often based on how the film represents individual history and trauma. These themes are, for example, personal and national healing (Douglas J. Weatherford 2020), unlived trauma (Mario Županović 2019), post-memory, transgenerational trauma and resilience (Adriana Rojas 2017), the embodiment of trauma (Enrique Bernales Albites and Leila Gomez 2017), and trauma and violence (Rebecca Maseda 2016). The film has also been defended as a creative filmic study of facts and fiction (Caroline Rueda 2015), and thought of as magical realism (Stephen M. Hart 2015), but it has also attracted criticism for its 'art film ambiguity over political coherence' (Patricia White 2015: 193). The director Llosa herself has been criticized for her previous film *Madeinusa* (2006) for perpetuating stereotypes of indigenous women and Andean life (Iliana Pagán-Teitelbaum 2012). Maseda, however, suggests that *The Milk of Sorrow* holds an 'ethnocentric view [that is] pro-indigenous' and that the film 'offers a [filmic] hybrid site of reconciliation' (2016: 2). Sarah Barrow (2013) suggests, however, that Llosa's appeal (to funders and transnational film festivals) is that each of Llosa's protagonists 'offers the possibility of a different kind of transformation and resistance within the context of repression' (198).[16] The fact that the film provokes commentary for its content, production and filmmaker is not unusual, but it suggests that understanding representation of women, of Andean culture, of nation and of trauma is not simply universal and my reading does not suggest otherwise.

In the film, although Fausta lives as part of an extended family with her uncle and cousins, she exists on the edges of their lives. She avoids unnecessary speech and eye contact with other people. The close relationship she has with her mother is established in the opening scenes where the spectator is told – by Fausta's mother Perpetua – in graphic detail about the violence inflicted on their family. The violence has imbued the bodies of Fausta and her mother with *susto* and this manifests itself in different ways. Perpetua's breast milk and nipples are contaminated by *susto*, and Fausta's entire body is infused with it making her prone to fainting and bleeding. The recollection of trauma is crucial to each woman as it justifies Fausta's physical and emotional demeanour, and it provides narrative continuity of testimony from the primary witness of trauma: her mother. The uterus becomes a shared embodied space that connects the two women. It is crucial for the spectator to understand the transposition of scale that allows Fausta, as an adult woman, to narrate her experience of being in the uterus. The shared history of daughter and mother creates an internal landscape which includes what the unborn (Fausta as foetus) can 'see' from the inside of the uterus, what is happening outside of the pregnant body and what is happening to the pregnant body. The uterus is turned inside out so that Fausta can become the embodied narrator of her foetal self.

Fausta narrates her embodied experience of her mother's rape – and her father's death – by describing what she saw and felt. She recounts this so that it becomes part of her present. Her narration is part of the grieving process for her mother, but it also enables Fausta to keep what happened in the past fresh in her mind. Her testimony presents a challenge to the spectator. She recalls historical events that may have been witnessed by others and may be corroborated, but the story she tells is from the point of view of the foetus. The reliability of her testimony, therefore, depends on the spectator being able to imagine the foetus as capable of seeing and feeling and to imagine its location in the uterus. Importantly, Fausta's memory suggests that the foetus has some objective understanding of what was happening while in utero. Even if the foetus was not capable of remembering or understanding and even if the recollection is an amalgamation of stories passed on to Fausta through her mother's storytelling, her biotourist testimony is one of an embodied witness (foetus) who was present when the events took place and is now narrating that past from her subjective point of view in the present.

The narrative dynamic between Fausta and her mother is initiated in Perpetua's dialogue at the beginning of the film, which creates a call and response not only in the present but also in the past, between the unborn, the living and the dead. Fausta's mother establishes that the foetus in utero could 'see' the physical abuse she was subjected to when she says that her attackers had 'no pity for my daughter watching them from inside'. This is an acknowledgement of the way this attack would mark Fausta in the future, and sets up a virtual narrative space, but Fausta's response to her mother's story takes place after her mother has died. Fausta strokes her mother's dead body in the same way she stroked her hair when she was alive (Figure 4.1).

FIGURE 4.1 *Fausta joins her mother beneath the blanket in* The Milk of Sorrow.

This touching brings them together physically and Fausta buries her head in her mother's blanket, stroking her body through the material in order to be as physically close to her mother as possible, even joining her under the blanket in death as if Perpetua was still pregnant. The physical closeness of mother and daughter emphasizes how important touch is in the transfer of memories. It is almost as if the sense of touch between daughter and mother invokes memory for them both. As Perpetua tells Fausta at the beginning of the film, 'I don't see my memories; it's as if I no longer lived.' Exchanging her embodied experience as memory is critical to Perpetua's sense of being alive; then, as she dies, she transfers these memories to Fausta so that they stay in the present. This means that the transfer and sharing of memory forms a bridge between past and future as if the two women have been on the same journey through life and that Perpetua's memory is Fausta's. The call and response of the two women develop a biotourist dynamic where there is a constant interplay between the inside and the outside of the body. The uterus becomes a virtual narrative space where each memory exists. Each woman provides a narrative by transposing the scale of the foetus and interpreting what it can see and feel.

The importance of the embodied testimony of the foetus is reinforced in the film as the spectator is brought into the action when Fausta directs her gaze to the camera. This happens after her mother's death where Fausta's narration is presented as an internal and extra diegetic monologue. She directs her testimony towards her mother's body lying next to her in the bed. She is talking to her mother, but it is important that Fausta's testimony is heard and understood by the spectator. This is emphasized by the way Fausta – in profile – sings her opening line (Figure 4.2). Fausta's lips are closed and this emphasizes that her memory is conceptual and visual as it forms her past-lived and present-living experience. Closing her lips isolates her testimony, highlighting the silence of trauma, and encourages the spectator to listen to her dialogue as she says, 'I saw it all from your belly.'[17] By removing her synch dialogue, the spectator is presented with Fausta's gaze, which is not only the gaze of an adult woman but also the gaze of the foetus. Yet, it is Fausta as foetus who tells the story. The singing voice gives narrative detail and takes the place of any physical proximity in this duologue between the living and the dead.[18] Fausta offers her conceptual and virtual narrative to interpret her experience in utero for the spectator. Her biotourist narrative confirms that her foetal self was capable of seeing and feeling. This is confirmed when she turns her head to look out at the spectator and moves her gaze to look directly into the camera saying, 'I felt the slashing of your body' (Figure 4.3). By facing out of the frame towards the spectator and telling her mother that she felt the slashing of her body, Fausta acknowledges her mother's testimony and forces the spectator to identify with the 'aliveness' of the foetus who is directing their testimony towards them. This short sequence establishes the foetal narrative and,

FIGURE 4.2 *Fausta narrates her experience of being in the uterus in* The Milk of Sorrow.

FIGURE 4.3 *Fausta faces the camera to describe the blows on her mother's body in* The Milk of Sorrow.

importantly, depends on the spectator's ability to transpose the foetus as narrator onto the body of the adult woman, Fausta. It also establishes the uterus as a virtual and metaphorical space, the home of the foetus.

The narrative strands that each woman describe include the history of violence within the wider community, but when Fausta's uncle insists, in the face of medical evidence to the contrary, that she does have *la teta asustada*, it is clear that Fausta's embodied condition is also an important part of how violence is remembered in the community. Fausta's body is important, and her physical responsiveness to intense emotions with frequent fainting and nosebleeds suggests that she is physically different from the other members of the family and extended community. Her embodied testimony, then, is a living reminder of collective trauma. Her embodied reaction to being anxious or frightened is to faint or to bleed from her nose, but physiologically the fainting and the bleeding are not related, she is told by a doctor. Both, however, are markers of *susto* and are considered part of the same embodied condition despite the lack of clinical importance. Her embodied difference gives her presence in the family a liminal and virtual quality where she is both part of and not part of their shared daily life. When Fausta displays melancholy characteristics emphasizing her sadness and anxiety, they are also part of the communal memory.[19] Although Fausta is physically part of the family and fully involved with activities they organize, her liminality comes from her emotional rather than physical distance from the rest of the family. The experience of rape shared by Fausta and her mother has repercussions for the rest of the community so that the biotourist narrative around the bioscape of the uterus becomes three things: the location that contains the unborn, a historical site for war crimes and the window through which the unborn can 'see' historical events.

As the film progresses, it is clear that this narrative is an important factor in Fausta's physical life and health. She protects herself from violation – rape – by inserting a potato into her vagina to place a physical barrier between her uterus and any possible rapist. Although it is the potato that is making her ill, Fausta has put it in in her body as a response to the historic violation of her mother's body.[20] Importantly, the potato is in her vagina and infecting the uterus, so it is not placed conceptually in the same location as any foetus.[21] The close proximity of Fausta as a foetus, however, places both her and her mother at the site of this abuse with Fausta inside her mother's uterus. Their biotourist narrative is a result of this closeness, the 'glorious vistas' of the uterus replaced by violent images. This biotourist journey begins with the voice of Perpetua singing her memories of war and rape. Although she sings this to Fausta as the only protagonist in the room, her song is also for the benefit of the spectator (the 'anonymous *tú*' according to Rojas 2017: 300).[22] Perpetua's voice-over monologue is sung over a blackout screen, which emphasizes her words and disarms the spectator with their own imaginative interpretation of who is singing (Figure 4.4). The ambient sound of the room, which includes the wind blowing, forms a quiet but distinct sonic background and establishes the physicality of the room. The mother's dialogue is prioritized and the use of voice-over, before vision, establishes narrative detail: that the story being told is important, that it is in the past tense, that it uses descriptions of extreme violence and violation, and that the victim was pregnant when she was raped. The tone of the voice

FIGURE 4.4 *Perpetua begins her song over a blank screen in* The Milk of Sorrow.

is high, and the black screen mean that it is not clear whether the singer is young or old, male or female. When the image of the dying mother fades up from black, the juxtaposition of the image and the sound is profound (Figure 4.5). The serenity of the ageing, dying woman in the care of her young daughter serves as a counterpoint to the violence in her story.

The physical and emotional tactility between Fausta and her mother foreshadows the significance that the loss of her mother is to Fausta. Fausta's mother tells her to sing to her so that she can 'freshen [her] drying memory'. This suggests that Perpetua's memory has not gone but depends on each other's ability to remember. The dialogue is accompanied by physical action as Fausta is seen in close proximity to her mother, rearranging her hair and repositioning her on the bed. Her mother's body is part of her everyday so that when she dies Fausta continues this close physicality, cleaning her mother's body and washing her clothes. She washes her mother's clothes so that she will not return to their village 'smelling of sadness'.[23] In a later sequence, although Perpetua is not producing breast milk, touching her nipple still represents the transference of the trauma – *susto* – through the frightened teat. The way in which the women from the community prepare Perpetua's body (Figure 4.6) establishes that she is not ostracized from the community and her body is touched by them all.[24] Fausta is directed to wash her mother's nipple so that the other women will not become contaminated by touching it. She appears under the sheet as an oval shape sitting upright, like an upturned pregnant belly, as if she is the foetus once more in adult size (Figure 4.7). Her mother's nipple is the main body part that represents the contamination of her uterus and reproductive system.

FIGURE 4.5 *In the fade-up from black, Perpetua is frail and dying in* The Milk of Sorrow.

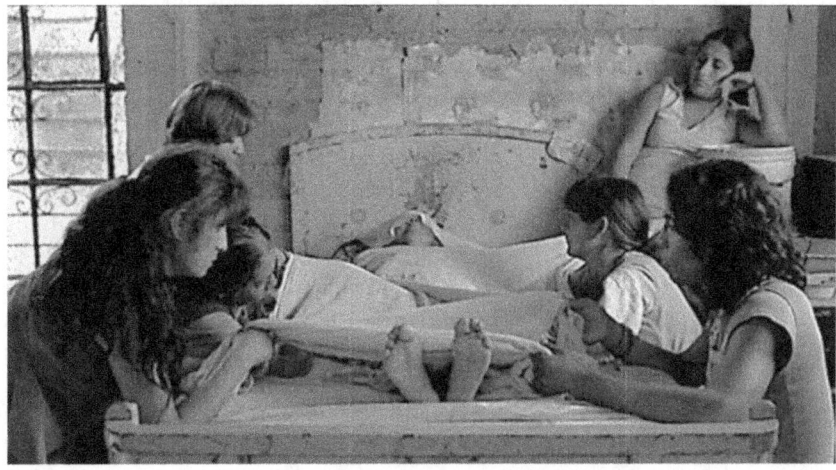

FIGURE 4.6 *The women communally wash Perpetua's body in* The Milk of Sorrow.

By contrast, *susto* affects the whole of Fausta's body. Fausta's corporeality as a foetus directly affects how she understands her corporeality as an adult. It is as though her experience as a foetus in the uterus remains part of how she sees herself and how she can accept her role in the community. Her lived body experience recalled as a biotourist narrative belongs to the whole community so that Fausta's body represents the traumatic effect on her whole family as well as the larger community of people traumatized and

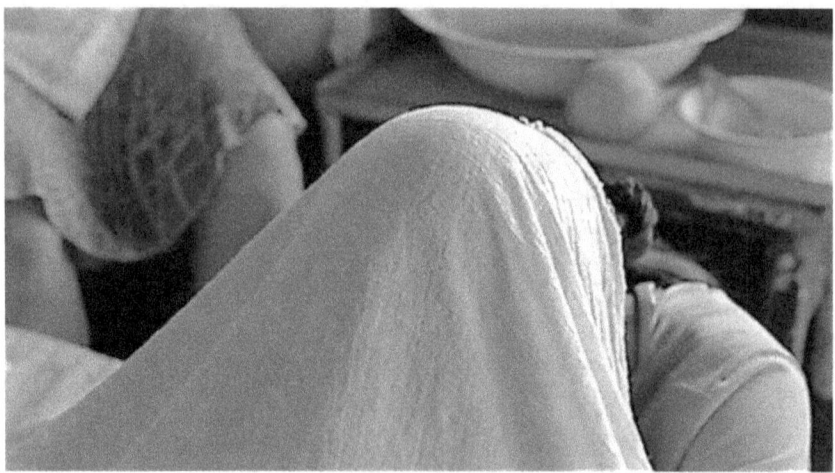

FIGURE 4.7 *Fausta washes her mother's nipple in* The Milk of Sorrow.

displaced by war. Fausta's corporeality, therefore, is an integral part of a community coming to terms with its past and becomes a way of preserving memory.[25] In this way, there is pressure from the community for Fausta to continue to display their trauma through her body as if they too are 'hungrily gazing' at and into her body as a reminder of their own past. The uterus in this narrative serves as a bioscape that not only unites mother and daughter, but it also serves as a virtual location for communal trauma. The spectator is encouraged to make sense of the foetal narration by identifying with Fausta as she recounts her experience of seeing and feeling while in utero as part of a biotourist narrative. The transformation in scale of the foetus from miniature inside the uterus to the life-size body of the grown woman is emphasized by the constant reference to Fausta's and Perpetua's bodies so that they can be thought of as landscapes and as conduits for narratives and memories of trauma. The film reflects the oral testimonies of many, but crucially the uterus becomes a narrative space that is virtual and communal.

Ain't Them Bodies Saints

Rather than the uterus functioning as a bioscape for communal memories, the uterus in *Ain't Them Bodies Saints* frames and encloses the foetus so that it can be voiced by one of the film's main protagonists. The film is set in an unspecified era, which might be the present day, in the southern states of the United States. The main protagonists are a young couple Bob Muldoon (Casey Affleck) and Ruth Guthrie (Rooney Mara) who find out they are expecting a baby just before they commit a robbery and Bob is arrested.[26] A policeman is killed and Bob takes the blame for wounding another police officer Patrick (Ben Foster), when it was Ruth who actually fired the gun. While Bob is in jail, he writes to Ruth frequently. Ruth, meanwhile, gives birth to Sylvie (Kennadie and Jacklynn Smith) and is settled with her daughter and watched over by her neighbour and guardian Skerritt (Keith Carradine). Three years later Bob, after other attempts, escapes from jail and makes his way on foot across the county to Ruth. Bob writes to Ruth who plans to leave with him. Patrick knows that Bob has escaped so he questions Ruth and takes her personal letters from Bob. Bob finds his way to Skerritt's store and Skerritt warns him to stay away from Ruth and their daughter warning him that there are people out to kill him. Bob visits Ruth but stays outside the house and just watches Ruth and Sylvie. Later, Skerritt is shot and Patrick takes Ruth and Sylvie to the police station for their own safety. Bob, meanwhile, is cornered by a group of bounty hunters and shot. When Patrick takes Ruth home, they discover that her front door is open. They find Bob lying on the floor of the bedroom bleeding heavily. Sylvie comes into the bedroom and she sees Bob who looks at her. Patrick takes Sylvie to another room and Bob dies in Ruth's arms.

Bob is separated from Ruth and his unborn child for most of the film, and the film charts his traumatic journey back to them. Their lives are, therefore, fragmented, but their narratives are intricately connected through their embodied history and the way they communicate with each other. Their embodiment is highlighted in the narrative in the juxtaposition of images, voice and music that bridge the physical and emotional spaces between them, and in the repeated sequences of actual touching between protagonists.[27] The film is positioned as a traditional Western, which includes small-town life, shoot-outs, jailbirds and the battle for the female hand. The film has not attracted much academic interest, and film reviewer Laura Kern (2013) suggests that '[w]hile it may not have a whole lot of plot, or even depth, Lowery's film – set in Seventies rural Texas – is so richly textured and visually exquisite that it hardly matters' (63). According to her film reviewer colleague Meredith Slifkin (2013), '[a]s befits any postmodern Western, *Ain't Them Bodies Saints* necessarily addresses the idea of the death of the West as we have known it', and she explains that the opening shots of the film 'illuminat[e] the mythic space in which doomed lovers Ruth [and] Bob [. . .] share precious moments together before they are separated by the law and fate' (66). This richly textured mythic place lends itself to the film's narrative core which is based on the spaces and silences between protagonists.

The nature of the film, with its slow pace and repeated scenes, means that the spectator experiences these spaces and silences as part of its corporeality. The corporeality of the film creates a frame for emotional connections through the rhythm or pace of the film and the use of naturalistic lighting that gives an air of authenticity. The musical soundtrack evokes an unknown era that, as mentioned earlier, is presumed to be the southern states of the United States. Corporeality is expressed through the closeness and distance of voice, close-up framing, protagonists touching, and where tactility is not always because characters are in close proximity. This establishes, for the benefit of the spectator, the close embodied connection that Bob and Ruth have already experienced. It also stresses tactile memories that can be understood to influence the intra-action between Bob and his unborn child. In my reading of the film, I concentrate on small moments in the narrative which, I argue, establish a biotourist narrative between Bob and his unborn child.

The opening and closing sequences of the film do more than mirror each other and bookend the film: they provide narrative information that at the end of the film makes sense of a conversation with the foetus. Bob and Ruth are physically separated at the beginning of the film, and their relationship is mediated by letters so that words, and the sound of the voice in the voice-over, become integral to their linked narratives around the uterus. The final sequence in the film illustrates how powerful Bob's spoken narrative has been throughout – describing his imagined relationship with his unborn foetus as his 'daughter'. This is reflected in the matching cinematography and mise en scène in the opening sequence (Figure 4.8) and the final sequence (Figure 4.9). The final sequence mirrors part of the opening to the film. Both sequences rely on Bob's voice. Each sequence gives narrative information, but the opening sequence only makes sense when the voice-over completes Bob's dialogue. The reason that this is complex is that the synch voice is

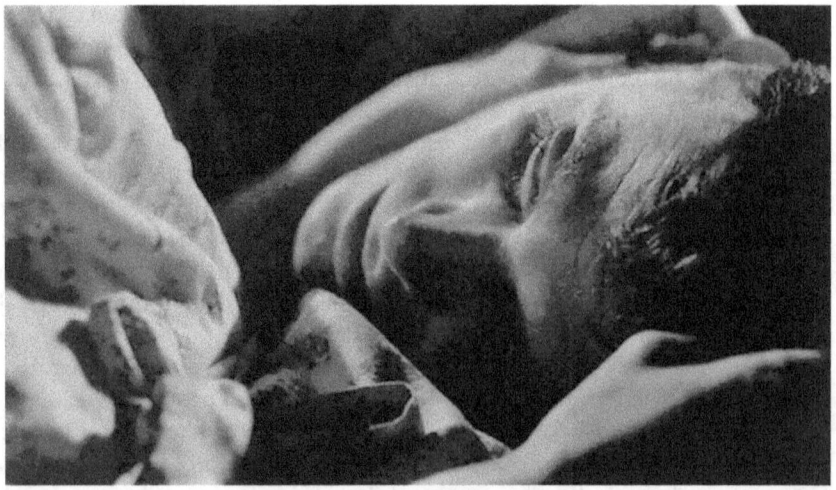

FIGURE 4.8 *At the beginning of the film, Bob talks to the foetus through Ruth's body in* Ain't Them Bodies Saints.

FIGURE 4.9 *Bob is cradled by Ruth as he dies at the end of the film in* Ain't Them Bodies Saints.

replaced by the voice-over, making Bob's narrative fragment. The voice-over provides missing dialogue from the opening sequence. Understood narratively as a conversation with Ruth, when the dialogue is voiced in full at the end of the film, it is revealed that she is not the person that he is talking to, it is the foetus.

Matching shots highlight the connection between events at the beginning and at the end of the film, but they also emphasize the physicality of Bob and Ruth's relationship. The final sequence includes a flashback to the opening sequence where Bob's head is cradled by Ruth in her lap as he sings through her dress to the foetus. The dialogue is from the opening sequence, which now plays over the matching shot at the end of the film, where Ruth cradles Bob as he is dying. In effect, the opening narrative is being filled in at the end of the film. In the flashback opening scene when Bob stops singing, he begins to talk, and we think he is talking to Ruth. He says, 'let me tell you about the future . . . in the future I am a very old man.' As soon as Bob says 'let me tell you about the future', there is an immediate cut to a close-up on Bob's blooded hand as Ruth takes his gun from him. His dialogue from the opening sequence carries on and forms an audio bridge between the two sequences. His voice-over says, 'we're in our house where everything is green and the sun's almost set.' The two sequences are briefly, but rapidly, intercut to establish a visual connection. The importance of this for the spectator is that this offers new narrative information. The pace of intercutting slows to allow the two scenes to become more defined, and the spectator is privy to additional information given in Bob's dialogue.

This intercutting is difficult to describe but what is important is its effect. Essentially a narrative space is being created that is guided by the filmic information on-screen. There is, however, another narrative space which I suggest is the uterus as premises for perception, the bioscape. As Bob's narrative is centred on the foetus – as actual in the opening sequence and as virtual in the concluding sequence – the narrative space becomes virtual. The strength of narrative space is how the foetus, or rather its virtual image, is framed by the uterus and coded by Bob as a foetus, then a child and a young woman. When Ruth takes the gun from Bob's heavily blooded hand, in the final sequence, his earlier dialogue describes the future, 'in the future, I'm a very old man. We're in [...] our house where everything is green and the sun's almost set. We're waving to someone and maybe that someone is you [and] we're really happy to see you.' This not only provides missing dialogue; it also creates a virtual image of the foetus in the future and in their family group. Bob codes the foetus not only as something that is meaningful to him, but he also creates an interpretative narrative that creates a living world with the uterus as screen. Technically, it is through reverse dramatic irony that narrative information has been kept from the spectator, but this does not explain how this biotourist narrative in a virtual frame with a virtual image is created.

The effect of the biotourist narrative throughout the film is in juxtaposing the past, the present and the future within this virtual frame. The dialogue that Bob attributes to a conversation with the foetus demonstrates that he has transformed the foetus in scale from a foetus in Ruth's body to an adult who has grown and is returning home. At the moment that Bob's voice-over says, 'We're waving to somebody and maybe that somebody is you and we're really happy to see you,' his daughter Sylvie comes through the door (Figure 4.10). Sylvie appears in the centre of the frame, but only just as she hides behind the door. The angle of their eyelines suggests that there is some recognition, although Sylvie is semi-hidden. The audio bridge of the dialogue is crucial at this point as in reality Bob, although looking directly at Sylvie, cannot speak to her and there is no diegetic dialogue (Figure 4.11). As Sylvie comes into the room and sees him for the first time and the camera cuts between mid-shots of both Bob and Sylvie, Sylvie is simultaneously the foetus who Bob was talking to in the uterus (through Ruth's body), the child standing in front of him now, and the grown woman of Bob's imagined intra-action. The reason to suggest that this is a biotourist narrative, initiated by Bob, is that the uterus has become a metaphorical space or landscape – a bioscape – where Bob has been able to 'meet' and 'greet' his unborn child. The foetus does not respond at any point, but in his imagined narrative, the foetus has 'come alive', and the uterine environment, as frame, has been turned inside out. By withholding information from the spectator at the beginning of the film and intercutting the opening and final sequences, and by transforming the foetus in scale, the arrival of Sylvie at the door is a profound moment of intra-action.

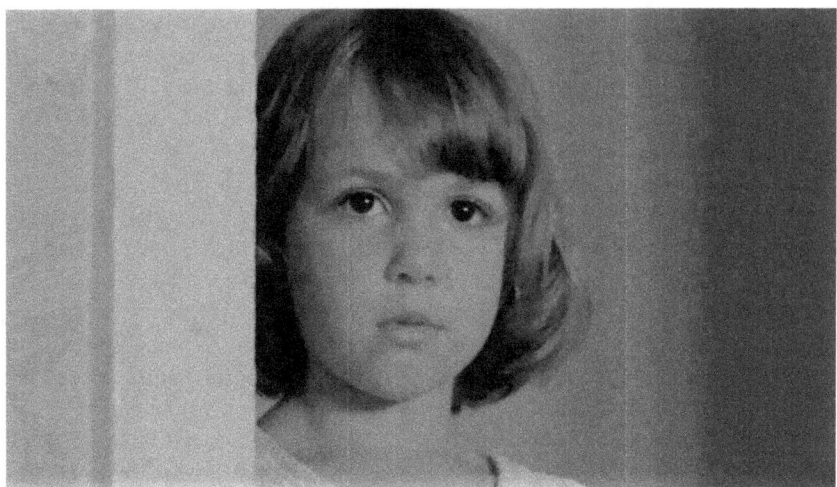

FIGURE 4.10 *Sylvie sees Bob for the first time in* Ain't Them Bodies Saints.

FIGURE 4.11 *Bob sees Sylvie for the first time in* Ain't Them Bodies Saints.

Bob's voice provides the narrative suture between sequences and signifies his embodied presence in the film. Because of the way his voice is used throughout the film, when he talks to Ruth's belly through her clothes, he also talks to the foetus. Throughout the film, the suggestion is that he touches Ruth when she hears his voice reading his letters. At the end of the film, when Bob is dying in Ruth's arms, their entwined hands mimic the image of them together inside their truck at the beginning of the film. Their tactility becomes an integral part of the biotourist narrative as it encourages the spectator to understand that there is a dynamic between the two characters that includes the internal body, the uterus, the external world and a virtual world. Returning to the opening of the film, when Bob sits in the truck with Ruth with his head in her lap, he opens her dress and sings to the foetus in her belly. He sings along to the radio and tells Ruth 'that's what you're supposed to do – sing 'em songs'. The scene is intimate. The camera begins in the truck with close-ups on the faces of the two protagonists, but then cuts to a tracking shot around the outside of the truck. The doorframes and windows of the car then obstruct some of the visuals, which means the spectator has only glimpses of their conversation. As it becomes clear later, this cut to a tracking shot also marks a temporal ellipse where the spectator loses access to information. This information is crucial to and is part of the intra-action around the uterus in Bob's biotourist narrative. It is an emotional intra-action around the uterus. Going back to the way that Barad describes the ultrasound transducer as the machine interface to the body, when Bob touches Ruth and speaks to the foetus through the uterus, the foetus becomes the phenomenon. There is no response from the foetus, but the uterus, by way of Ruth's body, acts like an interface through which Bob can talk to the foetus rather than to Ruth. The uterus becomes the premises for perception and the point of contact for his narrative.

Tactility in the film emphasizes the biotourist narrative as moments of contact, and this is essential to the reveal at the end of the film. When Bob returns to Ruth at the end of the film dying from a gunshot wound, he is found in her bedroom sitting on the floor holding a gun (Figure 4.12). Bob

FIGURE 4.12 *Ruth holds Bob as he is dying in* Ain't Them Bodies Saints.

is lying against the bedroom dresser, but it is obvious he does not have the physical strength to hold himself for much longer. Ruth supports his body, and he lays his head on her lap, mimicking the position they were in inside the truck in the earlier scene. The camera cuts to a close-up on their faces where the sound of their breathing accompanies their physical contact as they touch each other's mouths, noses, faces and hair and Ruth says, 'I've been waiting for you' (Figure 4.13). This scene reflects their reconciliation on-screen. Although the characters have been present throughout with Bob being represented by his voice on many occasions, their dialogue repeats the mantra of their separation, 'will you wait for me' and 'I'll be there waiting for you.' This is coupled with a musical leitmotif that plays when they are in the van at the beginning of the film and has been carried through the narrative by Ruth singing the song to Sylvie at bedtime as she recounts stories of Bob. The music is also used to signal to the spectator how the close-up aesthetic marks the progression of Bob and Ruth's relationship. A close-up on Ruth's face at the end of the film cuts to a tracking mid-shot of Ruth's smiling face in the truck from the earlier scene. Bob's dialogue then forms a diegetic and non-diegetic bridge between the two sequences to highlight the shift in temporality. Bob also establishes his relationship with the foetus, emphasizing that this relationship is separate from Ruth. When Ruth asks him to carry on telling her about the house, he tells Ruth, 'I'm not talking to you.'

The conversation with the foetus, therefore, is dependent on tactility but not proximity. Before Sylvie's birth, the last moment Bob and Ruth touch each other is when they are led away by the police (Figure 4.14). In this scene, they are separated from each other as they are led away

FIGURE 4.13 *Ruth kisses Bob as he is dying in* Ain't Them Bodies Saints.

FIGURE 4.14 *The last moment of touching before separation in* Ain't Them Bodies Saints.

by different people. The only physical contact they have is touching the sides of their faces, which they try to do for as long as possible so that only their skin and hair touch. In his letters, Bob talks about wanting to hold Ruth's face and he tells her that he thinks about her hair. Bob also narrates how he wants to 'take our baby girl in my arms'. When Ruth gives birth, the sequence is juxtaposed with other sequences of Ruth and Bob together. In these sequences, which have not yet appeared in the film, their arms and hands are entwined and then intercut with the birth images of Ruth and Sylvie's bodies together. Ruth's physical connection with Sylvie is established from pregnancy and birth, in complete contrast to the lack of physical contact Bob has with his daughter. Ruth carries Sylvie, she lies down with her as she reads, she holds her hand as they walk, and they fall asleep together with their faces and arms together. Bob, by contrast, describes how Ruth will know he is there even if she cannot see him and says, of Sylvie, that 'she'll feel me coming down the street'. Bob does glimpse Sylvie when he stands unseen and untouched outside their home, and later tells Ruth that he was 'so close I could touch your cheek'. This is the only other time until he is dying that he gets close enough to touch his daughter. Bob's ability to create a biotourist narrative that charts the journey of his relationship with Ruth and Sylvie demonstrates the strength of corporeal sensibility that permeates the film.

The uterus, then, is a narrative space in which a (one-sided) conversation with the foetus spans the whole film. Bob's relationship with the foetus is mediated by the corporeality of the film that establishes a tactility with Ruth and Sylvie through extended close-ups, use of the voice and music and the juxtapositioning of touching bodies. The use of the voice is critical to the way the film is structured, as it becomes an important narrative device at the end of the film. The diegetic voice provides a contrast between the voice of the expectant father looking into the future and the voice of the dying man looking back on his (virtual) past. The uterus provides the location for the extended conversation with the foetus by transforming the foetus in scale from an actual unborn to a virtual grown person. Bob 'speaks' to the foetus in a way that enables him to recognize her when he sees her, even though in reality he is not able to speak. The narration that he has provided throughout, therefore, makes it clear to the spectator that his imagined intra-action and close contact with the foetus is a biotourist journey.

Apio verde

In the film *Apio verde*, the stakes are much higher as the biotourist narrative of an imagined future child is created outside of the pregnant person and outside of the scan room. The film is set in present-day Chile. Adriana (Catherine Moyazer) falls in love with Diego (Cristián Gajardo), and they move in together and soon Adriana is pregnant.[28] All is well until she has a foetal ultrasound and she is told that the foetus has anencephaly, where part of the brain (and head) is malformed or absent. This condition, she is told, is not compatible with life, and the baby will not survive outside of the uterus. Adriana is horrified at the thought of carrying the foetus to full gestation. Diego, however, believes that they should carry on with the pregnancy. Adriana finds out about the reality of the foetus's condition by viewing images on the internet and then finds someone that will sell her abortion pills. She goes to collect the pills and returns home to find that Diego has organized a baby shower without telling her so that when she arrives home their friends and family are waiting to have a party. The room is decorated with balloons and images of babies. Adriana later dreams that she has a healthy baby daughter and that Diego is having an affair. Much later in her pregnancy, Adriana finds out she has cancer and that she cannot be treated while she is pregnant. Diego, meanwhile, is being pressured to speak against the abortion laws at a meeting of the Chilean Senate. Adriana is distressed and leaves home, and visits a nun, Mother Mariana (Sonia Mena), who organizes an abortion, but Adriana does not go through with the procedure and returns to testify at the Senate meeting. Adriana becomes increasingly distressed, and it is not clear if what is happening to her is her perception or actual, as Diego attempts an abortion in their home and attacks both Adriana and her mother.

Adriana runs the risk of being charged with a criminal offence and being imprisoned for three years if she has an abortion, so the film presents a domestic drama that is, from Adriana's point of view, a horror story. The laws around abortion in Chile at the time that the film was made stipulated that abortion was illegal under any circumstances.[29] The unborn foetus exists as a healthy 'baby' in the perception of other people, but for the pregnant person in the film, the foetus is considered as it is in reality, one that is incompatible with life. The film uses thriller tropes whereby Adriana's point of view becomes distorted, psychologically and in the frame, as she discovers that trusted people appear to be part of a conspiracy. She is both visitor and host of her own body and of her foetus. When she realizes that the foetus is gravely ill, she 'sees' it in a starkly different way to those around her. The film also uses horror tropes such as images of bloodstained medical instruments, in order to reflect Adriana's state of mind and the horrific nature of her predicament. Reviewer Andrew S. Vargas (2016) says that the film is 'a bit heavy handed, but one certainly can't underestimate the psychological toll such an experience can take on an expectant mother'. On the surface, the film appears to be part of the horror genre, but I read against this to discuss how the internal space of the uterus is reconfigured as a contested location, which allows the unviable foetus to become one that has a mediated personhood. The film centres on the distinct ways in which Adriana, Diego and others 'see' the foetus or rather understand its personhood. Adriana and Diego both think of the foetus as their child, and each one constructs a narrative that centres on its presence, but each has a different perspective. The different perspectives on what the foetus is creates competing biotourist narratives where Adriana understands the foetus and her 'baby' as unviable and those around her understand the foetus as a 'baby' with a future.

On the one hand, Adriana believes that 'a child would give its life for that of its mother' and believes that removing the foetus is a kinder action than leaving it to grow. Diego, on the other hand, says that as they both wanted to have a child, she cannot now change her mind based on the medical information they now have. For Adriana, the presence of an unviable foetus in her uterus that she will have to carry until the moment of its birth is horrific. The uterus in the film is a contested space in the eyes of the law as the foetus from the moment of conception is protected as if it were a person. This means that the uterus is a bodily space where the foetus, healthy or otherwise, is conceptually separated from the pregnant body. However much Adriana protests that it is her body, and it is up to her what she does, the reality is that she has to battle against the legal and social view that the foetus should be attributed personhood. The pregnant body is, therefore, negotiated differently by Adriana and by everyone else. The biotourist dynamic between the internal world of the uterus and the external world is influenced by the human and personalized narrative that surrounds the foetus. In this intra-action, the foetus in the bioscape of the uterus is 'alive' as much as it is terminally ill and dying. The pregnant body and the uterus form an embodied space whereby the foetus is interpreted as 'baby', 'son' and 'child' by other protagonists. Adriana also 'sees' the malformed foetus as 'baby', her 'son' and her 'child'. The horror that Adriana feels about having a foetus – and therefore, as she understands it, a 'baby' – that is malformed is shown in her response to images of babies from real life, as they appear outside of the uterus.

At the beginning of the film, one of the first sounds to be heard over the titles is the sound of slides going through a projector along with the sound of Adriana's voice panting and crying as if frightened and/or in labour. The sound mix foreshadows the slides in contextualizing the reality of the malformed foetus for Adriana. Adriana is looking at slides of actual foetuses with anencephaly on the internet. When the spectator can see what Adriana has been looking at, the images are stark. The slides are shown full screen as the computer screen fills the camera frame. The spectator must view the images alongside Adriana, and there is no extra diegetic music to provide a guide to the emotions that the spectator is encouraged to feel. The only sound in this brief sequence is the sound of the slides turning in a slide projector. The effect this has is to place the spectator in the position of Adriana's point of view and consider his or her own response to the foetus – or 'baby'. The computer screen takes the place of the uterus as Adriana, and the spectator can see what makes Adriana frightened. It presents a biotourist dynamic as both the spectator and Adriana are encouraged to renegotiate Adriana's uterus as a narrative space. The fact that Adriana has accessed these images suggests that it is important for her to see a true representation of her foetus's medical condition in order to understand the implications that this has for her own image of her own 'child'. The body of the foetus is also renegotiated in the juxtaposition of these images alongside Adriana's pregnant body.

There is no evidence in the film that anyone else, apart from medical professionals, understands what her foetus looks like in reality. The photographic images that she is looking at show babies with severe abnormalities of the head. The babies are shown in various positions: facing the camera, in profile, being held, dressed in baby clothes or simply with an identifying nametag. The photographs include a baby in what appears to be its mother's arms as well as another woman snuggling up to a baby, their heads held together and framed in a close-up. Adriana also looks at diagrams of pregnancy and reads about the medical condition anencephaly. Alongside the written information are black-and-white photographs of babies with severe spinal malformations. The images are of full-term babies, in contrast to the foetus inside Adriana that is less than three months of gestation. Her foetus is, therefore, a miniature version of these images even though it is only a few centimetres long. In viewing these images, Adriana is purposefully finding out how the foetus growing inside her might look like at birth. As a way to meet and greet her 'baby', this biotourist narrative includes the images that Adriana views as the actual images of full-term babies and the virtual image of what her own 'baby' will look like at birth.

The dissonance between the traditional images of pregnancy and the embodied reality of carrying a non-viable foetus is reflected in the cinematography when Diego organizes a surprise baby shower. From Adriana's point of view, the people who gather to wish her well are framed in wide angle, which distorts the image of their faces and bodies, making their heads seem larger (Figure 4.15). The wide angle also has the effect of distancing the group from Adriana's point of view, as their bodies appear to be disappearing into the hallway. This emphasizes the physical and emotional distance she feels towards the group who are celebrating and recognizing a foetus that does not exist. Adriana's friends and family create an image of a 'baby' by cutting out cardboard images of a baby and sticking them on the wall (Figure 4.16) as a way to celebrate the pregnancy, not knowing that the 'baby' is only alive because it is attached to Adriana's uterus. The cut-out baby has a head that is larger than its body which mimics real life, but also is a reminder of the way in which Adriana's foetus is malformed. This scene takes place immediately after she has collected abortion pills and is looking for somewhere to hide them in her bedroom, and she still has the packet of pills in her hand when she is confronted by her friends. Adriana, therefore, is still in the process of renegotiating how she 'sees' the foetus as 'baby' inside her uterus.

The group at the baby shower includes her obstetrician Tomás (Andrés Gomez) and his wife Lucía (Catalina Aguayo), and Tomás joins in the counting game where people take turns to spin Adriana for 'one month, two months, three months'. He takes hold of Adriana at four months and counts to five saying, 'Diego told me what you were planning. Do you know that if you wait you can donate its organs?' Later Lucía warns Adriana that 'if you take the pills, you might not be able to get pregnant again . . . you

FIGURE 4.15 *Adriana's friends, in a wide-angle shot which distorts the head, insist that she celebrates her pregnancy in* Apio verde.

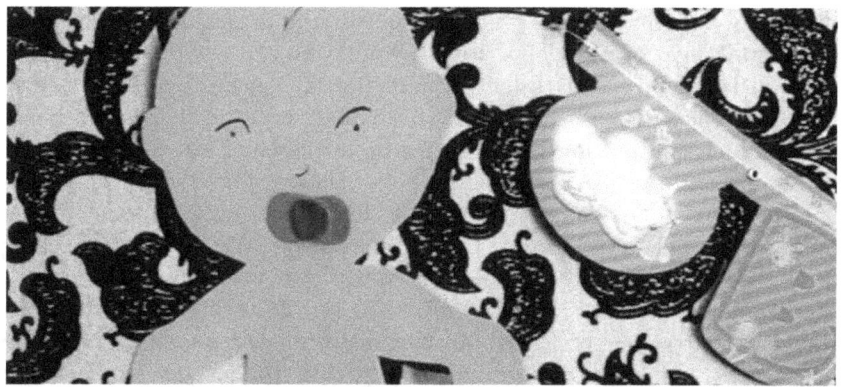

FIGURE 4.16 *The decoration stuck on the wall includes the image of a cut-out 'baby' with its head out of proportion with its body in* Apio verde.

might lose your dream of having a family'. As a final warning, Diego tells Adriana that Lucía had been told that her own baby would not be born and now he is a healthy boy. Adriana is now surrounded by the imaginings of other people based on an image of a 'baby' that does not exist for her at any point in her current pregnancy or in her uterus. Importantly, it is not the imagined 'baby' that she intends to abort. It is the actual foetus inside her uterus that she wants to terminate. The baby shower has been planned by Diego to present the imaginary interpretation of a healthy 'baby'. In this way, the uterus functions as a bioscape as a point of contact for his narrative, which intersects with others, so that he can attribute meaning where none is present. He does this so that he can persuade Adriana not to take the pills that will abort the inviable foetus.

The embodied reality that Adriana experiences contrasts with the fantasy sequences in the film. When Adriana is alone, she dreams or imagines alternative scenarios – Diego removes the foetus himself, Diego has an affair with Lucía, Adriana gets up in the night to take her turn comforting her own toddler in the next room. Some sequences show the contrast between Adriana's lived body experience and the reality of preparing for a child she will never have. For example, when Adriana imagines a child crying in the room next to her, she is shown alone while Diego sleeps. The static camera is positioned directly above Diego, who is sprawled across the bed. Taking up a quarter of the frame is a crucifix hanging on the wall. The feet of the figure of Christ point directly towards Diego's head. Adriana is placed at the top of the frame alongside Diego, but central in the frame. Adriana's hands are clasped as if in prayer. The soundtrack includes gentle piano, which is an audio bridge from the previous scene in a church. The sound of a baby crying is faded in. Adriana leans over to Diego and says, 'should you go or me?' but he does not wake. As she walks into the next-door bedroom, the piano is accompanied by a song and Adriana is filmed in soft focus in a pale pink light as she walks slowly around the bed where a young child is lying. The child has dark hair like Adriana and Diego and is dressed in pink patterned pyjamas, while Adriana is dressed in a high lace-collared dress, which is also pink-hued. As she picks the child up, it stops crying. Adriana does not talk, but her breath can be heard comforting the child. She breathes in small gasps and the child murmurs in reply touching her on the chest. Lights stream past them as the light is coming from the ceiling on a revolving lamp. The child looks directly at the camera as they are both framed in a close-up. This is Adriana's biotourist narrative whereby she renegotiates the space of her uterus transforming the foetus in scale from her uterus as its 'first home' into a small child in its bedroom. She creates a conceptual image of the child by fragmenting her own lived body experience of pregnancy, and visually objectifying the foetus as the living child that she wants to have.

The sequence of Adriana's imagined future child, her biotourist journey, contrasts with her real life as she is seen in a wide angle close-up leaning over her new – empty – cot. In this shot, Adriana is placed just off the centre of the frame to allow Diego to enter the back of the shot. The wide angle forces a distortion of perspective, which means that he appears further away from Adriana than he is, emphasizing their physical and emotional distance. A light source appears to be inside the cot and this shines on her face, focusing attention on her while showing the contrast between her smiling face in her previous fantasy and her closed expression in this scene. Ignoring Diego when he speaks, Adriana says, of the baby when it is born, 'on the day of the birth, we could buy him a little one-piece suit'. This piece of dialogue suggests that she knows that she will have to go through with the birth. As she says this, Diego walks towards her. He appears much closer to her as the perspective evens out, and he stands in the centre of the frame. At this moment, the couple is given equal prominence in the frame. Adriana asks Diego, 'do you think coffins exist for babies?' She does not wait for his reply, but it is clear that she is thinking ahead to the reality of giving birth to a baby who will be dead or die shortly after birth. This demonstrates that even though she has a strong image of her imagined future child, it does not distract from the image she has of the actual foetus in her uterus. Going back to the discussion in Chapter 3, the way that Adriana is shown, understanding the foetus as unviable, creating an imaginary image of the child she will not have, and preparing for the infant who will be born, demonstrates how the frame of the uterus is her premises for perception. The uterus becomes the point of contact for other narratives when it is constantly transformed into a narrative space by others who attribute alternative meanings to the foetus while it is inside the uterus. In a poignant moment, Adriana demonstrates her emotional attachment to the malformed foetus, which she understands as her actual future child, by saying, 'I want to have a place for them where we can visit and be a family.' This shows the gentleness of the frame of the uterus as Adriana moves from the actual image of the foetus on the scan to a virtual image of a toddler in her house, and from the healthy future of an imagined child to her future sick baby at birth.

Even though Adriana's foetus will not survive for long after birth, she and Diego create an image of a traditional family by painting on Adriana's growing belly. The belly is painted twice: at the beginning of the pregnancy before the scan is performed, and after a few months when they know their future child will not survive but the pregnancy continues. The paintings are similar. In the first painting session, Diego initiates a biotourist narrative, and superimposes it on the pregnant belly, of a house, a tree, a river and three people across Adriana's belly (Figure 4.17). In this way, he paints a 'glorious vista' in which they can 'meet' and 'greet' their child. The backlight emphasizes the swollen belly and highlights the human figures painted in dark blue. When the first painting is done, Diego says, 'here's where we'll live, near a river with grass ... you, me and our little baby.' Adriana's belly is shown in close-up, and the film is speeded up to reflect their impatience at becoming a 'family'. At this point, they have already bought a cot and talked about names. In the second painting, their mood is sombre. Again, Adriana's belly is shown in close-up and the film speeds up so that the painting takes shape more quickly. The pregnant belly in both sequences is not a prosthetic, so the consistency of the skin is lifelike, adding to the appearance of realism. In this second sequence, when the camera moves to reveal the two protagonists, Adriana's body is hidden behind one arm of a crucifix, which frames her head, and that of Diego. Adriana's body is hidden which cuts part of her body out of the frame (for technical reasons but also for effect). This separates Adriana from Diego, emphasizing their physical and

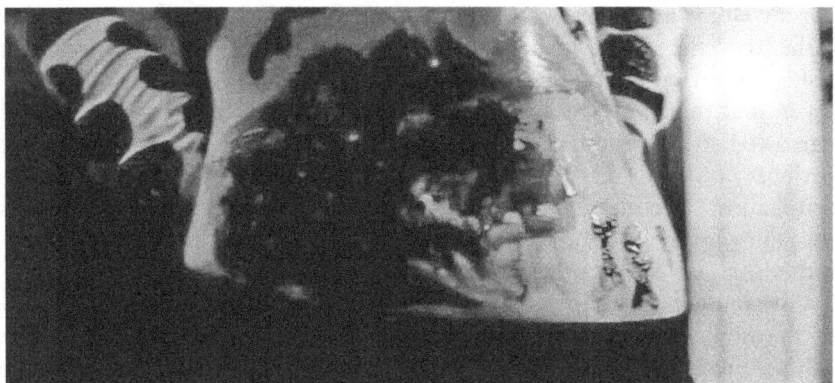

FIGURE 4.17 *Diego paints an imagined family on Adriana's pregnant belly in* Apio verde.

emotional distance. When Diego asks her if she likes the painting, she shakes her head and says that 'it (the child) looks more deformed'. This sequence shows how the imagined landscape of the foetal future is superimposed over the actual unviable foetus. The frame of the uterus is an actual frame that holds the unviable foetus; it is also an actual frame as seen and felt through the body. The painting emphasizes how the frame of the uterus, as pregnancy, creates a virtual frame for imagined intra-action. This sequence also demonstrates the fragmentation of the pregnant body and foetal image so that the uterine frame (and the foetus) is actual and virtual, and the perception of each image depends on the gentleness of the frame.

This figurative interpretation of what is happening in the pregnancy is also shown as an actual comparison when Adriana sits in the waiting room outside the scan room, and this sequence is intercut with a sequence in which Lucía is advised to have her dog euthanized. The two sequences are placed together and intercut to highlight the different medical approaches to a suffering animal and to an unviable foetus. It is made clear to Adriana that the foetus might survive for hours after birth and pain is not something that is explicitly ruled out. As Adriana sits waiting, she is foregrounded in a wide-shot but placed at the bottom of the frame to one side. The effect this has is to place Adriana as only one of many people waiting for medical appointments and to emphasize the everyday nature of receiving bad news. It also foreshadows the bad news by introducing a sound bridge between the scan room and the waiting room. A low, constant tone fades in over the end of the scan sequence and is then overlaid with the sound of a foetal heartbeat. As Adriana sits, the camera moves position and reframes in two jump cuts, gently echoing a heartbeat. The first jump cut advances the timeline, subtly changing the action of the character to signal the temporal ellipsis. The camera has moved position to a lower angle where Adriana remains at the right-hand side of the frame, but the low-angle makes her appear larger in the frame. Moving closer to Adriana, the focus is on her rather than the rest of the people in the waiting room. The second jump cut holds Adriana at the right-hand side of the frame in a wide angle mid-close-up so that the emptying waiting room can be seen. The depth of field has narrowed so that the few people left waiting are now out of focus in the periphery of the frame. This slow divide between Adriana and everyone else foreshadows her increasing isolation throughout the film, and emphasizes that the way she is treated throughout the film is a result of a legal reality rather than her lived body experience of pregnancy.

Adriana's dissonant perception of her baby is reflected in the corporeality of the film. Her pregnant body is fragmented when the belly is hidden behind props, the wide-angle shots of people's distorted faces echo the foetal condition and the parallel narrative of a sick animal is interwoven with images of Adriana waiting for her scan results. The jump cuts that progress time emphasize both how long she has to wait and how quickly time is passing. Time being the key factor in her subsequent desire for a termination. Importantly, the imagined healthy 'baby' that others interpret, and that she dreams about, is not the one that she wants to abort; it is the actual foetus inside the uterus. It is the imagined 'baby', however, that she is encouraged to think of as real. The personhood of the foetus is in conflict with this narrative as the imagined 'baby' does not exist. This dissonance arises from how the foetus is perceived while it remains on the uterus, not its physical reality. The personhood of the 'baby' is therefore mediated, and the uterus becomes an emotional and legally contested location. Although the medical condition that affects Adriana's foetus means that it is incompatible with life outside of the uterus, the perception of the people around her is that it is a living child. Moreover, although Adriana is the only character in the film who considers the implications of the physical reality of the foetus, it exists as a 'baby' for her despite being incompatible with life. While those around her prepare for the birth of her healthy 'baby', Adriana prepares for the termination of the foetus, or the birth of her actual baby that will die. This dissonance, created by individual acts of interpretation, can be understood by thinking of the uterus as a bioscape.

To summarise, there is a tension in the way biotourism is understood. On the one hand, it is a specific list of criteria as described by Sawchuk, which applies to the internal body as a whole. On the other hand, as Roberts and KrolØkke suggest, it describes the self-reflective intra-action between the spectator and protagonists in relation to the uterus. Sawchuk's notions of the transposition of scale and transforming anatomy into landscape have implications for reading the narrative space of the uterus as a bioscape. In each film, this bioscape can be understood through the intra-actions of characters when they interpret the foetus as existing outside of the uterus and the pregnant body by enlarging it to an actual person. Biotourism articulates the narrative around the uterus – as bioscape – by emphasizing how internal space in the body can be transformed by personalized narratives. These narratives are created around the uterus as a frame for imagined intra-actions. Introducing the notion of travel or tourism through the body helps to understand that this is an imagined journey of reinterpreting or retelling narrative. In each film in this chapter, the uterus has been thought of as a bioscape that allows the foetus to be voiced by its grown self or the foetal future to be voiced and recounted by another character. In this final film, other interpretative narratives create a cognitive dissonance between the actual unviability of the foetus and other virtual narratives that attribute meaning when none is present. Thinking of the uterus as a bioscape also makes sense of its properties as a premises for perception and orientation point, as discussed in Chapter 3. Adding the notion of biotourism helps to articulate the power of imagined narratives in creating meanings around the internal frame of the uterus that are in direct opposition to what is actually inside. Returning to the overall analysis in the book, thinking through the uterus as a premises for perception and as an orientation point has allowed me to think of how collaborative narratives are framed by the uterus. Thinking of the uterus as a bioscape has then allowed me to think about how the uterus becomes a point of contact for these narratives. In Chapter 5, I want to add Marks's notion of the recollection-object to investigate how objects inside and outside of the uterus are woven into the narrative landscape, particularly to propel narratives that signal the threshold of life and death, focusing on birth as a moment of transition.

5

The recollection-object, breaching the threshold in *Up*, *The Bad Intentions/Las malas intenciones* and *Birth*

This chapter adds the Marksian recollection-object to the analytical assemblage of my critical and textual analysis. I have already established the properties of the uterus as a frame for collaborative and intersecting narratives, and now I investigate how objects inside and outside of the uterus advance narratives of pregnancy that are not dependent on the pregnant body. Birth is a recognizable threshold that indicates a physical and temporal movement of the unborn into the world of the living, and the moment of birth signals how the focal point shifts from the pregnant body to the newborn itself. The recollection-object is a visual cue in each film that an embodied connection – or bond – is being made that could be said to invoke the memory of the foetus. The three films discussed in this chapter – *Up* (2009), *The Bad Intentions* (2011) and *Birth* (2004) – all have narrative similarities. Each film deals with questions of pregnancy and birth and experiences of childhood and memory. Yet memory is a complex process, and this chapter will introduce some critical discourses that clarify how narratives around the uterus can be at a distance from the uterus itself. Rather than thinking of pregnancy or birth as subjective experiences, this chapter will examine how birth is a threshold that imbues specific objects with meaning according to their proximity to the moment of birth.

A threshold can be understood as a physical space that connects two locations marking a moment of change or the next step in a journey; it can also be a temporal or emotional shift between the past, the present and the future. As Marks explains, the recollection-object is 'an irreducibly material object that encodes collective memory' through physical contact (2000:

77–8). This recollection-object can be a person or a thing, but, as Marks suggests, it is transformed or even erased in the process of encoding memory and memories or when it is interpreted by spectators as something that has meaning (122).[1] This could be called a process of bonding, but it is clear that being meaningful is not just a subjective point of view but can also be understood as a narrative construction. The films demonstrate the tension between the unborn and the living. It is the way that the narratives are constructed at a distance from the lived body and from the moment of birth that is so compelling and is the focus for this chapter. The tension is in the birth object itself – the foetus – as it provokes a different response from the spectator and other protagonists depending on its own proximity to birth. This means that the protagonists and spectators must negotiate the body not as it is but through the memory of objects in relation to the body. The growing foetus exists on the threshold of life, or perhaps more accurately on the threshold of viability, which suggests a precarious liminality between life and death. This liminality, physiologically, is dependent on the foetus remaining in the pregnant body and being nourished through the uterus: it is not independently alive. In each film, the foetus is absent or remembered though bonding with something, or someone, else.

Bonding, however, as I indicated in Chapter 2, has some flaws when it is applied to objects (the foetus) inside the uterus and interpretative narratives outside of the uterus. Although bonding could be thought of as suture, it is a more complicated concept than recognition or self-reflexivity, and this is demonstrated in each film. Furthermore, bonding is not necessarily a positive force. As Janelle Taylor suggests in relation to the foetal ultrasound scan, bonding 'can involve hate and fear as well as love' (2008: 78). Taylor suggests that the notion of bonding has become a 'catch all term' to describe an emotional, social attachment to the foetus, which is not always evidenced (78). This connection is based, she explains, on a miscorrelation between the pleasure of seeing the scan and the maternal relationship to the foetus.[2] This miscorrelation means that referring to bonding as a concept in relation to the foetus, or to birth, does not always take into account the way that the foetus as an object provokes a range of responses that are negative *and* positive.

As Marks suggests, 'when language cannot record memories, we often look to images. When images fail to revive memory, we may look to the well-kept secret of objects. Unpacking the secrets held encoded in images and objects, we find the memory of the senses' (2000: 195). Marks establishes the properties of objects to evoke memories. Although she argues for cultural specificity, the way that she explains how objects gain power from being circulated and passed around between people is particularly relevant to how memory is invoked in each film. Marks takes the Deleuzian notion of the recollection image and extends it to describe objects that, while they may not have a primary visual connection to an event, are capable of invoking a memory or an image of something else.³ In this, she stresses that 'objects are not inert and mute but [. . .] they tell stories and describe trajectories' (80). It is not, however, the objects themselves that tell stories; it is the embodied response to those objects that imposes a narrative trajectory. I suggest that Marks is talking about Jan Assman's (2011) 'communicative memory [. . .] that lives in everyday interaction and communication', and it is these everyday interactions that give objects their communicative value (18).⁴ Marks frequently uses collective memory to describe the way in which people with the same life experiences respond to images, perceived smells, textures and, to a lesser extent, sound. However, the use of the term 'collective memory' is problematic in the context of my discussion, and it is more accurate to talk about a shared, embodied memory (of things) rather than a collective memory.

According to Paul Connerton (1989: 6), the temporal layers of memory – particularly memories that are shared in communities – are formed by creating a context through recollection.⁵ Recollection, in this sense, is the way past experiences and knowledge are used to make sense of an object or person or situation. The act of recollection means that memories, particularly intergenerational memories, are in a constant state of negotiation and renegotiation. Michael Rothberg (2009) suggests that memories are multi-directional in that they depend on a constant movement between the past, present and future. Max Silverman (2013) also suggests that there is a depth to memory – the palimpsestic memory – where memories become layered and are interpreted through other memories to create life narratives.⁶ This suggests that memory has a materiality and is spatialized by being understood to have both breadth and depth. Life narratives, however, are not always remembered in the same way. According to empirical and theoretical research into intergenerational memory, there is a 'reminiscence bump' where recollected or remembered memories are more likely to come from late adolescence to early adulthood, and the most remembered events are likely to be positive ones (Steiner et al. 2014).⁷ This suggests that memory recollection and memory formation are dependent not only on the period when these memories are first formed but on the intensity of the period when the events take place. This imbalance in remembered events from different periods of life – life chapters – shows that memory is dependent on many factors for recollection. The reminiscence bump suggests that traumatic events are remembered in relation to positive events, and this is significant when the actions of protagonists in film to the foetus are understood as negative or positive. In effect, rather than thinking of negative and positive responses, these (re)actions are part of a more complex process of moving through thresholds when memories are negotiated and renegotiated as part of the lived body experience of everyday life.

The notion of the threshold suggests a precariousness between life and death that also marks the point where things begin to change. As Lorna Weir

(2006) argues, 'a threshold stabilises a relation between inside and outside', and by altering the nature of that threshold, between life and viability, the relationship between the internal and the external shifts (2). Robert J. Lifton and Eric Olson (2004) describe the process by which death is acknowledged to have happened but is then understood by its relatedness to life as 'symbolic immortality'. They argue that '[t]his relatedness is expressed in many kinds of symbolization that enable one to participate in ongoing life without denying the reality of death' (34). This is an important point to remember as in each film, there is no denial of death. The recollection-object 'disrupts the coherence' of the present when it is interpreted in different ways depending on who is looking at it (Marks 2000: 77–8).[8] This disruption of coherence implies that there is an interpretative relationship between objects and memory where memory can be real or imagined and part of an embodied experience. This blurring of images is usefully described by Marksian haptic visuality as 'mutuality', in which the spectator becomes lost in the images on screen and 'implies a tension between viewer and image' (184–5). This tension or mutuality is a key factor in understanding how narrative around the embodied space of the uterus implies a 'social relationship formation' (Taylor 2008: 78). In my readings of the films in this chapter, I stress the importance of the recollection-object to narrative construction around the threshold of birth, but this chapter is not specifically about the concepts of life and death.

Understanding the concepts of living and dying is highly personal and based on lived experience, age, background and beliefs. Nevertheless, my readings offer a way to understand narrative structures that are attributed to life and death, particularly as they apply to memory. The films in this chapter depend on the understanding that pregnancy and birth have happened, and this is crucial to narrative development. In *Up*, the foetus can be understood as a memory object, but it is the adventure book filled with photographs that becomes a recollection-object through which to remember pregnancy loss. In *The Bad Intentions*, the pregnant body is less important than the foetal presence which is (re)created as an adversary to the main character. In *Birth*, the reincarnated person threatens to overwhelm a memory of the deceased. These narratives, however, do not depend on pregnancy or the pregnant body as a central narrative thread.

Up

Pregnancy and pregnancy loss are important emotive themes in the film *Up*. Although the film is primarily for children, it tackles the unspoken grief at the memory of miscarriage and infertility.[9] Desmond O'Neill (2009), writing in the *British Medical Journal*, calls the film a 'gerontological Trojan horse' which 'combin[es] the hero role [. . .] with the pains of ageing, bereavement,

[and] intergenerational solidarity', and goes on to say that there are few films which tackle 'courtship, infertility and death in the opening 10 minutes' (922–33).[10] O'Neill explains that the opening sequences are designed to have an emotional impact on the spectator, and I might add that this might be particularly resonant for the adult who accompanies the child to the cinema.[11] In the main body of the film, Carl (Ed Asner) is widowed and lives in the house he originally bought when he was newly married to Ellie (Elizabeth Docter). Early in their marriage, Ellie has a miscarriage, and they have subsequently have no children. After Ellie dies, Carl refuses to talk to anyone including Russell (Jordan Ngai), a young boy scout who arrives at his door offering services to the elderly. When city developers try and convince Carl to move so that they can demolish his house and build new apartment blocks, Carl refuses. He is then embroiled in a confrontation when the developers destroy his brightly painted postbox, a precious reminder of Ellie who painted it. When Carl attacks the site manager, he is visited by the community services with details of a retirement home. He agrees to move but instead attaches balloons to his house and flies out of the city in the direction of Paradise Falls in South America, a place Ellie had always dreamed of visiting. As Carl flies, he discovers Russell is on his porch and they end up travelling together. Carl tries to ignore Russell, but eventually must save his life and bring him back to the city. During their adventures, Carl finds a note from Ellie in her adventure book that tells him to have his own adventure. Ellie had placed the note in the adventure book before she died. It is only after he finds this note and once his adventure is completed that Carl begins to engage with the world around him once more.

For the purposes of my analysis, I am going to focus on the four-minute sequence at the beginning of the film which concertinas the lives of Carl and Ellie from young newlyweds to Ellie's death. The sequence is not placed at the absolute beginning of the film, but it appears a few minutes into the narrative after the two main characters meet as children. Importantly, this sequence establishes the presence of the foetus in pregnancy and the subsequent loss in miscarriage. This loss underpins the narrative subtext so that the foetus becomes a recollection-object for each character, although this is not expressed explicitly. The recollection-object that has most strength, I suggest, is the adventure book that Ellie carries throughout her life, which becomes imbued with the memory of their pregnancy loss. But it is not straightforward to explain how the book operates as a recollection-object without first describing how pregnancy and pregnancy loss are developed narratively and expressly visually.

The sequence at the beginning of the film has a sophisticated narrative structure which functions as a complete narrative with a beginning, middle and end. It also acts as the apparent inciting incident for the film. The conventional and stereotypical story of a young couple setting up a nursery in their home is quickly and starkly stripped back to reveal the key moment in their life when they learn they will not have children. The sequence is played with music but without dialogue or sound effects, which means that the embodied dynamic between the two characters is an essential element of the narrative construction. This embodied connection not only emphasizes their emotional bond, but it also draws the spectator into the narrative around the uterus. This is demonstrated in a transition between the scene where Carl and Ellie paint the nursery ready for their baby and the scene when they receive bad news in the hospital. The two scenes become a sequence as they are linked both visually with a tracking shot from one to the other and acoustically by the slowing of the musical soundtrack. The tracking action of the camera (incorporating a screen wipe to change the scene) acts as a temporal shift and demonstrates how the mise en scène in the nursery provides a visual counterpoint to the following image in the hospital. The tracking shot changes the content of each scene, but the way the two scenes are edited emphasizes the gentleness of the frame. The first scene operates as a vision of the present and the second scene operates as an embodied memory of the past in one change of frame. The threshold of life and death is crossed in this ellipsis, and the spectator only shares this moment of change through the affective way the characters respond.

Before the camera tracks from the bright colour of the nursery, the static shot with an open frame suggests the outdoors off-screen through the window to the left of the frame and the rest of their house as off-screen through a door that is ajar at the right of the frame (Figure 5.1). The pregnant body is prominent in the frame and in the mise en scène. It is important to note that the frame of the uterus is present in Ellie's embodiment and in the centre of the frame in the form of the metaphorical stork painted on the

FIGURE 5.1 *Carl and Ellie preparing the nursery in* Up.

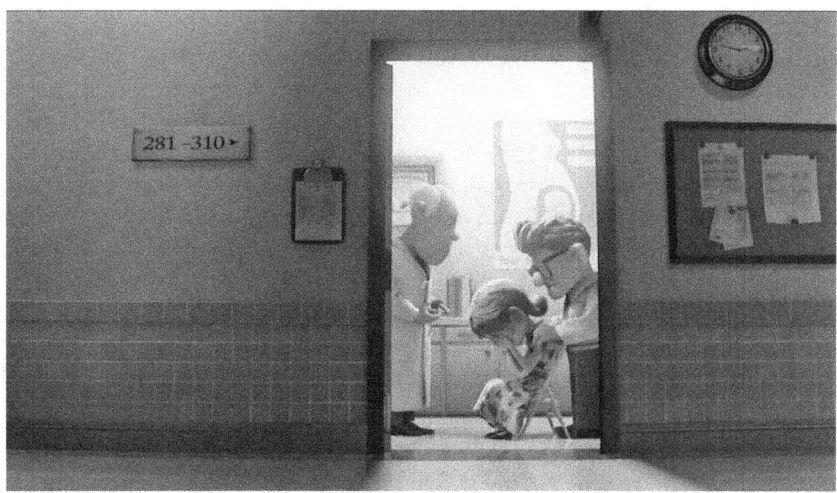

FIGURE 5.2 *Carl and Ellie in the hospital, receiving bad news in* Up.

wall flying towards Ellie bringing the 'baby' in a sheet. With the nursery door slightly open at the far right of the frame, it looks as if the stork is ready to take the uterus out of the door. The linking door, however, does not lead Ellie into her house, but it takes her to her miscarriage. As the scene changes, the stork is replaced in the centre of the frame by the anatomical position of the foetus in the uterus which hangs over Carl and Ellie's heads (Figure 5.2). The miscarriage has happened in the narrative gap and is now a private event that the spectator can only glimpse through the doorway. This highlights the threshold between public and the private in relation to their lived experience of pregnancy and birth. It also establishes that the foetus as a recollection-object exists in a conceptual shift from public to private and from one embodiment of pregnancy to another of pregnancy loss. In the second scene, the shot is more closed. The corridor that runs alongside is in semi-darkness, and the characters are squeezed into the space in the centre of the frame by the doorframe. Although the hospital room opens onto the corridor, suggesting that there is a world outside off-screen, the way that the characters are framed suggests that this is not relevant to the moment that they are experiencing.

The tracking camera between the two scenes is crucial as it indicates a passage of time wherein the journey to hospital, the telling of bad news and medical procedures have all taken place. The ellipsis creates a dynamic between the past and the present where 'the image has to be present and past [. . .] at the same time' (Deleuze 1989: 76). This temporal and emotional shift is created through the gentleness of each frame. In the elliptical moment that marks the threshold of life and death, the actual foetus disappears or disintegrates. The uterus can be understood as the site of change and the foetus becomes a hidden recollection-object as it is encoded in the memory of the miscarriage. The miscarriage initiates action in the narrative but is a weak inciting incident as this narrative strand is solved very quickly. The miscarriage creates no narrative obstacle. For the presence of the foetus to have any additional meaning, the miscarriage must be remembered as a bond in their life chapters as well as part of the threshold between life and death. If the sequence had been longer and with dialogue, the visceral response would be significant but not so important.

As Carl and Ellie enjoy a fulfilled life doing very ordinary things such as going to work and enjoying their own company, the sequence of the miscarriage functions primarily to construct backstory. Importantly, Carl and Ellie had already created a virtual image of their 'baby' before the miscarriage, the one that was being delivered by the stork into the new cot. But the 'baby' has already been constructed as a recollection-object before the pregnancy begins. On a trip to the park, Carl and Ellie lie in the sun and Carl imagines the shapes in the cloud as shapes of a 'baby' (Figure 5.3). They both create a vivid image of a baby floating in the sky, disembodied, and separated from the uterus (Figure 5.4). This establishes that the image of the baby is their perception of a virtual 'baby' rather than something that exists. For Carl and Ellie, the virtual image of the 'baby' is strongly associated with the tactility of their relationship. They climb up the hill and Carl holds Ellie's hand; they maintain their close physical contact lying down with their heads placed alongside each other on the rug. Importantly, the haptic quality of the sequence matches the scene in the nursery. The vivid green of the moving grass coupled with the bright colours of their clothes matches the

FIGURE 5.3 *Carl points to the sky and Ellie looks up in* Up.

FIGURE 5.4 *Carl and Ellie look at the shape of a baby in the clouds in* Up.

colour palette of the nursery and later matches the colour palette of their garden following the miscarriage when Carl gives Ellie her adventure book.

There are many objects associated with Carl and Ellie's shared memories such as the grape juice bottle-top that Ellie gives Carl when she first meets him, the mismatched chairs they always sit in and the painting of Paradise Falls that has centre place in their living room. Nonetheless, it is Ellie's adventure book that becomes strongly associated with the memory of miscarriage. The book becomes part of their communicative memory shared through physical contact. When the adventure book is first seen, Carl and Ellie are children. Ellie shows Carl her book (Figure 5.5) and shares with him her dreams of travel to South America and Paradise Falls. When Ellie's face peeps over the book, it looks as if she is giving him something that is precious and secret. Taking almost the whole frame, the book is presented to Carl as something that he cannot escape. This is emphasized by the way he is pushed into the right-hand corner of the frame. The next time the book is seen, Carl is offering it to Ellie as a comfort after her miscarriage (Figure 5.6). Again, the book takes up the centre of the frame, but there is an equivalence as Carl's hands place the book into Ellie's hands.

In each interaction, the adventure book is imbued with an embodied memory (reflected in the worn-out colours and curled edges of the book) that instantly becomes part of their shared past. It also becomes a visual cue for the spectator. Later, when Ellie realizes that she is dying, she gives the book to Carl (Figure 5.7). The exchange of touch and movement is echoed here when she strokes his chin, touches his tie and holds his hand, all gestures relating to their everyday life together. This time, their hands touch beside the book. The book is worn but as intact as it was when they were

FIGURE 5.5 *Ellie takes the centre of the frame as Carl is pushed to the right side of the frame when she shows him her private adventure book in* Up.

FIGURE 5.6 *Carl gives Ellie her well-worn adventure book to give her comfort after her miscarriage in* Up.

young. This time, Ellie's bones protrude under the skin of her hands showing her increasing frailty. It is only later in the film, when Carl is at a turning point in his adventure (the final turning point in the narrative of the film), and on the point of giving up, that he opens the book to find that Ellie has placed photographs of their life together in her section of 'stuff I'm going to do' (Figure 5.8). Alone this time, the book is in the centre of the frame but

FIGURE 5.7 *Carl touches Ellie's hand as he passes her adventure book in hospital before she dies in* Up.

FIGURE 5.8 *An emotional turning point for Carl is opening Ellie's adventure book to find that she has written him a note in* Up.

in a long shot as Carl sits beside Ellie's empty chair. This emphasizes Ellie's physical absence, but the adventure book remains important as a reminder of her and the miscarriage in the centre of the mise en scène.

The adventure book becomes an object imbued with memories of Carl and Ellie's childhood, the miscarriage and the unborn foetus, Ellie's death, and

Carl's own adventure. It becomes a recollection-object that evokes embodied memories of all these life chapters. The strength of this recollection-object is that it evolves and becomes absorbed by objects that are associated with – but are not representative of – the original memory. As I have said, Carl and Ellie's relationship is marked by their physical contact before and after the miscarriage. Their easy physicality is demonstrated when they arrive home from the hospital following the miscarriage. Ellie sits with her face to the sun in a chair that is placed in the garden but is facing away from the house. It is as if she is looking out of the garden, but her eyes are closed so she is not even looking out of the frame. She is still wearing the dress that she had on in the hospital, and Carl is also wearing the same clothes, which suggests that this physical and emotional reaction is very immediate. The movement of the breeze in her hair (Figure 5.9) is echoed in the subtle animation of Carl breathing (Figure 5.10). When Carl watches Ellie in the garden, his point of view becomes the spectator's point of view. At this moment, although Ellie is in the centre of the frame, Carl is prominent to the front of the frame. This emphasizes Ellie's emotional distance from him and from the spectator. Almost imperceptibly, Carl can be seen breathing. His chest moves in and out in a slow rhythm. The slow pace of movement of Ellie's hair coupled with Carl's slow breathing forms a rhythm which gives the impression of an embodied empathy. While Carl watches Ellie, the slow breathing suggests Carl's embodied response and contributes to the pace of the film at this point. It is in these moments that the adventure book is exchanged, see Figure 5.6. It becomes a recollection-object because of its proximity to the miscarriage. It also emphasizes how the sequences in the

FIGURE 5.9 *Ellie sits quietly, letting the sun fall on her face and the breeze blow through her hair when she returns home after the miscarriage in* Up.

FIGURE 5.10 *Carl watches Ellie from the window, his breathing echoing the movement of her hair in* Up.

park, the nursery and the hospital resonate over this sequence. There is a gentleness, and mutuality, to these images when they are read as imaginative superimpositions. The images of a virtual 'baby', being pregnant with a 'baby' and losing the 'baby', are important to how this image of Ellie and Carl in the garden is perceived by the spectator and how the adventure book becomes a crucial element in the narrative.

Associating the miscarriage with the adventure book allows narrative continuity. The book marks the temporal shift from the moment of miscarriage without it being materially part of the pregnancy loss. As a collection of embodied memories, the adventure book is critical to the narrative. The adventure book, positioned as part of the close emotional bond created by the couple, is part of the recollected narrative around the uterus. It could be argued that the foetus is the recollection-object, but it is not mentioned or shown. Instead, the actual foetal image is replaced by the virtual imagery of a 'baby'. Later in the film, when Carl surrounds himself with objects which remind him of his life with Ellie, his home effectively acts as a place 'imbued with memories and palimpsests of relationships' (O'Neill 2009: 922). In this palimpsest is the memory and imagery around their shared experience of losing a foetus. When Ellie dies, those memories resonate through objects, including the adventure book. This can be understood as mutuality where remembering and forgetting are part of gathering memories. The foetus only exists for a short time in the film, but the embodied experience of miscarriage, where the foetus becomes virtual, remains throughout the film in the transfer of recollection-objects between the protagonists.

The Bad Intentions

In *The Bad Intentions*, the main character Cayetana (Fátima Buntinx) creates a virtual image of a 'baby' that is distinctly different to the traditional images created by Carl and Ellie. Although the uterus is a premises for perception for Cayetana, she uses her imagination to construct a virtual image of her unborn sibling as her heroic rival. She incorporates the history and myth of her revolutionary heroes into her lived experience, which now includes a love/hate bond with the foetus. Set during the 1982 and 1983 civil war in Peru's capital city Lima, Cayetana is the film's main protagonist. She lives a middle-class life in the city. Her mother Inés (Katerina D'Onofrio) travels frequently away from the city and her biological father Francisco (John-Paul Strauss), who is separated from her mother, does not always arrive for his scheduled visits. Her stepfather Ramón (Paul Vega), although more affectionate, spends long hours in his painter's studio. Cayetana, then, spends most of her time in her room or being fed and dressed by staff. She explores the grounds of their gated house by herself and the only time she leaves is to be driven to school. While at school, she is interested in the stories of Latin America's revolutionary heroes, and she incorporates them into her everyday life as lucid dreams, engaging with her heroes as if they were real. On one of her trips home, her mother Inés reveals that she is pregnant.

Cayetana is devastated by this news and believes that when the baby is born, she will die. She spends the time leading up to the birth, preparing for her own death. Eventually, when the baby is born and she does not die, Cayetana refuses to follow her heroes, explaining that she must stay and get to know her brother. Cayetana's embodied emotions of love, fear and death are experienced through her lucid dreams of heroes and heroic sacrifice. Cayetana's imaginative dreams surface at the very opening of the film during the credits sequence and emphasize the importance she attaches to the concepts of heroism, liberation and valour. Her dreams establish that her character is highly imaginative, and that her imaginative state of mind influences her emotional and embodied engagement throughout the film. Her dreams encourage her to have a visceral response to her mother's pregnancy. She understands the foetus to be her heroic adversary, involving the foetus in the complex system of images and objects through which she makes sense of the world around her.

Although she dreads the birth of her sibling, Cayetana creates a heroic character for the foetus while it is in the uterus. Cayetana fetishizes the foetus so that it becomes a recollection-object that she understands as real and is something of value to her. This helps her to position the foetus in her everyday world, as she understands it, which includes the foetus's role in her revolutionary battle. She spends long hours cutting out figures of Latin American revolutionary heroes and pasting them into battle scenes,

which she then narrates with graphic details of killings and torture.¹²
Cayetana experiences the material presence of her revolutionary heroes. As
the narrative progresses, she steps into the world of her dreams to become
a revolutionary character herself. It is helpful here to think about Marks's
suggestion that the 'optical perception privileges the *representational* power
of the image, haptic perception privileges the *material* presence of the image'
(2000: 163; my emphasis). Cayetana experiences her heroes as if they were
in the room with her: she touches them haptically with her eyes. This is
reflected in what Cayetana says at the beginning of the film when she tells
the figure of José Olaya, 'I want to be a hero, like you.'

She places herself in the threshold between the life and death that
she references in the context of the life and death of her heroes. This
explains her anxiety over her own embodiment. She identifies her daily
life, including with the anxiety about her own health, with their visceral
battles for liberation. Her embodied connection to them, therefore, becomes
increasingly real. Cayetana recreates images not only from what she can
see but also from what she can hear and feel. She hears voices shouting and
horses galloping. She mimics the way fingernails are torn off, pulling at her
own fingernails as she narrates the images. This establishes not only that she
has an embodied connection to the story of her heroes but that the spectator
is also encouraged to witness the haptic quality of her lucid dreams. She
has been told in history lessons that when Latin American heroes Simón
Bolívar and José de San Martín met to liberate Peru, Bolívar said that 'two
suns cannot shine in the same sky'. Although this did not necessarily mean
that one of them had to die, Cayetana translates this into meaning that she
cannot exist in the world at the same time as her sibling when it is born.
Her mortality, as she understands it, depends on the foetus remaining in
the uterus. While the foetus is in utero, she remains alive. The foetus, then,
becomes a yet-to-be-born recollection-object for Cayetana that is a marker
of her own mortality.

Although Cayetana's negative thoughts about the unborn foetus are seen
by the other protagonists in the film as jealousy and malice, these feelings
can be read differently, and as positive, if it is understood that Cayetana
believes that she and her sibling are both heroes awaiting their first meeting.
Cayetana's lucid dreams are crucial to the way she experiences the world.
Her visceral response is to the actual embodied world around her and
the imagined bodies of revolutionary heroes. For Cayetana, mortality is a
threshold she must cross. It is this certainty of her own fragile mortality that
she has learnt from historical narratives, and it creates a visceral, embodied
intra-action that she shares with the heroes. Cayetana cuts out images of
historical heroes with scissors, and her collages fill her wardrobe and cover
her desk. The overlapping pictures are tactile and visual connections to her
lucid dreams. Sarah Thomas (2014) explains that 'this imaginative realm
serves not only to demonstrate Cayetana's progressive claiming of agency,

but also to align the adult spectator with the child's perspective, bringing the adult viewer into the child's world rather than the other way around' (54).[13] The recreated battle scenes become a way for Cayetana to escape the equally bloody and violent reality of the life around her. The use of a sharp razor blade, rather than scissors or a pencil, demonstrates how easily the body can be cut. She pours red paint onto the picture that shows the capture and torture of indigenous leader Túpac Amaru. The picture shows that he has ropes tied around each limb and is then pulled in opposing directions. His body, as she says, is so strong it does not separate. She takes her razor blade to make cuts across the pictures of his limbs (Figure 5.11), as if she were cutting them apart. The imagery in this sequence is visceral. The bright red drops of paint echo the vivid primary colours of the picture with the strip of daylight prioritizing the act of cutting. Cayetana takes this violent moment in history and places herself in the action, slicing through the limbs of the hero who is being tortured. In this way, it can be understood that Cayetana understands the threshold between life and death, but that crossing this threshold involves her own embodied sacrifice.

To understand her actions in relation to the foetus, it is crucial to understand this visceral embodied connection. When Cayetana cuts her finger with a razor blade later in the film and then smears her blood across the fresh linen of her baby brother's new crib (Figure 5.12), it is because she is anticipating her own death rather than wanting to harm the foetus or the baby when it is born. Her mother has gone to the hospital to give birth, and it is not only the thought of the baby that is causing her distress, but the fact that the birth of the baby, if it is born alive, is a threat to her own mortality as

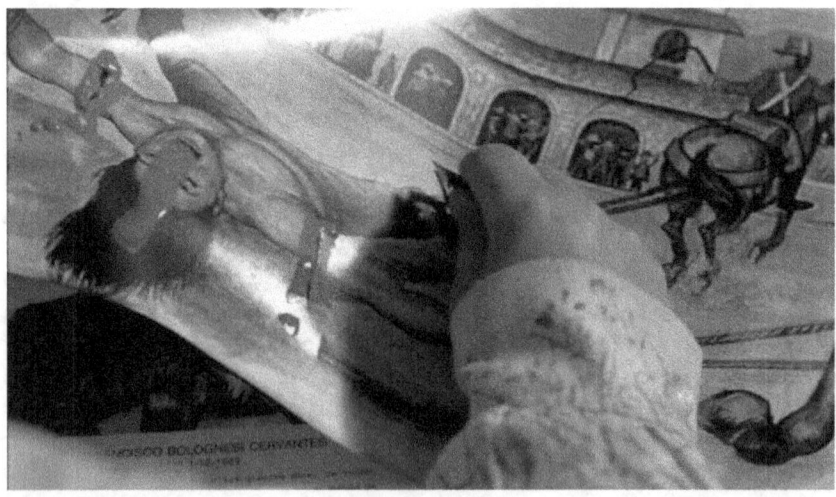

FIGURE 5.11 *Cayetana drips red paint and cuts the picture in* The Bad Intentions.

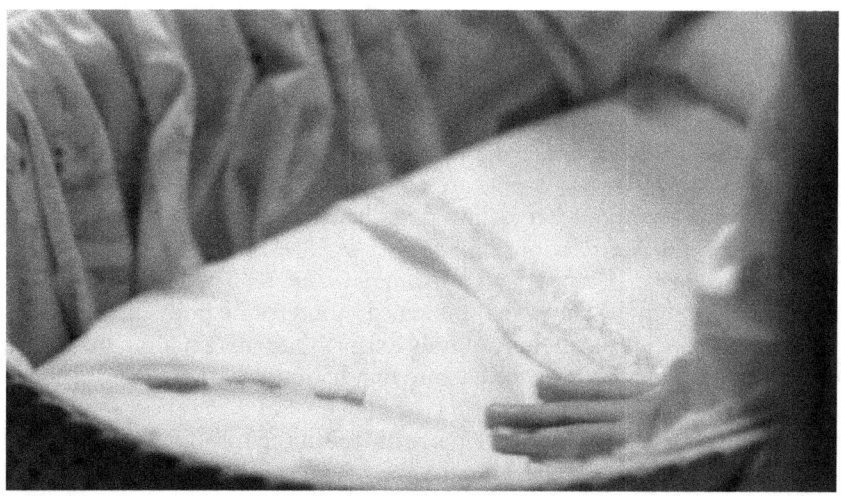

FIGURE 5.12 *Cayetana smears her blood onto her brother's crib in* The Bad Intentions.

she has imagined it. So, there is a context for her action. Cayetana's mortality and that of the baby are, in her mind, entwined. This also explains an earlier sequence where Cayetana is taken to school by her mother in the car. They are late and travelling at speed. Suddenly, when Inés feels the movements of her foetus, she takes Cayetana's hand and places it on her pregnant belly. Cayetana becomes distressed and removes her hand immediately. It is as if this tactile experience is too visceral or real for her and it overwhelms her. In this moment, she is forced, physically, to experience the foetus from the embodied frame of the uterus as something that is alive inside the body as well as the imagined and interpretative narrative that she has created for it. Crucially, the actual foetal movements through her mother's body reinforce the likelihood of her own death. When Inés asks if she can feel the baby move, Cayetana says no and asks if it is dead. By touching her mother and feeling the movements of the foetus, the separation between the unborn and the living is brought into sharp relief for Cayetana, and her own notion of the threshold between life and death is simultaneously reinforced and destabilized.

Cayetana's fascination with death and dying is not only in relation to how the body works but also in relation to how the body dies. Her fascination is influenced by her embodied anxieties about her own health. When she first mentions Túpac Amaru, she says that he fought for the rights of the miners who, among other hardships, suffered from asthma. Cayetana has asthma and thinks that her mother and everyone else want to swap her for a healthy child. She asks herself, 'why do they want a new baby, what's wrong with the old one? Is it no good because it's got asthma?' While she is asleep, and before the baby is born, Cayetana dreams that the medical members of staff who are caring for her newborn brother meet her in the garden. They explain that the newborn needs blood and vital organs to survive and that they have her parent's permission to take them from her as the baby's closest relative. She has no desire to die by choice to save her brother, so she tells the medical staff that her organs are no use as she is adopted. The fact that Cayetana dreams about her bodily parts being used to protect her sibling gives insight into her relationship with her own body and suggests that she understands the difference between fantasy and reality. She understands that her own body has an actual biological bond to the body of the foetus, which suggests that the foetus not only exists in her imagination, but it also exists as a material presence for her and that her understanding of death and mortality is sophisticated.

Cayetana repeatedly experiments with the mechanics of the body and she uses tactility to discover how it works. When her grandmother's blind maid brings her a glass of milk, Cayetana stands in her way so that she can bring her finger close to the maid's eyelid (Figure 5.13). She does this so that she can see how close her fingers can be before the maid is aware of what she is doing. The implication is also that she could hurt the maid as her fingernail is almost touching the maid's eye. Cayetana's finger is framed in the centre of the shot, emphasizing that she is holding it in front of the maid's eye. It is Cayetana's eyes, however, that are the focus of the shot. As she knows the maid is blind, this suggests that it is her own eyes and her own sight that she is trying to understand, not that she is trying to harm someone else. In a similar way, when she is alone with her newborn baby

FIGURE 5.13 *Cayetana brings her finger towards the blind maid's eye in* The Bad Intentions.

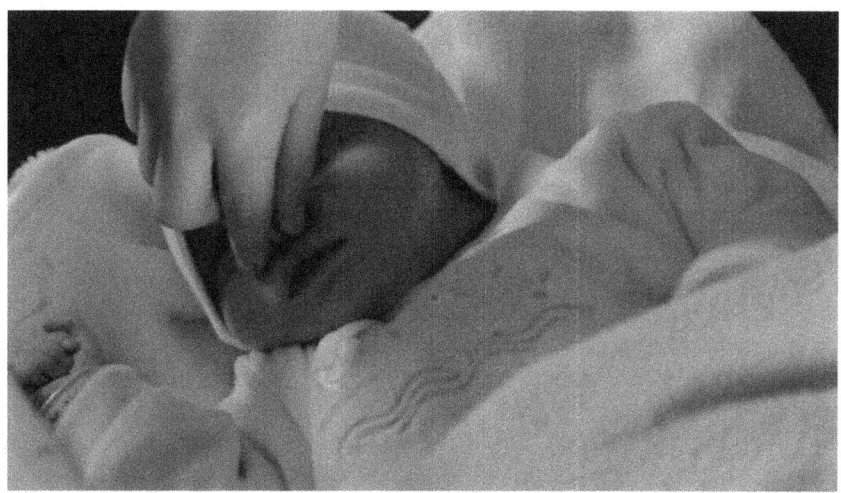

FIGURE 5.14 *Cayetana pinches her baby brother's nose to stop him from breathing in* The Bad Intentions.

brother in the hospital, she pinches his nose to see if he will stop breathing (Figure 5.14). Her hand, in the centre of the frame, covers part of the baby's face as if her whole hand is covering his face. But she holds his nose only with her fingertips until he moves uncomfortably, struggling to breathe. She then takes her fingers away and desperately blows in his face so that she is sure he is breathing. This also suggests that she is not sure whether the baby, now that it is born and outside of the uterus, is alive or dead. Again, this demonstrates a sophisticated knowledge of how bodies in general, and hers in particular, work.

Throughout the film, Cayetana appears to be trying to understand the materiality of both kinship and mortality by pushing people away physically or psychologically on the one hand and trying to find physical and psychological closeness on the other. Cayetana understands loyalty, friendship and kinship by experimenting with her collages, re-telling heroic escapades and recreating scenes of violence and torture, but she is constantly surrounded by conflicting images in her own life. When she creates her own vivid imagery, of heroes and the foetus as recollection-objects, it affects her on a visceral and emotional level that is haptic as well as embodied. Taken from many sources, the images, along with her narration of accurate historical detail, provide a counterpoint to the actual images she sees around her every day. When she travels to school, she sees the body of a dog hanging on a street corner, a hammer and sickle in flames on the outskirts of the city and the sculptures of war heroes in every plaza. Cayetana understands the couple, who live just outside the walls of her house, as neighbours, but she must physically climb a ladder to wave to them. When the wall is raised, for the protection of her own family, she is unable to see the couple and they are removed visually from her everyday life. She speaks to the man who begs in the street and who approaches the car asking for money. He says he cannot sleep, so she offers him her asthma medication because it makes her feel sleepy. She is, therefore, both physically removed and immersed in a world that she understands through fragmented snippets of conversations that sit alongside images that she sees from the inside of a car, over the wall of her house and through the car window. Her understanding of kinship is constantly being complicated, and it is her revolutionary heroes that provide emotional stability for her and give her what she understands to be an embodied presence in her own life.

Cayetana's images of heroes make her feel safe in an environment that is becoming increasingly dangerous, and they function as transitional objects as well as recollection-objects, unlocking memories of her own cultural history, making sense of her present world and readjusting her own embodiment to the imagined foetus born as a live baby. The emotional detachment that Cayetana has from actual people, including her sibling, shows that she identifies more closely with virtual figures and strangers. In her relationship with her unborn sibling, she forms an emotional attachment (not necessarily positive but an embodied emotion nonetheless), but her emotional disconnection, which is both psychological and physical, is shown visually. When Inés first arrives home from her travels, she wants to see Cayetana, but she cannot be found. Cayetana is hiding in a kitchen cupboard. She comes out of the cupboard, then views the scene in the lounge through a set of glass French doors. She moves the glass door backwards and forwards so that the images are clear, then dislocated and blurred, mimicking her embodied distanciation, aware that she is watching the people in the room. She does this again when her mother comes into her room. Cayetana looks at her mother through a plastic stencil (Figure 5.15), so that her image is blurred and fragmented. Even when she removes the stencil, her mother's pregnant body is framed in the doorway. The perspective makes her mother appear on the same plane as the doorway, the dolls on the bookshelf and the pictures on the wall. This creates an unreal quality to the image as shadows obscure her face (Figure 5.16). Cayetana is experimenting with her own haptic visuality, creating a distance between what is actual (what she can see) and her virtual life that she understands as real and that she feels viscerally. Towards the end of the film, it is clear that Cayetana has some insight into her lucid dreams. Despite her experimentation with seeing and imagining, she does not follow her heroes into their final battle. She knows, from her history lesson, that their final battle is doomed. When her sibling is born, and she does not die, a threshold has been crossed whereby she can distance herself from her imaginary heroes and her baby brother ceases to be her adversary.

Cayetana contextualizes her mother's pregnancy, with the foetus as her heroic adversary, as part of her lucid dreams, and she engages in this fantasy

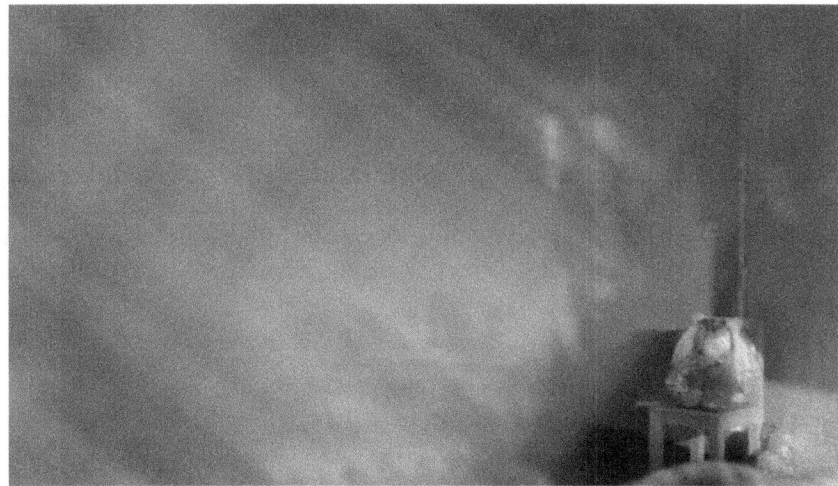

FIGURE 5.15 *Cayetana looks at her mother through a plastic stencil in* The Bad Intentions.

FIGURE 5.16 *Cayetana's mother is framed in the doorway in* The Bad Intentions.

to make sense of her everyday world. She conflates historical facts and her everyday life so that she can position the foetus in utero within the context of her everyday reality, which is living a sheltered life in a city that is in the midst of a civil war. In her virtual life, the foetus demands her personal sacrifice and death. In reality, she experiences an embodied disconnection from the real object in the uterus. It is only when she is forced to confront the reality of the foetus, by touching it through the frame of her mother's body and the uterus, and finally touching the baby when it is born, that reality and fantasy come together, and this affects her profoundly. While the foetus is in the uterus, it remains a fetishistic image, and a powerful recollection-object with which she understands her own world. The foetus as a recollection-object, however, is re-embodied at birth so that it disintegrates once the baby has been born (see Marks 2000: 122). The foetus as recollection-object for Cayetana only exists while it is in the uterus. She also turns her back on her virtual heroes when she has passed her threshold of mortality and survived.

Birth

In, *Birth*, the threshold between life and death is embodied in the character of the young boy who claims that he is the reincarnation of the main protagonist's dead husband. The film is set in present-day Manhattan. The main protagonist Anna (Nicole Kidman) lives in an apartment block with her upper-middle-class family. At the beginning of the film, her husband Sean (Michael Desautels) is shown collapsing and dying while running in Central Park. The present day of the film is ten years after his death and his death is shown as a flashback. Anna's current fiancé Joseph (Danny Huston) announces their engagement at a family party. Her late husband's sister-in-law Clara (Anne Heche) is also invited to the party, but when she arrives, she makes an excuse and goes into the park to bury a parcel. A ten-year-old boy follows her and digs the parcel up. Later, the boy turns up at Anna's apartment claiming to be her dead husband. Nobody believes that the boy, who is also called Sean (Cameron Bright), is a reincarnation. Slowly, however, Anna begins to believe him and spends increasing amounts of time with him, and they make plans to live together when he turns eighteen. Clara eventually confronts the young boy, claiming that she had an affair with Sean, and that the boy should recognize her. As a result of this confrontation, the boy eventually admits that he is not Sean. He returns to school, and Anna marries Joseph. Some of the other characters in the film believe that the boy is an imposter who has memorized details of Anna's late husband's life from stolen letters that he has found in the park. The drama in the film, therefore, comes from the tension that results from the boy's claim to re-embodiment as it challenges their beliefs about the living and the memory of the dead.[14] The dramatic tension centres not only on the validity of the young boy's testimony but also on the emotional impact that the suggestion of reincarnation has on the protagonists.

The main protagonist Anna moves between disbelieving and believing the boy's testimony, which causes her emotional trauma that is both disturbing and comforting for her. The adult relationship that Anna develops with the young boy – which, seen in isolation, is inappropriate and negative – is part of her emotional re-bonding with her deceased husband.[15] The young boy becomes a vivid recollection-object for Anna, offering her a way to remember and communicate with the person she still loves. At the beginning of the film she is sceptical that her dead husband has been reincarnated, but her emotional journey is punctuated by significant events that remind her of her husband, that make Anna question the threshold of life and death. This means that at the end of the film Anna is grief-stricken on her wedding day as she recalls the boy's final letter to her. This letter tells her that when young Sean returns to school, and to being a child, he writes to her to say that 'I've been seeing an expert [. . .] they said I'd been imagining things [. . .] it's a good thing it's gone away now [. . .] I'm really sorry I made you sad. The good thing is that nothing really happened [. . .] I'll see you in another lifetime.' Her palpable grief implies that the experience with the young boy throughout the film provokes a response in her that brings deeply held feelings and memories of her dead husband close to the surface of her present-day life.

The film heavily signposts the threshold of life and death by beginning with a sequence set ten years in the past, where the adult Sean collapses and dies underneath a bridge in New York's Central Park (Figure 5.17). The location is matched to the present day when Anna meets the boy (Figure 5.18). The two sequences appear at different points in the film, but the mise en scène in each forms a graphic match in the framing of the bridge and the movement of the camera. In both sequences, the camera begins with a static long shot of the characters' journey towards the bridge and then tracks backwards underneath the bridge, keeping the protagonists in the frame. Along with

FIGURE 5.17 *Sean runs under a bridge where he collapses and dies in* Birth.

FIGURE 5.18 *Anna meets ten-year-old Sean at the location of her husband's death in* Birth.

a low bass rumble, this framing gives the impression that the camera is drawing both Sean and Anna towards it – Sean to meet his death and Anna to meet his reincarnated self. The young boy chooses this location for his first private meeting with Anna. To prove that he is her reincarnated husband, he tells Anna that she will know where he is going to wait for her. The meeting of Anna and the boy under the bridge suggests that he understands the importance of the location to Anna as the site of her husband's death. Knowing the site of her husband's death suggests to Anna that young Sean is telling the truth. The boy asks Anna if her brother-in-law, a lawyer, were to ask him some questions and he were to answer correctly, would she then believe him. Although she remains doubtful, Anna asks him who told her that there was no Santa Claus. Unable to give a name, the boy insists that he will know them when he sees them. At this moment, Anna begins to doubt her own judgement, as the boy claims to recall events that happened before he was born. She tells him 'you're just a little boy' and rushes away. It is only later, when Anna sees the physical effect of her rejection on the boy, that she begins to consider that he might be telling the truth.

For Anna to believe the boy, she must accept that her husband's death coincided with the boy's birth and that there was an embodied moment when the dead body of adult Sean entered the body of the foetus in utero. She is visibly shaken by this possibility but remains unconvinced by the boy until she rejects him and tells him to leave her alone. As a consequence of her saying this, young Sean collapses. At this point in the narrative, Anna and Joseph have already confronted the boy and his father to warn the boy to stay away. Anna is telling the boy, 'you are hurting me, do you understand that? I don't want you to bother me.' Importantly, his consequent physical collapse – knees buckling and falling to the ground (Figure 5.19) – is only witnessed by Anna. The boy's father is looking away, but Anna turns her body slightly and glances back in time to see the boy drop to his knees. Sean's collapse is synchronized with the opening bar of the opera's overture.[16] This musical bridge continues over the sequence and follows Anna's journey in the lift from her apartment building to their late arrival at the opera. This physical collapse sparks a visceral reaction in Anna and is one of the most striking moments in the film.

The sequence ends with a four-minute-long close-up on Anna's face in which she tries to stifle her conflicting emotions while watching an operatic performance. The camera picks out Anna and her Joseph but closes in and focuses on Anna as she takes her seat. Once seated, Anna is framed in close-up (Figure 5.20). Importantly, there are other opera-goers sitting behind her, and their bodies remain out of focus but remain at the edges of the frame. The slow rhythmical breathing of these bodies emphasizes Anna's frantically stifled breathing. Anna's expression changes subtly and appears to move from fear to sorrow to affection which suggest that she is beginning to believe that Sean might be telling the truth. If so, he becomes a living recollection-object that is, in fact, her dead husband. As Marks suggests, an object or an image that resurfaces from another place or culture can 'disrupt the coherence' of the present (2000: 77). This is what is happening to Anna as her physical and emotional equilibrium is disorientated. The camera is static but handheld so that it follows any slight movement to keep Anna in centre frame. Anna's face moves briefly and sharply when her concentration is broken by Joseph's quiet comments in her ear. It is

FIGURE 5.19 *The boy collapses when Anna tells him to leave her alone in* Birth.

FIGURE 5.20 *A close-up highlights that Anna is distressed but must remain calm in* Birth.

only the camera and the spectator, however, that witness Anna's embodied response. The light reflecting the gloss on her top lip guides the spectator's eye from her lips to the light shining on her earrings, which in turn draws the spectator's attention to the beaded necklace on the person behind her. This draws the spectator's eye to the breathing bodies beside her. The effect is to emphasize Anna's embodied response, the tactility of the moment and the haptic quality of the scene, so that the spectator shares the moment of Anna's physicality. The implication is that she is considering the possibility that her husband Sean has crossed the threshold between death and life, in a moment that has taken place in utero.

The transfer of the dead adult into the foetus (reincarnation) takes place while the foetus is in the uterus. This threshold between life and death is signalled visually by the suggestion of an embodied exchange of adult and child immediately after Sean's death in the opening sequence of the film as the young Sean is born (Figure 5.21). At this point, there is no reference to the pregnant person. The pregnant body of the mother cannot be fully seen and at the birth remains out of the frame by the narrow depth of field that focuses on the baby's body. The specificity of the moment of reincarnation is reinforced visually by a temporal ellipsis with the foetus being born under water. The foetus, at this point, is on the threshold of life. Even though it is on the point of birth, the shift to the moment of reincarnation can be understood to happen when the foetus is still submerged, as this marks the time between Sean dying and the foetus leaving the uterus and taking its first independent breath. The moment of birth, as the point of the baby's first breath, is signalled by the same musical motif of plucked violin strings, flute

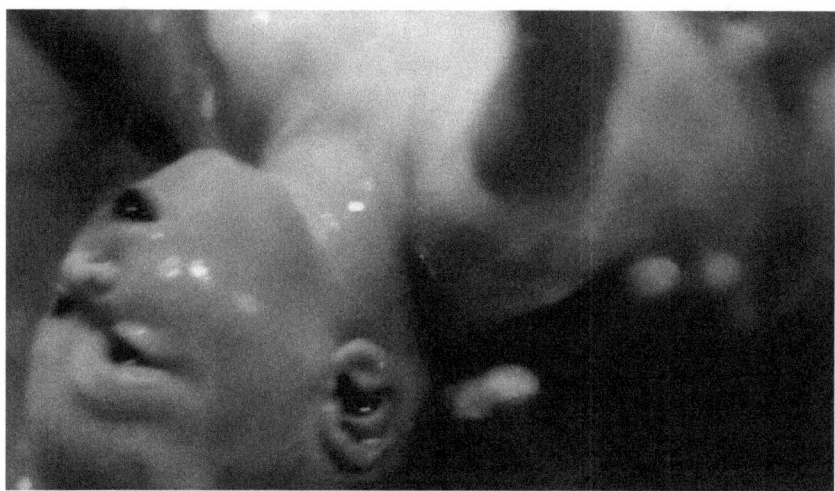

FIGURE 5.21 *The first breath of air for the boy as he is born in* Birth.

and triangle that began the film, but without the sinister bass undertones of brass, woodwind and cello strings. This musical bridge links the two sequences of Sean's death and the birth of the baby and gives weight to the suggestion that some essence of Sean has been transferred to the foetus.[17] The bridge where Sean dies is framed like a tunnel that, when juxtaposed with the birth scene, makes metaphorical reference to the birth canal. Importantly, this sequence of death, reincarnation and birth is witnessed by the spectator, not by the protagonists. This moment, however, is not marked by any reference to maternity. There is no additional visual or audio information about the baby or its biological heritage. The only thing that is seen in addition to the baby are the hands that lift the baby out of the water bath, which implies that this reincarnation is separate or separated from the maternal body and the uterus. The importance of this sequence is to establish reincarnation, but also to establish that this change in the foetus enables it to become a recollection-object for Anna, suggesting that the future bond between them is present in the foetus while it is in the uterus.

The bond that occurs between Sean, the foetus and Anna has an effect on Joseph who, even if he does not believe the boy is a reincarnation, understands that his ambiguous presence is 'disrupting the coherence' of the present and is having a negative influence on his own relationship with Anna. As Joseph waits for Anna in an apartment they are viewing, he realizes, as he looks out of the window (Figure 5.22), that she is with the boy and that they are taking a carriage ride around Central Park. Joseph's mood changes when he stares out of the window at them. He concentrates on what he is seeing, and his body remains still as if the image has rooted him to the spot.

FIGURE 5.22 *Joseph is framed by the window as he sees Anna and Sean in the carriage in* Birth.

This is seen in the aesthetic of the sequence. Joseph stands by the window of the apartment, and the grey sky is reflected across his body, creating what appears to be a dissolve. This suggests his embodied, emotional response to the boy's presence. It also marks his anxiety and anger that the boy represents to Anna her dead (but now alive) husband. The reflection of the leafless trees in the park surrounds his body. The branches are reflected across his body and around his head, which creates the impression that he is slowly disappearing within them. The railings outside of the apartment form part of the lower frame of the image. Their pointed arrows draw the eye towards Joseph, but also direct the slow zoom. As the zoom starts, the low bass tones of cello mixes into the flutes, violin and xylophone, which is then gradually replaced by the full strings. This signals the musical motif that connects all the protagonists.[18] The sweeping score builds in intensity with the slow zoom so that by the time the camera stops in an extreme close-up of Joseph's face (Figure 5.23), the image is overwhelmed by the volume of the theme music. Both Anna and the boy are the focus of Joseph's point of view and the reason for his static stance. In this moment, the uterus can also be described as a premises for perception, the location where the threshold between life and death that Anna's husband and the boy have crossed.

The moment that the boy draws Joseph's gaze to the window signals that the boy functions as a recollection-object for him and compounds his unhappiness. This is written on his face. As the boy had suggested, Anna has not shared with Joseph every detail of her previous romantic life. The implication is that Anna's loving memories of her husband are only shared with the boy and that these private memories have resurfaced for Anna

FIGURE 5.23 *Slow zoom into a close-up of Joseph as he watches Anna and the boy in the carriage in* Birth.

and threaten the relationship she now has with Joseph. In this way, Joseph is forced to confront Anna's memories, even if he does not know what they are. By implying that the boy knows what Anna's memories are, the boy becomes a powerful recollection-object for each of them, imposing a narrative trajectory that for Anna is positive and for Joseph is negative. That the boy is the object of their attention is emphasized in the cut from the close-up on Joseph's face to a long shot of Anna. The close-up on Joseph is not static when the cut happens, so the zoom has not quite finished and the cut is on the camera's movement towards his eyes. The long shot of Anna is also cut on movement in an extremely slow tracking shot where the camera moves towards her. The effect of this transition is to focus the spectator's gaze on Joseph's embodied reaction, and then carry his gaze through to Anna as the frame moves towards her. The tracking shot does not end up on a close-up of Anna, but it gets close enough to her to see that her eyeline shows she is looking out of the left-hand side of the frame, and that her gaze is on the boy playing in the park. By editing the shots on this movement, the point of view of Anna and Joseph and the spectator ends on the boy, emphasizing his emotional power over the two protagonists.

Although young Sean functions as a recollection-object, when he returns to be a child, his own embodiment as the recollection-object changes, it disintegrates. This is the reverse process of the body of the boy disappearing as he is replaced by a man who has been dead for ten years. The young boy is not only a vehicle for memories, but he is also a catalyst for those memories, and he is transformed through them so that he becomes something different to who he actually is. The recollection-object, however, remains a part of Anna's memory and part of her shared narrative with the boy. The recollection-object that is embodied by the young boy has a powerful effect on Anna. She wades into the sea at the end of the film – it is his letter confirming that he will leave her alone that has a profound emotional effect on her. Although the boy rejects his role as the embodiment of her dead husband, Anna remains emotionally connected to him or rather to the recollection-object that he had become. The bond that has been created between them is physical and emotional, but it relies on Anna believing that her husband returned from the dead. When the boy as recollection-object disappears, Anna's emotional connection to the recollection-object does not diminish. Young Sean, then, becomes a recollection-object many years after his own birth.

Sean as a recollection-object can be contrasted with the recollection-objects in *Up* that are centred around the lived body experience. The lost foetus in *Up* is a hidden recollection-object that remains an unseen part of the subtext of the film. In *The Bad Intentions*, virtual images of revolutionary heroes are understood as recollection-objects that mean something to the main protagonists, but they too disappear, or dismissed at the end of the film when the baby is born. The recollection-object has a transient quality where any bonding depends on it remaining meaningful to protagonists. Although Marks uses it as a way to explain specific cultural artefacts or objects that are redolent of another time, place or culture, it is a useful concept when thinking of how objects link narratives of pregnancy when they are not wholly dependent on the pregnant body. This is an important factor in thinking of the uterus as a narrative space. The pregnant body is not necessary for a discussion on reincarnation, neither is it completely necessary to a narrative of pregnancy loss. The pregnant body in each film may only be important as the place that keeps the foetus alive. It can be sidelined once that function has concluded whether in a live birth or birth loss.

The recollection-object, therefore, adds to the conceptual framework of the book as it articulates how the threshold of the body, the uterus, is crossed in the aftermath of miscarriage, in the fear of mortality and in the belief in reincarnation. The recollection-object makes sense of how narratives that originate in the uterus can become separated from the body. When there is a temporal gap between the birth moment and its memory, the pregnant body (and by implication, the pregnant person) is given less significance. The recollection-object, then, makes sense of how pregnancy, and the lived body experience of pregnancy can be fragmented. Chapter 6 will investigate pregnant embodiment and engage with how Eugenie Brinkema understands the space outside of the frame as *mise n'en scène*. Brinkema's discussion returns the focus of the book to formal structure and off-screen space to think about what else is not in the mise en scène or what is not put into the scene enough to think of pregnant embodiment as a presence–absence that is embedded in the narrative structure of *Arrival*, and how the uterus functions as a palimpsest in *Ixcanul*.

6

Pregnant embodiment as *mise n'en scène* in *Arrival* and *Ixcanul*

Throughout the book I have stressed that the narrative space of the uterus should be considered as off-screen space, but in this chapter I want to add the lens of Eugenia Brinkema's (2014) *mise n'en scène*, what is not put into the scene, to discuss pregnant embodiment as presence–absence.[1] As I have mentioned throughout the book, the lived body experience of pregnancy is a state with which many people intra-act, either with the body or through technological visualization. But how pregnancy is experienced or felt is not the same as how pregnancy appears on screen. This chapter offers ways to understand how pregnant embodiment can be constantly inferred but not present in *Arrival* and be hidden as a lived experience in *Ixcanul*. I argue that pregnant embodiment in *Arrival* exists in temporal gaps and is suggested in action rather than as embodiment. In *Ixcanul*, pregnancy is physical and visualized on screen, but the lived body experience of pregnant embodiment is hidden as part of the pregnant and post-partum body. In each film, the foetus is understood to exist or have existed, but it remains unseen. Brinkema's *mise n'en scène*, I suggest, contributes additional depth to this discussion by articulating not only what can be understood as on-screen or off-screen but what is left out of the scene to make sense of what is missing from each film. As Brinkema argues, 'we have not yet asked enough of form' (40), and she suggests that, without turning away from other theoretical ways of analysing film texts, returning to questions of form can unearth surprises. In these two films, the surprising link is pregnant embodiment.

The visual cues in both films are suggestive of the lived experience of pregnancy, but pregnant embodiment is absent or missing even though it underpins each narrative. As I mentioned in Chapter 2, *mise n'en scène* demands that close analysis attends to what is put into the scene and what is left out or put into the non-scene, and although Brinkema says that the spectator is not the focus of her analysis, it helps to explain how the affective nature in each filmic text is an interplay between on-screen and off-screen space. Importantly, Brinkema expresses a desire to return to form to understand the 'more ephemeral problematics such as duration, rhythm, absences, elisions, ruptures, gaps and points of contradiction' in close analysis (2014: 37). As being pregnant suggests a temporality that is linear, as time moving forward, but also as time-limited or paused, pregnant embodiment can be understood as filling the gaps in temporality. Pregnant embodiment as an expression is rich and complex as it indicates physical and conceptual presence–absence. Being 'pregnant' can describe the materiality of the uterus with the presence of a growing embryo or foetus. Being 'pregnant' can also be used to suggest something more ephemeral that is less like a presence but as something that is full of meaning or has an importance that has yet to be expressed or understood. Being 'pregnant' can also signify a pause or a period of expectation, and it can also be used figuratively to express emotion or feeling as the materiality of a moment that is full or swollen.[2] Embodiment, by contrast, can be understood as what it means to have a body or an idea that is inscribed on the body or even a personification that functions within a representation. By placing the two words together, pregnant embodiment expresses that which is grounded in physicality and that which is conceptual.

Before thinking about pregnant embodiment, it is important to say that there is no simplistic analysis of pregnancy as present or absent in either film in this chapter, nor can pregnancy be explained only as subjectivity or representation. However, I do want to acknowledge that the theme of pregnant embodiment for many people involves their own subjectivity as an emotional response to the materiality of their own bodies. Imogen Tyler (2000, agreeing with Christine Battersby (1998)) explains that pregnant embodiment is not only an actual subjective lived body experience, but also an embodied potential. Tyler argues that we should be conscious of multiple subjectivities rather than just the individual pregnant person. Being pregnant, she explains, is not a metaphor; it is a lived body experience that has a transitional and transient subjectivity that includes the non-pregnant. As I discussed in Chapter 1, and as Iris Marion Young (2005) points out, pregnancy is commonly understood as belonging to the foetus, not the pregnant woman. Pregnancy, as Young explains, is often considered as 'a state for the developing foetus, for which the woman is a container' which is partly, she suggests, as a result of pregnancy becoming a medically 'objective, observable process' (46). The separation of bodies indeed silences the subjective experience of pregnant embodiment when the pregnant subject becomes 'decentred, split, or doubled'. The question is, where does this separation of bodies sit within philosophical thinking, and how might this be addressed in close textual analysis? As Tyler (2000) argues, the separation of bodies is difficult to reconcile with philosophical notions of the self as individual. She emphasizes that thinking about pregnant embodiment philosophically must include the implications for non-pregnant bodies. This is a critical point and in my discussion of *Arrival* and *Ixcanul*, I consider pregnant embodiment as something more than individual subjectivity and more than a fleeting state of a few months. To return to Tyler's point, the subjective experience of pregnant embodiment expresses the now-ness of maternity but also expresses a subjective and objective not-yet or not-ever. As the main protagonist in *Arrival* appears to have no lived body experience of pregnancy, yet she has a daughter who lives and dies, the question that this film and the main character ask is 'who is the child?'

Arrival

The filmic world of the characters in *Arrival* is defined not only by the circularity of time but by the complexity of language structures, and this has encouraged a range of interdisciplinary critical discussion. Jane Stadler (2017) refers to the Sapir-Whorf hypothesis that explains how different structures of language influence perceptive and cognitive understandings of the world, to argue that the film's language shows how cinema itself is an effective conduit for understanding other world views.[3] David Evan Richard (2018), taking a phenomenological approach, says that *Arrival* is 'self-reflexive of film as a sensuous event', and describes how human and alien bodily gestures enforce the filmic language and the spectator's response to it (41). David H. Fleming and William Brown (2018) focus on how the film 'throws up a counterintuitive model of time', which they base on Deleuze's (1995) discussion of a 'third synthesis' of time and John M. Ellis McTaggart's (1908) notion of 'unreal time'.[4] Fenty Kusumastuti (2019) explains that polysemy, when the same words and phrases are interpreted as meaning different things, is significant to the linguistics in the film, particularly when the protagonists are trying to understand what the aliens are really saying. The human characters in the film look for ways to communicate with the aliens, but as Kusumastuti says, they do not necessarily understand each other. She also explains that it is important to recognize 'the interrelation of polysemy *in* the film and the polysemy *of* the film' (75, my emphasis) so that although interpretation of language is a key thread in the narrative, the overarching theme in the film is polysemy. My reading of the film differs from those above in that while I appreciate that the narrative deals with interpretation (or translation) of language and the complexity of time, the film makes sense of what is missing from human reproduction when it is reconstructed in chronological order. In my analysis, I consider how pregnant embodiment as lived body experience can be discovered in the film through the gaps, elisions and ruptures created by the narrative structure. Looking to the *mise n'en scène* allows me to reveal how pregnant embodiment exists as something that has not happened and has yet to happen once the narrative structure is unravelled.

Arrival complicates the notion of pregnant embodiment by presenting a non-linear narrative whereby a 'not-yet' born child dies before conception, leaving a 'not-yet' pregnant body. The question of the unborn, as Barbara Duden (1993) explains, is that it 'is never there with certainty. In spite of many signs and intimations of its presence, one can never be sure about it' (9). Duden suggests that with no reassurance of survival outside of the body, the foetus is 'a "not-yet" [with] a peculiar temporal dimension' (10). The term 'not-yet' is used by Duden to describe the complex historical, cultural, social and legal processes that establish the status of the foetus and to the way that medical verification attributes presence and personhood. She says that medical verification replaces the subjective embodied sensation of quickening, where the pregnant person first feels the first movements of the foetus and where this feeling is only experienced by the pregnant person. In the film, the 'not-yet' foetal presence can be said to exist in off-screen space, present in the *mise n'en scène* but absent on screen. The narrative of *Arrival* is constructed to show the biological and emotional relationship between the main character, a mother, Louise (Amy Adams), and her daughter, Hannah (Julia Scarlett Dan, Abigail Pniowsky, Jadyn Malone). Throughout the film, Louise works closely with an interdisciplinary team, including her colleague Ian (Jeremy Renner). While Ian works on mathematical calculations of alien language, Louise concentrates on the practical issue of understanding how their language works. Ian becomes increasingly visible as a physical presence in Louise's narrative of reproduction, which includes Hannah. Although the narrative of the film suggests the existence of a child, by the end of the film the lived body experience of pregnancy that is implicit in the main protagonist's maternal representation has 'not-yet' happened. The conceit of the film's narrative is that the past is a vision of the future, which can only be understood retrospectively by re-ordering the narrative chronologically.

Importantly, although the aliens' concept of time is a recurrent motif in the film, the film does not show time as the aliens see it – as happening simultaneously. The language of the film remains linear: it has a past, present and future. Time, however, is arranged as non-linear which prompts Tijana Mamula (2018) to argue that the prolepsis, the flash-forward, can be thought of as 'temporally unplaceable' (542).[5] The prolepsis does, however, offer fragmented or liminal moments of time that appear as a series of events that are meaningful to Louise. The suggestion is that these are events that she remembers and are in her past. The threshold of life and death, however, is continually being crossed as each time Louise 'sees' Hannah, she does not exist. As the spectator is encouraged to read these moments as concrete events that have already happened, the ellipsis created by the narrative structure challenges the position of the spectator in relation to the lived body experience of Louise and Hannah. There is no evidence in the film that Louise wants a child or thinks about having a child. Pregnant embodiment in *Arrival* is assigned to Louise in her maternal representation as a biological mother who is grieving the death of her child. Seeing herself with Hannah, however, does not make any sense to Louise. Although the lived body experiences of 'circumstantial childlessness' (Lois Tonkin 2017; Leslie Cannold 2000) may involve the presence of an imagined unborn child, this is not what is happening in this film. Importantly, it is over halfway through the film that Louise, after seeing herself with a baby, then a child and then an adolescent, says to the aliens, 'I don't understand, who is the child?' This moment around the mid-point of the film's narrative confounds any notion the spectator might have had that Louise was ever pregnant. Louise's presumed pregnant embodiment encourages the spectator to believe that the lived body experience of the pregnant person exists in the film and that her experience as a biological mother is an expression of her maternal subjectivity. It is overly simplistic, however, to understand Louise's character development as maternal without considering how the corporeality of the film upends the linearity of pregnancy and embodied subjectivity.

As Lisa Baraitser (2014) suggests, understanding reproduction and non-reproduction as temporality can help to understand what is meant by 'stilled time' or the expectant time of pregnancy that ends when birth begins (1). She argues that temporality is always thought of in terms of a linear progression to the future, and this is defined by dominant cultural narratives linked not only to social and economic specificity but also to markers of time that bring people together such as birth and death. Baraitser (referring to Lee Edelman's (2004) discussion of how queerness has been positioned with 'no future' in reproductive futurism) suggests that we must rethink many timelines including reproduction and birth, so that they can be thought of in terms of an 'infinitely expanding present' (Baraitser 2014: 3). For example, in *Arrival*, the language of the aliens, Louise is told, 'is free of time [and like their bodies] it has no forward or backward direction'. This notion of time as expanding in the present speaks to both the movement and the stillness of time and could be aligned with McTaggart's (1908) argument about the 'unreality of time' when events have fixed moments in a timeline but time itself is always moving through past, present and future. Thinking of time this way means that there is always a deferred affectivity, a 'not-yet' that signals a rethinking, Baraitser suggests, of how the timelessness of death and grief is understood as subjectivity. Insofar as the film lands on questions of subjectivity and embodiment, it can only be read as such after repeated viewings. It is almost impossible to register the detail of each shot and to discuss what the film does when Hannah appears on the screen unless there is a constant freezing of the frame. As Laura Mulvey (2006) suggests, it is only by stopping and starting any film repeatedly that the detail within the film's corporeality can be seen. My reading of *Arrival*, then, unearths the tensions between the text on first view and the meaning that is read into it through repeated viewings. By slowing down the film and investigating its corporeality 'so that time itself becomes palpable', *Arrival* can be said to add a Mulveyan 'something extra and unexpected, a deferred meaning, to the story's narration' that demands critical attention (150–1). This something extra, I suggest, is the presence–absence of pregnant embodiment.

Pregnant embodiment, although not seen on the screen, is a presence that cannot be ignored in the film; the question is, how is this presence achieved formally? Returning to the opening sequence, the moments after Hannah's birth appear at first viewing to be a clunky, over-laboured backstory that provides exposition in the narrative of the main character Louise. The aim of this sequence is to establish that a baby has been born, and it forces the assumption of pregnant embodiment. The spectator must believe that pregnancy has happened to the body even if, narratively, pregnancy has 'not-yet' happened and the foetus does not exist. When Young argues that 'pregnant existence entails, finally, a unique temporality of process and growth in which the woman can experience herself as split between the past and the future', (2005: 47) she is talking about the embodied state of pregnancy as it is experienced by the pregnant person. In *Arrival*, it is pregnant embodiment that is split and decentred. When Louise is first seen in the film, she appears to be post-partum, holding, stroking and smiling at a baby. The close framing and narrow depth of field allow the spectator to see what is happening but from a distance. There is no establishing shot, no orientation in the room. A relationship is suggested by another unidentified person in silhouette. There is evidence of a marriage with rapid close-ups of a gold ring on Louise's ring finger that matches a ring on the hand of the silhouetted figure. This sequence establishes quickly and aesthetically a traditional, biological mother. It is not clear whether the unidentified person is the father, a friend, a relative or medical personnel. The montage that follows shows the baby growing into a young girl and dying as an adolescent. This opening sequence influences the way that Louise as a character is read in the narrative which, we are led to believe, is in the present. This sequence, however, is from Louise's future. In the plot of the film, she is not-yet pregnant, and she is not-yet with the biological father. Her daughter, therefore, is not-yet conceived so can not-yet die. The spectator is encouraged to understand that her character is a grieving mother. In effect, Louise's character is not understood as she is but only as something that she has the potential to become at the end of the film.

The process of persuading the spectator that Louise is becoming a parent is achieved by conceptualizing Hannah as a child. In the two-minute montage that follows her birth, Hannah is shown growing up and beginning her journey to adulthood. Becoming an adult, however, is halted in her adolescence, so that she is in a constant state of 'not-yet' being born, not-yet 'being' a child, but nevertheless dying. In child development Emma Uprichard (2008) says that the process of being a child always involves 'becoming the adult' where the 'will-be' is more important than the 'is' (304). The film, however, demands that the 'is' of being a child is crucial to the spectator orientation. This is clearly shown in the sequence where Hannah and Louise play outdoors. In the shot-reverse-shot, Hannah is seen from Louise's point of view, but when Louise is framed, her eyeline shows that she is looking left out of the frame towards Hannah. The handheld camera pivots along the axis of Louise's body so that Hannah runs from side to side around Louise (Figures 6.1 and 6.2). This anchors the scene formally around Louise's body. Hannah appears in the centre of the frame, out of focus, in a long shot, all from Louise's point of view. Finally, Louise remains in the centre frame in a mid-close-up, but as part of a long shot whose subject is Hannah. The spectator is left looking beyond Louise to Hannah who is in the distance such that when Louise's head bows into the frame, it covers Hannah from view. Formally, this sequence orientates the spectator around Louise and her point of view of Hannah.

FIGURE 6.1 *The camera pivots along the axis of Louise's body in* Arrival.

FIGURE 6.2 *Hannah is seen to run left to right of Louise in* Arrival.

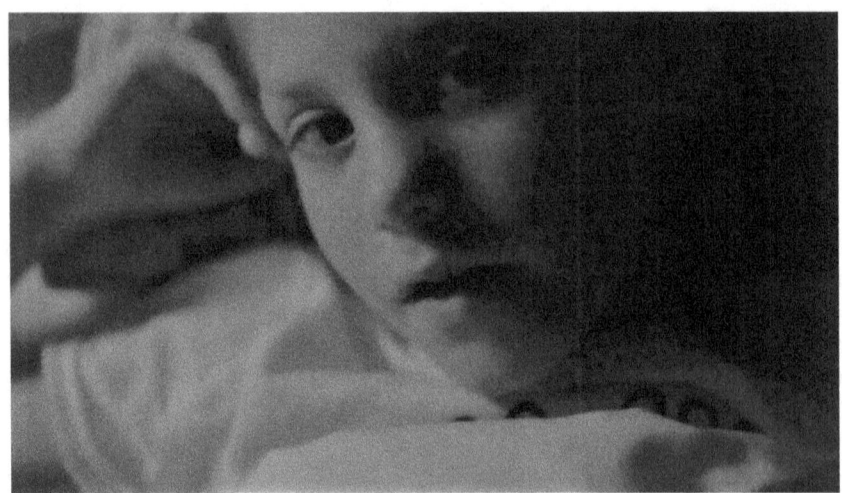

FIGURE 6.3 *In soft focus, Hannah faces the camera to say 'I love you' in* Arrival.

This formal arrangement encourages spectatorship to appear as collaborative and collusive. This collusion is most evident when Hannah is shown in a close-up as a young girl. She is lying down, facing the camera, the light is soft as if it is night. Her eyeline is slightly off-centre but she is facing the camera when she says, 'I love you' (Figure 6.3). The soft key light highlights the bridge of her nose, her eye and her mouth. Her fingers tickle the side of her head where she rests her hand. The softness of the light on the folds of her shirt in turn emphasizes the softness of the child's face. The film then cuts to a wide-angle close headshot of an adolescent Hannah with harsh hospital lights behind her, framing her furious face as she screams, 'I hate you' (Figure 6.4). Hannah's dialogue is directed at Louise, but her eyeline is designed to provoke a reaction from the spectator. It is as if she is shouting at us, the viewers. The sequence propels the dramatic tension of the narrative, as the push-me, pull-you parent-child relationship is given extra poignancy when Hannah dies. It also encourages the spectator to enter into the *mise n'en scène*. It is crucial that the spectator has a vested interest in Hannah, to believe that she exists as a character from Louise's past and to understand this series of events as narrative progression, but the aim is also for the spectator to understand Hannah as a physical presence.

Physicality is an important way in which Louise's character experiences her visions of Hannah. Louise experiences disturbances in her own embodiment when she becomes aware of Hannah's presence. Almost an hour into the film, Louise is at her desk when she hears pages being turned, and it is not her. In mid-close-up, the mise en scène establishes Louise's physicality as she works actively (Figure 6.5). The camera is above and to

FIGURE 6.4 *With the harsh hospital light behind her, Hannah screams 'I hate you' in* Arrival.

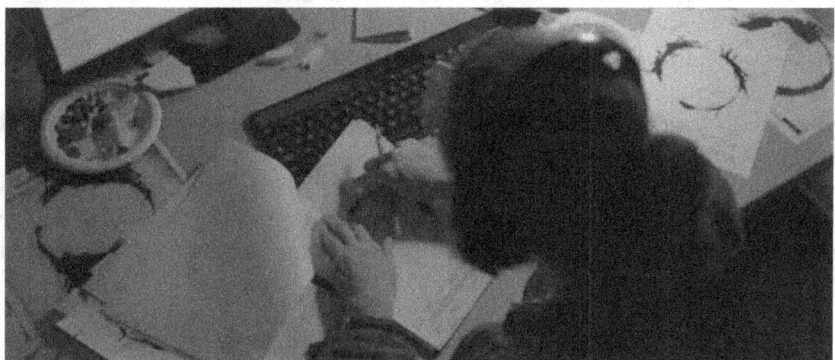

FIGURE 6.5 *Louise's physicality is echoed in the way her desk is covered in her notes, designs and snacks in* Arrival.

the side of Louise, so that her desk appears at an angle in the frame. Her keyboard is at an angle to her screen. Her paper notes on the design of the heptapods' language partly cover her keyboard. Her snack of segmented orange and nuts on a take-away plate implies she is too busy to sit and eat a meal. She rips a post-it note from the pad, writes something and sticks it onto her note. The voices of other people working can be heard. The camera cuts to a side-view close-up on Louise with her headphones on. The ambient sound does not drop out, but there is a close-to-mic crisp sound of paper pages being turned. There are two things happening here formally:

the mise en scène of the first mid-close-up establishes her physicality; the second close-up relies on exaggerated sound in the *mise n'en scène* to signal an additional physicality. It is not clear where this sound is coming from; it might be Louise's headphones, but the audio from one sequence to another establishes a change in embodiment for Louise as well as sensing another physical presence. When Louise stands up, she is unsteady on her feet and falls into a chair, and while it would be exaggerating to say that this is a moment of pregnant embodiment, the way the narrative is arranged and the way in which Hannah is being conceptualized suggests that this could be an event outside of the immediate mise en scène. The turning of pages, which appears out of nowhere, has an effect on Louise that is embodied. She hears her own voice talking before the camera cuts to the pages of a child's book being turned. Rather than it being an expression of pregnant embodiment, I suggest that this formal transition from one temporality creates an off-screen ellipsis in which pregnancy and pregnant embodiment must exist.

Louise's embodied 'feeling' and the appearance of a child's book establishes a parallel narrative of Louise and Hannah talking. In this sequence, the spectator has an extended view of Hannah. The mid-close-up on Hannah shows the texture of her hair woven into plaits. The mid-shot also shows the soft texture of Hannah's dress as it folds and rides over her shoulder blade, her half-empty pencil case slumped on the table, the school bag flat on the table and the out of focus landscape in the background. The child is being conceptualized through the aesthetic of the film. Matching eyelines and point-of-view shots establish the close relationship between Louise and Hannah. Importantly, the detailed side-shots of Hannah (like the recognizable images of a foetus in a scan) demonstrate that she is being conceptualized for the spectator. Hannah's embodiment is an important component of her conceptualization, and she is given a physicality, an aliveness, as she is seen

FIGURE 6.6 *Hannah appears to close her eyes in response to being touched in* Arrival.

playing, running, painting, drawing and shouting. This reflects an active body, one that is engaged with the environment and with the people around her. This aliveness marks every sequence with Hannah, including her physicality when she is with Ian and Louise as her hair is stroked, she is picked up and twirled around, her hand is held and she responds to having her hair stroked by closing her eyes (Figure 6.6). Hannah has a physical presence within the diegesis of the film that is emphasized by the corporeality of the film as she takes up more film time. There are moments when Hannah is seen as if in a flowing or ebbing consciousness that might be understood as a memory. This is shown in soft-focus shots, at canted angles in the frame, and as an unrecognizable silhouette. This gives the appearance that Hannah is appearing through the movement of time, in the way memories resurface repetitively. When this happens, Louise's body anchors the narrative so that even though time is fragmented, it appears linear.

It is this grounding of linear chronology in Louise's narrative arc that allows Hannah's presence to be read as a memory. In a sequence that occurs forty-seven minutes into the film, Hannah appears to be a memory. The whole sequence is less than a minute long, and Hannah is in two shots that together last just twenty seconds. These shots are bookended with a tracking shot around Louise leaving the spacecraft, on her way to the decontamination and medical inspection tent. When she gets out of her jeep, the camera follows her towards the medical tent. As she doubles up as if dizzy or in pain, the camera begins to track around her in a mid-shot and the bass rumble of the soundtrack continues over the first shot of Hannah. The handheld shot is a person in a darkened room who appears to be looking at an indecipherable moving figure (Figure 6.7). As the shot progresses, the figure at the front of the frame appears to be a child and the blurred figure in the distance becomes more animal-like. In the second shot, the camera moves in close-up from the animal's body to focus on the child's face. This second shot also has the synch audio of a horse's hooves on a hard surface emphasizing the physicality of the moment. As the camera travels, Louise's body appears in the sequence and she says, 'I know' in a calm voice as if to reassure the child. The tone of her voice establishes that the child and Louise have a caring relationship. In this complex sequence, the moving handheld camera emphasizes the intimacy of the moment. The lack of synch sound in the first shot gives an ethereal air, as if it might be a memory, understood as fleeting. The added sound of the horse in the second shot grounds the images in what appears to be real-life action. The sequence suggests Louise's changed embodied state, which links the two characters physically, but also highlights how memory appears as a presence that is physical even if that memory has yet to be experienced.

Louise's embodiment is crucial to the narrative, but I suggest caution with the temptation to apportion her embodied changes that are seen on screen as pregnant embodiment as Louise experiences intense changes to her embodiment as an integral part of the film. She is doubled up, bending forward,

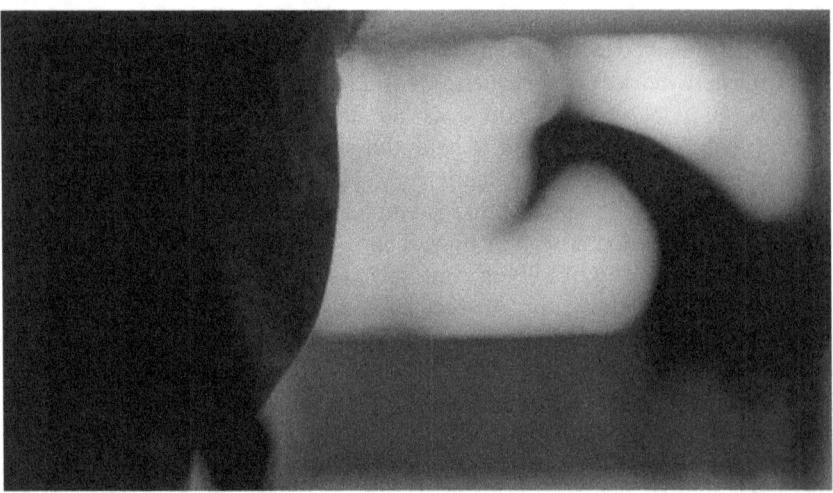

FIGURE 6.7 *As the image sharpens, the blurred figure becomes more animal-like in* Arrival.

before she sees Hannah, and this could be read as mimicking a contraction or foreshadowing the deliberate movements of the heavily pregnant person. Again, when she revisits the alien's spacecraft alone, she appears as if she is underwater with her eyes barely open and her hair flailing slowly around her head (Figure 6.8). In another context, and a different critical discussion, her embodied experience could be described as embryonic. Embodied experiences are, however, part of the aesthetic of the film. Before she ever sees Hannah, Louise's hands shake. She absorbs the language of the aliens through her fingertips and feels faint while breathing through an oxygen mask in her spacesuit. When in the spacecraft, Louise floats upwards only to be thrown sideways by the altered gravity or atmosphere of the spaceship. If some of her movements echo pregnant embodiment, then it could be argued that Ian is similarly experiencing pregnant embodiment as he stumbles when leaving the astronauts' cage, falls upwards in the altered gravity (Figure 6.9) and vomits into a bin when he enters the changing room on his return. As the two characters are so intimately linked through the corporeality of the film and through their future reproductive bodies, perhaps they are both capable of experiencing the bodily symptoms of pregnancy. As pregnancy is absent as embodiment in the present for both characters, this cannot be discounted. Overall, the film implies through its narrative and aesthetic construction that pregnancy and reproduction exist and that they are fundamental to the story. My argument is that the narrative cannot make sense without understanding that pregnancy, although absent from the screen, must be considered as having a presence. Pregnant embodiment exists in the *mise n'en scène* of the film, I suggest, as a presence–absence. This raises important

FIGURE 6.8 *Louise appears as if she is underwater, with her hair floating around her head in* Arrival.

FIGURE 6.9 *Ian floats upwards, stumbles and is thrown sideways in* Arrival.

questions about the shareability of pregnant embodiment and whether it can always be understood as a subjective experience. In the next film *Ixcanul*, pregnant embodiment is present on-screen and the main character's pregnant and post-pregnant state drives the narrative. My discussion returns to the question of how pregnant embodiment appears in the gaps and elisions, not only of the narrative but as part of the images that, although clearly seen, have something missing that relates to what pregnancy does and how it leaves a palimpsestic mark on the body.

Ixcanul

Pregnant embodiment is a central feature in *Ixcanul* but is not presented as the subjective experience of the main protagonist María (María Mercedes

Coroy). The narrative of *Ixcanul* pays attention to the political, social and historical context of the film's topic. Working with Kaq'chikel speakers on script development, using non-professional actors, setting the film in real locations and adapting real stories of indigenous lives, the director Bustamente creates an authentic narrative. At the same time, according to Debra A Castillo (2019), the film pushes to one side the aesthetic inconveniences of indigenous modern-day living (a nearby US chain-food store, for example, is not included in the landscape of the film) to provide a backdrop more appropriate, according to Castillo, to 'authentic exoticism' (120). The discussion of indigenous representation is of great significance to analysis of this film and others, such as *The Milk of Sorrow*, and there is a fine line between representing authenticity and creating a colonizing approach through traditional representations. Castillo argues that there are many absences in the film: absences, for example, of the actual voice of the actors and the communities that they represent.[6] Importantly for my discussion, one of Castillo's concerns is that the foetus/child becomes part of 'biomedical waste' whether, as the film suggests, it has been sold for body parts or given as a gift in adoption.[7] When Castillo talks about the foetus/child who is missing, she explains that '[t]he child then figures a certain kind of surplus reproductive material – living or dead, boy or girl – and this figure is at the heart of this plot, even as s/he is shunted to the side, never seen, the very epitome of a semiliving object' (131). I agree with Castillo's argument about absences, but I also think differently: the foetus/child does exist on screen. We do not see it, but it exists as a presence–absence in off-screen space while it is in utero as part of the young protagonist's body and even when it is removed from body.

In the film, María becomes pregnant when she has sex with her boyfriend Pepe (Marvin Coroy) for the first time. Although she has been promised in marriage to the owner of the coffee plantation Ignacio (Justo Lorenzo) where she works, María agrees to have sex so that Pepe will take her away from her village when he leaves. When María's mother Jauna (María Telón) realizes that her daughter is pregnant, she tries to help her abort the foetus. When this fails, she tells her husband Manuel (Manuel Antún) about the pregnancy and Manuel then tells Ignacio. When María is stung by a snake, her parents take her to hospital. The family speak Kaq'chikel, an indigenous language, and cannot understand the medical staff at the hospital who all speak in Spanish. They must rely on Ignacio to translate for them, and he uses his position as translator to tell María and her family that the baby has been born dead. María gives her fingerprint to sign a form, which, it is suggested, gives permission for the baby to be taken away. Later, when María believes that she has been tricked, she digs up the baby's coffin to find that it is weighted with a brick which is covered in cloth.

One of the most compelling moments in the film in terms of *mise n'en scène* occurs after the supposed death of María's baby. María and her parents walk alongside their community as mourners, and their dialogue suggests the baby is absent from their vision. The baby, however, is right behind them in the frame in its coffin (Figure 6.10). María is held by her mother and her father walks alongside. The child's coffin is carried at head height and it moves in time with the procession across the back of the frame. As the handheld shot continues, the coffin, draped in white cloth, moves in and out of focus. María asks her mother, 'why couldn't I see the baby?' and her mother replies that 'the venom deformed your baby [. . .] It's better that you didn't see it.'[8] The baby, as they understand it, is in the coffin, which is in plain sight in the frame. Of course, the dramatic irony of the narrative is that there is some doubt about whether the baby is in the coffin. What is in the frame is María's post-partum body with her uterus as a palimpsest to mark the presence of the foetus. The frame also includes the past post-partum body of Juana with her uterus as a palimpsest of María's foetal presence. The frame, therefore, includes pregnant embodiment as something that has already happened to the body. Narratively, this is an absence. Rather than a focus on the presence–absence of the foetus, it is the interaction of the two post-partum bodies that I find significant. Technically, post-partum signifies a limited amount of time from giving birth, but I use the term here to acknowledge that the uterus is always marked by pregnancy. The presence–absence of the foetus is at the centre of the frame, but pregnant embodiment, as presence–absence, is also in the centre and front of the frame. As Brinkema (2014) explains, often the process of grief is a productive narrative theme in cinema 'because its form has an intrinsic arc of resolution; mourning demands and brings forth a story' (95). Her critical point is that that loss is often difficult to show on screen, so the processes associated with grief are presented. She says, 'absence is made present visually to the film by displaying the materiality under or behind any being,

FIGURE 6.10 *The baby's coffin appears in the centre of the frame behind María and her parents in* Ixcanul.

replacing the substance of a body with the substance of the environment in which that body once existed' (95). Although Brinkema is talking about the cinematic tropes of the empty chair or bed, it serves to explain how the post-partum body in the frame, when thought of as pregnant embodiment, is an important marker of loss.

Yet, there is no evidence that María engages with her own pregnant embodiment in any meaningful way. For example, when Ignacio and Manuel return from fumigating the land against the snakes, María serves them coffee. When she rushes out to vomit, she is seen in the left-hand the corner of the frame. Her figure is blurred as she places her hand over her mouth to suppress her nausea (Figure 6.11). The camera does not follow María, but it stays on a mid-shot of Ignacio. This allows the men to have a conversation about whether either of them has been affected by the substance that they have used for fumigation. Manuel says that María is reacting to the product and that he too feels nauseous. Ignacio says he does not feel anything at all. Neither Manuel nor María are given time in frame to express their nausea. The moment of pregnant embodiment, as nausea and vomiting, for María is absent from this mise en scène even if it is understood to be happening off-screen. It is notably that there is a later sequence of vomiting after María drinks the abortifacient tea[9] which also begins outside of the frame, off-screen. Manuel even asks Jauna to tell María to move further away from him because she is waking him up. María is moved further out of the frame into a silent *mise n'en scène*. María is only briefly seen as her final vomit ends the sequence. The act of vomiting here is a useful narrative device of transition. After the sequence where María has sex with Pepe, the film must establish that she is pregnant. A reference to vomiting is one way to do this. Crucially, vomiting, when used as a sign of pregnant embodiment, means that the pregnant body does not have to be present in the frame.

FIGURE 6.11 *María is seen leaving the frame to vomit. The vomiting takes places in off-screen space in* Ixcanul.

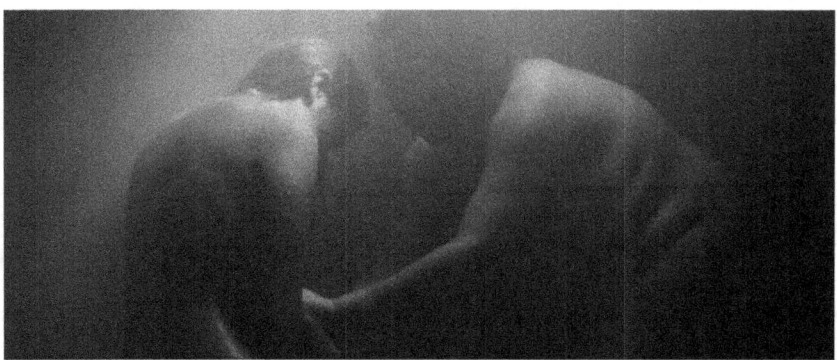

FIGURE 6.12 *Jauna in centre frame touches María's belly and realizes that she is pregnant in* Ixcanul.

Pregnant embodiment is shown explicitly in the swelling of the pregnant body, seen for the first time in the sweat bath – *temazcal* – where Juana notices that María is pregnant. Juana realizes as she strokes and feels María's belly and asks her whether she has counted her moon cycles (Figure 6.12). The two women are placed in the middle of the frame. The light from the top of the *temazcal* catches the side of María's head, her ear, the side of her face, just glancing the swollen belly at the side of her torso. Juana leans into this light as she holds María's arm, revealing her own post-partum body. Juana is more active, rubbing and smoothing the skin on María's arm and belly. The belly is hidden behind María's arm but is a focus for Juana. It is a moment for Juana to explain that they need to 'get rid of it'. This is a complex sequence in terms of pregnancy embodiment. The pregnancy is discovered by touch, but María has already been experiencing embodied changes, like vomiting. Although the movement in the frame suggests a tender moment between mother and daughter, the dialogue points to the importance and danger of the foetal presence. When Juana later prepares her herbal tea abortifacient, she asks María where Pepe is now. Juana is suggesting that Pepe's absence highlights his lack of responsibility and she uses this to persuade María to drink the herbal tea. The biological father is now effectively erased from the narrative of the film.

Although the father is erased, the foetus is continually present in off-screen and on-screen space and is also present for María as a girl and for Manuel and Juana as a boy. At the point of burial, María has to be distracted so her mother tells her that the branch that had been sitting on the top of the coffin is to be planted and grow strong, 'thanks to the breath of the baby'. When María refuses to let go of the coffin, she says, 'let me see [. . .] I want to see her.' The personification of the foetus as a gendered being, as such, is part of its liminal quality: it can be both genders at once. Once she is pulled away, María remains by herself in the frame watching the burial. She has not been allowed at any point to see her baby, yet she believes strongly that the baby is a girl. The following sequence begins with the branch planted on the top of the grave alongside a homemade wooden cross, as if the plant is a visual reminder of the baby that she has never seen (Figure 6.13). At this point, they assume that the baby has been buried and so this mise en scène also includes the contents of the coffin as the silent *mise n'en scène* of 'biological waste'. Later, Manuel narrates the life of the baby as they return, empty handed, from their battle to get the authorities to find the baby (Figure 6.14). Their bodies are connected through touch as Manuel consoles Jauna and Juana consoles María, the absent foetus/baby missing from the framed intergenerational group. Manuel says of the foetus, 'surely, he went

FIGURE 6.13 *The wooden cross and branch provide a visual marker for the foetal/baby presence in* Ixcanul.

FIGURE 6.14 *The post-partum María listens to Manuel construct a narrative for the absent baby in* Ixcanul.

to the US, in a house with a garden like in the magazine.' He goes on to say that 'he'll have to speak English'. María does not add to this conceptual narrative but counters it. She tells her father that 'she is a girl and she's too young to speak'. This indicates that María now has greater agency, but only after the end of her pregnancy and loss of her baby. In a previous sequence, she is shown digging up the grave of her baby with her hands, desperate to prove that the coffin does not contain her baby. She throws down the bricks wrapped in cloth that are inside the coffin in front of Manuela and Juana, as if the heaviness of the bricks weighing down the coffin has been masquerading as the product of her pregnant embodiment. María's agency, however, is sporadic throughout the film. When her father creates a narrative for the foetus, it is his narration, not María's. Her subjectivity, as post-partum, is not part of her father's narrative, even though her uterus was the last place that the foetus/child existed for anyone in the family.

Although pregnancy is actively happening to María's body, the way that the pregnant body is stroked, carried, dragged and laid out suggests that the pregnant body is passive. Rather than an active way of being, pregnant embodiment in the film is shown as vomiting, bodily growth and heaviness, all outward signs of a foetal presence. When Juana makes María hop down the volcano to help the abortion process, for example, despite her mother's insistence, María can only hop lightly, her feet landing softly and with little noise in the volcanic ash almost as if she does not have the heaviness that is demanded of pregnancy. In a later sequence in the *temazcal* when María is heavily pregnant, Juana massages the pregnant belly, telling María to massage it every day so that the baby's head will be in a good position (Figure 6.15). Juana pushes with force, while María sits passively. There is something missing here about the way a heavily pregnant body responds to having the belly massaged. There is no indication that the baby is moving in

FIGURE 6.15 *The camera tilts down and the pregnant belly takes the centre frame between Juana and María in* Ixcanul.

response to touch and there is no outward sign that María feels anything. As with the earlier sequence in the *temazcal*, María sits passively in a mid-two-shot so that the two women are given equal space in the frame. This time, however, the camera tilts down so that María's pregnant belly takes up the centre of the frame. When María voices her body's reaction to the pregnancy by saying that she has an acidic stomach, her mother tells her that it is because the baby's hair is growing. The foetus is in the centre of the frame off-screen, and its hair is growing inside María's pregnant belly causing heartburn, but María does not move. Moreover, María's symptoms of pregnant embodiment are explained away. The camera then tilts up but not to the equal frame of the two women. The camera returns to place Juana in the centre of the frame, as if despite the focus of massage on María's belly, the pregnant subject has been erased in a screen-wipe.

Pregnant embodiment is not only a subjective experience of pregnancy, but it also expresses what it is to be pregnant, what it is to have been pregnant and what it will be like to be pregnant. There are moments when pregnant embodiment is clearly seen as belonging to the pregnant body in the frame as it is in *Ixcanul*, but often pregnant embodiment is implied by a series of bodily reactions such as dizziness (*Arrival*) or vomiting (*Ixcanul*). The recognizable visual tropes of pregnancy are often used as a shorthand for the experience of pregnancy not just in these two films but in films about pregnancy in general. The lived body experience of pregnancy as pregnant embodiment is much harder to show on screen, and even harder to include in analysis without reverting to pregnancy tropes. I suggest pregnant embodiment appears in the gaps, absences and ellipses in narrative. A more complex close analysis of the frame and the narrative space beyond the frame can be achieved by thinking about what is not in the scene but is clearly in the *mise n'en scène*. This chapter suggests that as well as thinking of the uterus as a premises for perception and as a bioscape, paying attention to the formal qualities of *mise n'en scène* offers more options for a close analysis that is not based on representations of pregnancy or the pregnant body. And it is this attention to the formal qualities of narrative in on-screen, off-screen and non-scene space that enlivens the critical discussion about pregnancy and the pregnant body. In my concluding remarks, therefore, I offer some thoughts on why the analysis in this book is important not just as a formal discussion of meaning-making in film, but also as a serious contribution to redefining close textual analysis of pregnancy and reproduction.

Conclusion

This book has argued that the uterus is a narrative space. The overarching discussion, however, has been to redefine close textual analysis of pregnancy, the pregnant body and reproduction. Taking the Americas as a starting point, the analytical focus has been on the uterus, rather than the cultural, social, political markers of reproduction or gender-specific representations. In doing so, the critical discussion has been widened to consider the lived body experience of pregnancy. This has highlighted the lack of variety in some films where pregnancy is often only a small part of narratives rather than a central driving force. The argument, therefore, uncovers omissions in film narratives about pregnancy as much as it explores alternative narrative analyses of pregnancy.

Importantly, a new corpus of films has been introduced. Bringing together disparate films recalibrates critical discussions of reproduction. When seen in dialogue with each other, this new corpus encourages complexity in analyses of pregnancy and reproduction by uncovering small moments that are worthy of textual attention but would ordinarily go without critical comment. The presence of the post-partum and the unpregnant body, for example, is rarely considered for in-depth analysis. This lack of complexity, I suggest, is because pregnancy, the pregnant body and reproduction are commonly understood in terms of their aesthetic role in mise en scène or their social, cultural, historical or ideological specificity. The difficulty here is that these analyses can rely on representation, which all too often results in analytical shorthand for the generic woman. Sustained investigation into the uterus as a frame creates more analytical possibilities, which I suggest can then be used to revisit specific genres such as horror or to rethink questions of gender. As I discussed in Chapter 1, pregnancy is so often linked to narrative and generic conventions that it is not enough to assume an identifiable pregnancy genre without also considering the lack of variety and repetition in fiction films. The new corpus thus demands new methods of critique.

My phenomenological approach, outlined in Chapter 2, has prioritized film theories of the frame and off-screen space and brought them into dialogue with feminist discussion of the pregnant body in the foetal scan. Empirical research into the foetal scan offers another way of looking into the body that I have found useful when thinking about the frame in film.

Roberts's notion of collaborative coding, for example, expresses how narratives around the body intersect and has been helpful in Chapter 3 when investigating the uterus as a Sobchackian premises for perception. Adding Sobchack's notion of the gentleness of the frame helps to understand how images continue to resonate with the spectator even when they are no longer on the screen. I have also added Deleuze's notion of an Elsewhere to describe off-screen space as it demonstrates how virtual images are understood alongside actual imagery in negotiated, collaborative narratives. This has led me into thinking of the uterine frame as a bioscape, a point of contact for intersecting narratives, in Chapter 4. Collaborating coding and the bioscape can be understood as in conversation with each other demonstrating how the uterus becomes a frame for negotiated narratives.

The analysis has been extended to include the Marksian recollection-object in Chapter 5. The recollection-object articulates how objects that are associated with pregnancy or the moment of birth circulate between people to create positive and negative kinship bonds. Brinkema's notion of *mise n'en scène* in Chapter 6 then adds another dimension. Even though the uterus has been understood as a premises for perception, a bioscape and as a frame for the threshold of birth, *mise n'en scène* brings additional depth to the formal analysis of the frame. Investigating what is not put into the scene or what is not limited to off-screen and on-screen space encourages more exploration of perceived absences from the screen such as pregnant embodiment. Each chapter, therefore, has provided a slightly different element to understanding the uterus as a frame to define its properties as a narrative space. When assembled, each critical discussion advances the textual analysis, thus offering a distinct way to investigate each filmic text.

Focusing on the frame has meant moving beyond a phenomenological enquiry that is only 'documenting the stirrings of the skin', as Brinkema suggests that we should (2014: 38). The investigation has been into ways of looking and how, as Sobchack explains, 'the film transcends the filmmaker to constitute and locate its own address, its own perceptual and expressive experience of being.' Importantly, as Sobchack explains, film theory often prioritizes the screen and 'only indirectly [the] dynamic activity of viewing [. . .] engaged in by both the film and the spectator' (1992: 9, 15). The metaphors of cinema used in classical film theory – the screen as a picture frame, a window or a mirror – assume an analysis of *active* viewing that, Sobchack argues, side-lines the *dynamic* quality of the embodied experience in the viewing process. I agree with Sobchack, but I am also inclined to heed Brinkema's caution against the navel-gazing theorist always returning to the 'I' of the affective encounter. As she argues, this often results in being 'complicit with the explicit marketing of feeling' (2014: 32). On a personal note, I have taken Brinkema's advice to be mindful of the affective encounter while asking more of form and of formlessness to offer new textual readings of narrative space in pregnancy. As Laine (2013) suggests, however, it is impossible for a researcher to leave behind their own emotions when they embark on a phenomenological approach to analysis.

Certainly, I have written this book as a way to write myself and my own intersubjectivity into film critique, but I do this because I cannot always recognize the narrative and textual analyses around the reproductive body in film scholarship. I take the spirit of Laine's meaning when she says that the strength of a phenomenological perspective is to 'set in motion, put into context and [be] shared by others' (18). As Sobchack also suggests, phenomenological readings may well be informed by a particular experience, but should be resonant and applicable to other possible or future experiences of other spectators (2004: 5). Returning to the way that form presents pregnancy and the labouring body demands that historical, political or socially informed philosophical enquiry should also be attentive to the richness of possibilities in the filmic text. Phenomenology, Frampton points out, describes, 'our *experience* of things' where there is an interconnection between the subject and the object (2006: 39, emphasis in original). Focusing on the textuality of pregnancy and reproduction as part of a phenomenological and philosophical investigation not only offers solutions to the difficulties of reading pregnancy in filmic text but also opens up critical enquiry of reproduction to more analytical possibilities.

Finally, as Sarah Cooper (2013) points out, when Sobchack was thinking about the film experience in the 1990s, she was 'swimming against the tide of prevailing theoretical trends' such as post-structuralism (110). This is a reminder that we have not yet exhausted the implications of phenomenological enquiry. As Cooper says, '[t]he screen and the film are no longer only to be understood as objects subject to the gaze of spectators; rather, they are in a dialogical, mutually implicating, relationship' (111). This has been the focus of the book, to address the ways in which pregnancy, the pregnant body and reproduction connect bodies and people, through collaborative narratives. Crucial to my analysis has been to consider the pregnant and labouring body as normal rather than normative. This stresses the importance of the lived experience. As I emphasized in the Introduction, any specific imagery of the normality of pregnancy and the labouring body demands discussion and should not be ignored in the race for ever more elaborate close analyses of pregnancy. My point is that, alongside any analysis of a birth sequence or any comment on the social and political nature of birth, pregnancy and the labouring body should be framed as normal. My hope is that my approach will encourage writers to produce more diverse scripts about pregnancy and reproduction in the future. I also hope film scholars will understand the importance of normality in any questions of reproduction, and I suggest that understanding the uterus as a narrative space is one way to achieve this.

NOTES

Introduction

1   In *Mediático*'s special dossier on *Roma* in 2018, Deborah Shaw explains that Cuarón makes amends to the people who worked for his own family by 'tak[ing] us to the spaces of [Cleo's] existence that her employer-family never see'. Shaw argues that Cleo's stillbirth and later confession that she did not want the baby symbolize the hidden consequences of a live birth. Shaw explains that Cleo, in real life, would not necessarily have been able to keep the baby if she wanted to stay employed. Olivia Cosentino (2018) then explains in the same dossier that the film is about the 'missing parts of stories that are typically told by (privileged) people who have the platform and opportunity to tell them'. Cosentino argues that the film is about Cleo's intimate and emotional labour, part of which is to keep her emotions under control while her baby is dying. Pedro Ángel Palou argues that the most important element of the film is that way in which Cleo's voice is given prominence by prioritizing her point of view and framing her gaze, particularly when she is delivering her baby. In another special dossier on *Roma* in *Film Quarterly* (2019, which includes a useful bibliography by Marc Francis), interpreter Carla Marcantonio notes that in public question and answer sessions with actress Yalitza Aparicio, the sequences of Cleo's water breaking and her stillbirth were of great interest. Marcantonio suggests that the politics of motherhood were of equal importance to the audience as the broader political backdrop of the film. Her point is that women saw their lived experiences of mothering and motherhood reflected in Cleo's character. Sergio de la Mora (2019) gives a comprehensive overview of the reactions to the film in the same issue of the journal. The film, he suggests, exposes class and race not only onscreen but in the reaction to the film's narrative and to Aparicio herself. The undercurrent of racial hierarchies, he suggests, have fuelled debate about the film's political positioning most particularly in the way that it perpetuates the narrative of indigenous subjugation. Importantly, he goes on to suggest that Cleo's experiences in the film such as stillbirth may be the subjects in a future narrative in a new cinema.

2   A search for 'uterus' in IMDb in May 2020 produced these top results: *The Uterus* (2017, Pedro Antoniutti, Brazil); a US TV series *The Uterus* Part 1 (2010) produced by Wellington Chiu and Nicole Wright; and *Uterus Independence Day* (2019, Kayla Baken), episode 6 of US TV series *New Yorkers in LA*.

3   A history of the ultrasound scan is beyond the scope of this book, so I recommend Nicolson and Fleming's book as it engages with the implications for women's lives and for feminist critique as perception of the technology constantly moves between being understood as a visualizing or as a diagnosing technology. As they note, in the late 1950s, the obstetric team at Glasgow University (led by Ian Donald, regis professor of obstetrics and gynaecology and formerly regis professor of midwifery) which was made up of physicians, technicians and engineers discovered the fourteen-week-old foetus during an ultrasound examination of a uterus (and woman) thought to be enlarged due to a fibromyomata, a benign tumour often found in the uterus. The discovery of this early foetus was not casual or an epiphenomenon as such: the early scan was used to identify differing body tissue such as tumours and cysts and viewing the foetus was also part of this journey of discovery. Once the team at Glasgow realized that they could recognize foetal life at a very early gestation, they could provide appropriate care to the pregnant person who might otherwise be advised to have a dilation and curettage D and C for uterine bleeding.

4   Nicolson and Fleming note that the 'iron curtain of the maternal abdominal wall' is a phrase used by the obstetrician Professor Ian Donald (1955: 5). The 'iron curtain' originally refers to the curtain lowered onto the stage as a fire precaution. They explain that 'by the 1930s [it had] acquired the metaphorical meaning of a barrier to communication', rather than the physical and political barrier it has come to signify in the present day (2013: 285). They reference Patrick Wright's work, which charts the history of the iron curtain (2007). They also say that in 1937, the UK Ministry of Health's investigation into maternal mortality found that half of the deaths of women in childbirth were avoidable; one of the causes being medical mismanagement in the use of obstetric instruments (Nicolson and Fleming 2013: 58).

5   See Stuart Campbell's (2006) lecture for OBGYN.net conference. Campbell is professor and head in the Department of Obstetrics and Gynaecology at St. George's Hospital Medical School and was previously a research registrar with Ian Donald in Glasgow.

6   Although there are promising signs of a willingness to amend legislation, abortion is prohibited completely, with no exceptions, in the Dominican Republic, El Salvador, Haiti, Honduras and Nicaragua. In 2017, the Senate in Chile approved changes to the law so that it now allows abortion if there is a threat to a woman's life, an unviable foetus or the pregnancy is a result of rape. In August 2018, the Senate in Argentina rejected an extension of abortion laws beyond the threat to the mother's life or in the case of rape: the campaign had wanted abortion to be freely available up to fourteen weeks of gestation. In 2020, the Argentinean president Alberto Fernández committed to putting forward an abortion bill to the Senate. The bill, for abortion up to the fourteenth week of gestation, was passed by the Senate in December 2020 and became law in January 2021. Countries where abortion is allowed with few or no restrictions are Cuba (with parental consent for minors), Guyana, Puerto Rico, Uruguay (with parental consent for minors), see www.guttmacher.org/f act-sheet/facts-abortion-latin-america-and-caribbean.

7   The fragility of abortion rights has come into focus while I prepare this book for publication. The Covid-19 pandemic of 2020 has been used as an excuse to limit abortions in some states of the United States with closures across many states forcing women to travel huge distances to have their abortion. See https://www.guttmacher.org/article/2020/04/covid-19-abortion-bans-would-greatly-increase-driving-distances-those-seeking-care. The reason for this is that abortion is not considered as an 'essential' medical need.

8   See www.guttmacher.org/state-policy/explore/overview-abortion-laws.

9   The referendum in the Republic of Ireland in June 2018 allowed for the relaxation of strict abortion legislation. This has been understood as a moment of global significance primarily because it is a nation that has never had liberal laws on abortion. This marks the nation out as significantly different from other countries such as Chile where parliamentary political changes have constantly influenced the restriction or relaxing of abortion law.

10 An important factor in any discussion of gender is the lived body experience of trans men and women who find conception difficult because of the way their bodies function physiologically and this challenges the way that pregnancy and reproduction is bound up in notions of being a woman. Even if the politics of gender transition are put to one side, for some people pregnancy is complicated by medical and social expectations (influenced by representations) of the pregnant body. See Margaret Besse, Nik M. Lampe and Emily Mann (2020) for a literature review of US experience-based research into trans men achieving pregnancy and giving birth.

11 There are other scholars working on questions of pregnancy and the body. Rosemary Betterton (2014), for example, offers an in-depth discussion about maternal bodies, including the uterus, and ways of looking across the visual arts. She says that '[a]s a process that occurs within a woman's body, pregnancy is structurally located in the personal and private sphere, but it is always also public property' (4). Betterton also engages with the research of Julie Roberts (as Julie Palmer) on the non-diagnostic scan. She notes that Roberts (Palmer 2009a, b) suggests caution in attributing the presence of the visualized umbilical cord and placenta to the material presence of the mother. The suggestion is that this can also contribute to side-lining a woman's reproductive physiology.

12 For a discussion on marginal cinemas and mainstream critical theory, see Julianne Burton-Carvajal (2006: 17–35).

13 Chanan and Podalsky suggest that it was Alejandro González Iñárritu's multi-protagonist film *Amores Perros* (2000) from Mexico that signalled a shift in how Latin America cinema and its filmmakers were seen in the rest of the world. The film gained its international popularity from its viscerality which, according to Stephen M. Hart, signalled that '[t]he "New" New Latin American film was typically located in a generic (often urban) non-traditional site [. . .] thereby making a clean break with films of the 1990s, which were located within a recognizably national space' (2015: 108). Podalsky gives an extensive account of the reaction to Iñárritu's film not only internationally but also by critics from South America who saw the film as 'Tarantino-lite'.

14 For discussions on New Latin American Cinema, Cinema Novo and Third Cinema, see Zuzana Pick (1993), John King (2000) and Anthony R. Guneratne and Wimal Dissanayake (2003).

15 Chanan uses Jacques Derrida's notion of *différance* to signify diversity, but he uses the term in a different context to Derrida's original meaning. Derrida's term accentuates the linguistic similarity of difference and deferral and could be most closely related to the system of signs and signifiers that marks linguistic theory (which itself forms the roots of European cinematic theory, particularly of the *Cahiers du Cinema* group). Derrida uses the term to describe the pause or the gap that exists in the process of understanding – a deferral. Margrit Shildrick (1997) explains that *différance* suggests that meaning is 'deferred or detoured, always in some sense somewhere else' (103).

16 The term post-national, I suggest, recognizes the complexity of discussions that began in critical movements, theoretical approaches and understanding of film aesthetics associated with a national consciousness such as Third Cinema in Latin America that articulated the importance of political filmmaking as separate from Hollywood (First) and European Auteur traditions (Second). See Octavio Getino and Fernando Solanos's manifesto *Toward a Third Cinema* (1970–71), which is also discussed by Michael T. Martin (1997: 33–58). Post-national also acknowledges the diversity of exilic, diasporic and postcolonial 'accented' film production and filmmakers where the nation is seen from the differing viewpoints (Hamid Naficy 2001).

Chapter 1

1 Gustavo Subero (2016), writing about Latin American horror films, points out that some representations of the female in Latin American film run counter to the importance of mothers in political activism: for example, *Las madres de la plaza de mayo/The Mothers of the Plaza de Mayo* in Argentina. He argues that 'the image of the *madre abnegada* (self-sacrificing mother) that is often portrayed in film and other media – especially in soap operas – bears no necessary relation to the politicised group of mothers who have mobilised political change in many parts of the continent' (112).

2 Narratives of pregnancy and reproduction as they apply to China's one-child policy appear as non-fiction in the US documentary *One Child Nation* (2019) by Nanfu Wang and Jialing Zhang, and two documentaries by Fan Jian, *The Next Life* (2011, Japan/China/UK) and the forthcoming *A Second Child*. Both films follow a couple who have another baby following the death of their daughter in the Sichuan earthquake in 2008.

3 Boswell investigates nineteenth- and twentieth-century (north) American literature such as Nathaniel Hawthorne's *The Scarlet Letter: A Romance* (1848) and Harriet Ann Jacobs's *Incidents in the Life of a Slave Girl* (1861) as well as Hollywood cinema such as D. W. Griffiths's *Way Down East* (1920, USA) *Rosemary's Baby* (1968, Roman Polanski, USA), *The Handmaid's Tale*

(1990, Volker Schlöndorff, USA/Germany), *Look Who's Talking* (1989, Amy Heckerling, USA), *Juno* and *Precious* (2009, Lee Daniels, USA).

4   These figures are taken from IMDb's (Internet Movie Database) listings. While these weekend gross figures do not indicate how a film's popularity changes in the aftermath of its distribution, it is a marker of the level of interest that a commercial audience (fee-paying) has for that film on first release.

5   In Oliver's argument, it is the pregnant body rather than romance that provides comedy not motherhood. This type of film, therefore, is not strictly a mom-com; it is more accurately – using her criteria – a preg-com.

6   Amy C. Chambers (2020), writing about Alice Lowe's *Prevenge* (2016, UK), explains that it subverts the horror genre (or gynaehorror genre) as it is written by, and stars, a pregnant woman who is also the director. Lowe, Chambers argues, 'interrogates the tensions apparently inherent in the pregnant body and de-fetishises them', by playing specific tropes, such as pregnancy and nature, for comedic effect. This chapter is in a forthcoming book. I thank Amy C. Chambers for allowing me to read the article before publication.

7   Fischer first published this essay in 1992 in *Cinema Journal*. She also notes the importance of Ingmar Bergman's film *Persona* (1966, Sweden) as a film about maternity even though this is not expressly a thematic strand in the film.

8   This also applies to the Mexican/Spanish film *Pan's Labyrinth/El laberinto del fauno* (2006) which the director Guillermo del Toro explains is a uterine fantasy world with 'a fallopian palette of colours: we used crimsons and golds, and everything in the fantasy world is very rounded while everything in the real world is cold and straight' (Kermode 2006).

9   Clover also explains the phenomena of 'dual focus narratives' in the occult film, whereby the female narrative is there to 'open up' the male narrative (1992: 70).

10 Rødje refers to W. J. Thomas Mitchell (2005) who suggests that images have a vitality which he calls 'vital signs' where they are not alive but they are attributed life in the form of symbolism or representation (e.g. the Twin Towers). Mitchell calls this a 'double consciousness' that 'vascillat(es) between magical beliefs and sceptical doubts, naïve animism and hard headed materialism, mystic and critical attitudes'. He also explains that this aliveness in images is often explained as something that 'someone else' wants or thinks: for example, 'primitives, children, the masses, the illiterate, the uncritical, the illogical, and the "Other"' (Mitchell 2005: 5–27).

11 Rødje refers to films from the 1950s such as *The Return of Dracula* (also known as *The Fantastic Disappearing Man*, 1958, Paul Landres, USA) and *The Tingler* (1959, William Castle, USA). Rødje and Sobchack both mention two films directed by Sam Peckinpah, *Bonnie and Clyde* (1967, USA) and *The Wild Bunch* (1969, USA). Sobchack says that in the 1960s there was 'blood everywhere' in US films, which she suggests reflected the fear of mortality as high-profile murders (Martin Luther King, Malcolm X and Robert Kennedy) were reported on US television. She says that although *Bonnie and Clyde* was

'not the first film to overly bathe itself in blood, it was the first one to create an aesthetic, moral and psychological furor' that 'stylised death' (2000: 114). She suggests that in more recent films, such as Quentin Tarantino's *Reservoir Dogs* (1992, USA) and *Pulp Fiction* (1993, USA), 'bodies are more carelessly *squandered* than carefully stylized' (121, emphasis in original).

12 Rødje refers to historian Melissa L. Meyer (2005) who insists that blood is not particular to any one culture; rather, it is of universal significance, which is partly because of its symbolic role of reproduction.

13 The recently published Palgrave Handbook of Critical Menstruation Studies (Chris Bobel et al. 2020) indicates the importance of interdisciplinary research into menstruation.

14 According to Sharra L. Vostal (2005), menstrual products such as mass-produced sanitary towels introduced a 'new aesthetics of waste and a new attention to the female body' when they arrived on the mass market in the United States after the First World War. They were introduced in response to modern ideas about personal hygiene and an emerging class of women working outside of the home. They also hid the practical inconvenience of menstruation.

15 See Bettina Bildhauer (2005: 67–8) for a discussion on medieval text *De Secreta Mulierum/The Secrets of Women* (1483) where she notes that the belief in 'humours' suggested that all bodily fluids including menstrual blood, semen and breast milk were believed to be by-products of blood, which in turn was digested food.

16 Documentary filmmakers are also charting the pregnancy journeys of trans men. Leeds University Trans Pregnancy Project has compiled a list of recent documentary films from the United Kingdom, United States and Ecuador on their website https://transpregnancy.leeds.ac.uk/resources/documentaries-and-short-films.

17 Erica P. Teichert (2019) '*Pañuelazo*: Visual Strategies of the Legal Abortion Campaign in Argentina', LASA Annual Conference, 25 May.

18 The campaigning group *Las Tesis* took the phrase from Rita Salgado and performed it as a flash mob on Valparaiso, Chile. This performance was then taken up by a national protest in the capital Santiago outside the Supreme Court during the International Day for the Elimination of Violence towards Women.

19 Katherine Farrimond (2017), talking about the fantasy texts *Jennifer's Body* (2009) from Netflix, the HBO television series *True Blood* (2008–) and The WB series *Supernatural* (2006–), explains that it is the hymen that attracts attention when talking about virginity. She argues that as well as this practically unwarranted attention to the hymen, notions of female and male virginity are often 'rooted in the body' and in heteronormative ideas about penetrative sex. She explains that as virginity is often considered as symbolic, she suggests that 'a move to abandon the term and its mythology altogether might be a more worthwhile endeavour than an attempt to examine its complexities' (162).

20 It was not until 2014, thirty-six years after his birth, that de Carlotta found her grandson, Ignacio Hurban (now Montoya Carlotta), who had volunteered to have his DNA tested.

Chapter 2

1 Kroløkke's empirical ethnographic research, noting verbal and non-verbal exchanges in the scan room, was carried out in ultrasound clinics offering a foetal ultrasound as part of regular antenatal check-ups in Copenhagen (Denmark) and Albuquerque (United States). The clientele in Copenhagen was largely white middle-class women, and in Albuquerque the clientele was mainly Native American and Hispanic.
2 Deleuze capitalizes the word 'Elsewhere' and I will follow this convention.
3 Although Deleuze does not speak about the embodied spectator, it is important to recognize that he does speak about spectatorship. Felicity Coleman (2017) explains that '[as] Deleuze articulates it in the *Cinema* books, the "spectator" is always a part of the image, but not as a singular entity or individual subject. Rather the viewer is an image among images' (329).
4 Sobchack takes this term from Richard M. Zaner (1971) who reflects on consciousness and the animate object in the work of M. M. Gabriel Marcel, Jean-Paul Sartre and Maurice Merleau-Ponty.
5 James Pomeranz and Edward A. Pristach's (1989) work on human perception uses the term to describe selective and divided attention in how line segments are understood. Perceptual glue is also used as a way to express how speech is understood (see also Robert E. Remez and Philip E. Rubin (1992)).
6 José van Dijck suggests that interpreting the sonogram is a straightforward process, which can be accomplished by an ultrasound technician. Decoding, she suggests, is a more complicated and highly skilled process, usually performed by specialist sonographers where the full medical implications of what can be seen on screen are understood (2005: 105).
7 Roberts's research is concerned with interchanges that take place in the 3D and 4D bonding or boutique scan (as opposed to the more usual greyscale 2D diagnostic ultrasound scan). Despite this kind of scan often described as non-diagnostic, ultrasound technicians are trained to look for abnormalities. It is simply not possible to describe them as solely non-diagnostic.
8 Janice McLaughlin (2003) has noted that the ultrasound's medical purpose (to find soft markers of abnormality and measuring probabilities) is at odds with the expected outcomes of the patient (to provide reassurance and a first picture of the baby). She asserts that despite the medical profession having some reservations about its routine use in antenatal care, it is thought impossible to carry out in-depth random control trials (RCT) of ultrasound use as women are unlikely to consent to *not* being scanned (274).
9 Despite its critical connection to the foetus and the pregnant person, the placenta is considered – along with the umbilical cord – a barrier to seeing the

foetus during the ultrasound scan, especially when a keepsake picture is being taken by the sonographer (JaneMaree Maher 2002; Palmer 2009b; Roberts 2012b).

10 Luc Boltanski explains 'techno-foetuses' as 'new beings' brought about by new procreative technologies (2013: 136). He suggests this complicates the wider discussion about the status of the foetuses that are thought of as worthless, and the foetuses that are thought of as priceless, where status is not only of personhood but also of legality.

11 Steve Robson (2010) suggests that it is not yet shown that the 3D/4D scan has additional benefits for diagnostic and prognostic assessment although he suggests that the high definition scan will be used increasingly in the future in specialist departments dealing with abnormalities of the face, nervous system and the brain (696–8).

12 Barad takes physicist Niels Bohr's work on observation in quantum physics and uses it to develop a feminist framework for discussing the piezoelectric crystal in the ultrasound scan. She discusses materiality, technology and embodiment – including the way the ultrasound transducer acts as both a transmitter and a receiver – to examine the 'relationship between the material and the discursive' that is, for Barad, the central element to agential realism. She argues that agential realism is a feminist framework that 'challenges the disciplinary divide between epistemology and ontology', and she names the process as 'epistem-onto-ology' or an 'epistem-onto-logical framework' (1998: 120).

13 Roberts takes the idea of the foetal scan as part of 'an act of translation' from Mitchell's work on the foetal ultrasound (2001: 108).

14 Stephen Heath (1976) describes the outside of the frame as how film works at a loss where the 'discontinuities, the absences [. . .] structure it' (80).

15 Merleau-Ponty likens the gradation of looking to an animal in a cage 'whose freedom gently comes to an end' (1968: 100). Freedom, Merleau-Ponty suggests, is beyond the frame of the cage, and is not part of the animal's everyday existence, but it exists nonetheless as part of its perception.

16 Sobchack considers Deleuze's work as parallel to her own, even though he rejects the position that his work is a phenomenological study of cinema. Sobchack argues for the similarities, suggesting that Deleuze uses semantics to distance his study from 'existential phenomenology'. One of the reasons Sobchack provides for this distancing is that Deleuze does not recognize the embodied experience of the spectator (1992: 30–1).

17 Braidotti accepts, however, that the increased autonomy of smart technologies increases the agency of these technologies. She suggests that the development of military technologies, used in warfare and peacekeeping, raises profound legal and ethical considerations when these machines are programmed to make decisions (2013: 44).

18 Sympathetic imagination is a philosophical term and Mills is not the first, nor the only, person to talk about it. She notes the definition given by Peter Goldie (2000: 194–204) where he calls it 'in-his-shoes' imagination. The issue of pain,

Mills notes, is exploited in *The Silent Scream* when the narrator, obstetrician Nathanson, uses emotive language to describe foetal pain during abortion. The film plays on the idea that the foetus is vulnerable to pain and combines the medical authority of the narrator with the technological image of the foetus to create and ascribe meaning. The foetal ultrasound images are manipulated to highlight rapid movements when medical instruments encounter the foetus, which suggests the foetus reacts to pain. In addition, when the foetus is seen with its mouth open Nathanson suggests it is screaming silently.

19 Mills also notes that the abortion lobby have long used the ultrasound image as a way to express their views. She argues that, as 3D and 4D imagery increases, it is important to consider the process of its reception as a tool in these moral and ethical arguments (2011: 101–20).

20 Roberts notes that the use of possessive pronouns is not common when referring to the foetus. She mentions this in reference to Julia Black's documentary *My Foetus* (2004, UK), which investigates whether knowing the 'realities' of abortion can change the decision to be pro-choice. Roberts recognizes the importance of Black's film – showing an actual termination – as a counterpoint to the rhetoric of the anti-abortion lobby in the United States. Black, Roberts explains, subverts the rhetoric and imagery of the anti-abortion lobby by showing an early termination as quick and containing no identifiable body parts (2012a: 62).

21 Mills explains that, within the anti-abortion lobby, 'hyperbolic claims to personhood can and often do operate in the absence of images of the early embryo' which makes the argument about the forcefulness of foetal images more complex (2011: 104).

22 I thank Roberts (personal correspondence) for pointing out that interacting with the technology is an integral part of the scan process. As she says, the technician can position the screen and the transducer in order to get a better picture, and the pregnant person has prepared their body for the scan and helps by moving their body into position so that the scan is successful in recording clear images.

23 The documentary film shows an ultrasound scan image of a foetus during a suction abortion. Narrated by pro-life physician Dr Bernard Nathanson, it claims that the foetus can be seen screaming. Petchesky (1987) describes the emotive film as belonging to 'the realm of cultural representation rather than of medical evidence' (267).

24 Roberts (as Julie Palmer) writes about the connectivity of the placenta in her empirical research on ultrasound scans. Roberts refers to Maher's (2002) notion of the 'placental body' as a way to give agency to the pregnant woman and as a 'reminder of the location of the foetus in the gestating body' (2009b: 78). More recently, Maria Fannin (2014) has written about 'placental relations as a model for the negotiation of difference' as a way to counter negative interpretations of the fetal–maternal relationship (289–306).

25 This is how Dziga Vertov saw the film camera. He describes the camera as Kino-Glaz, or Cine-Eye where the camera, as the eye, could be placed right next to the action, but also placed in locations where the human eye could not reach.

26 The definition that I use of 'symbiosis' is taken from the *Oxford English Dictionary* of 'two different organisms [. . .] which live attached to each other whether mutually beneficial or not' (1989: 451).

27 Duden calls this the 'Nilsson effect' and explains that his foetuses were taken from corpses and (fallopian) tubal pregnancies. Importantly, she explains that fetoscopy (inserting a camera into the body to see the foetus in situ) was not sufficiently developed for Nilsson to capture these images from live foetuses (1993: 11–24).

28 For more on the historical context of Nilsson's photographs of the foetus and his book *A Child Is Born* (1965), see Solveig Jülich (2015), and for a discussion of Nilsson's images and fetal remains, see Suzanne Anker and Sarah Franklin (2011: 103–25).

29 Stormer's work relates to medical practices in the nineteenth century and the idealized foetal image of the twentieth century linked with abortion.

Chapter 3

1 Rachel McLelland (2013) discusses the narratives of *Juno* and the 1999 novel *Push* by Sapphire, and its adaption as a filmic text *Precious* (2009, Lee Daniels, USA), to argue that the notion of adolescence is determined by genre but also by the social expectations of young characters. She argues that adolescence is experiential and theoretical and that it is 'contained by various narratives and uncontainable within narrative', but she also explains that the label 'adolescence' is not necessarily one that each young protagonist would use to describe their experiences, even if their character journey is often analysed as such. Pamela Thoma (2009) and Heather Latimer (2009) include *Juno* in their list of films about unintended or unwanted pregnancies. Thoma views *Juno* (and the other 2007 films *Waitress* by Adrienne Shelly and *Knocked Up* by Judd Apatow) as a film about the commodification and depoliticization of motherhood which includes, or rather excludes, the absent biological mother of Juno. Latimer (2009) reads *Juno* and *Knocked Up* (2007) through the lens of reproductive politics. She argues that these films echo the circular debate around abortion rights that Margaret Atwood began in her 1985 novel *The Handmaid's Tale*. The 1980s in the United States and Canada, Latimer argues, is where the language of abortion began to revolve around words like 'freedom', 'choice' and 'privacy' and the concept of foetal personhood. This language, she argues, has come to define the pro-life and pro-choice movements. Each film, she suggests, reflects an uneasiness with reproductive realities as they are both coy about engaging with abortion in any meaningful or controversial way.

2 The uterus at this point is still above the pelvic cavity, and even when it returns to the pelvic space, the uterus will not return to its pre-pregnancy size.

3 Abortion is illegal in Costa Rica. Even therapeutic abortion, which is allowed under the Costa Rican Civil Code, is seen as socially unacceptable which

reduces the number. The legal repercussions of abortion are, therefore, very serious for both Teo and Jessie. This qualifies my use of the word 'choice'.

4 Her physical response could be called 'sublime' as an overpowering emotional and corporeal experience that must be controlled. The notion of the sublime is relevant here, but it forms part of a much wider discussion about creativity and the senses that I am not able to give justice to in this book. It is worth mentioning, however, that Sawchuck talks about the sublime when she talks about biotourism, as one of the factors that creates a powerful connection with the internal body. James Kirwan (2005) who writes on the history of the sublime describes the process as 'the self-provision of pleasure through an act of the imagination that is the nature of the sublime' (163).

5 An adult would normally use the familiar second person *tú* (to *tutear*) when speaking to a child. The use of *tú* is also used in addressing the Christian God in prayer.

6 In the Catholic Church, the rosary is used to recite specific prayers and is associated with the life of Mary, the mother of Jesus. The beads are arranged on a string in a particular order so that prayers can be recited in pattern. It is traditional for a pattern of prayers to be said in repentance for specific sins: the more serious the sin, the greater the number of prayers.

7 Note that this sequence does not depend on the flawed notion of menstrual synchrony, which was first investigated by Martha McClintock in 1971. She concluded that women in close contact synchronized their menstruation as a result of pheromones that affected the length of cycles. McClintock's methodology, however, was repeated and questioned by H. Clyde Wilson in 1992, who identified flaws in the collected data. McClintock's methodology was repeated by Anna Ziomkiewicz in 2006 who concluded that menstrual synchrony could not be proven.

8 Neonaticide in the United States is defined as the killing of an infant within the first twenty-four hours of birth (United States, United Kingdom, New Zealand literature review by Theresa Porter and Helen Gavin 2010: 99–112). This is distinct from the killing of an infant under the age of twelve months – infanticide. The specificity in the film of neonaticide is important as this is often linked to the mental health and age of the birthing person, and, in the United States, is overwhelmingly committed by women under the age of twenty-five. A review of the literature on neonaticide in the United States describes the difficulties of definition: neonaticide can be a result of premeditated violence or a result of passive neglect. The report emphasizes that neonaticide is not a modern-day phenomenon and that there is no specific law in the United States which treats it any differently from homicide (Krista Marie Drescher-Burke et al. 2004).

9 The definition of stillbirth varies according to country, but in the United States a stillbirth is defined as foetal loss after twenty weeks' gestation. For more information, see www.cdc.gov/ncbddd/stillbirth US government website.

10 Roger Ebert (2007) speaks to this dichotomy in his review explaining that there is a tension between the symbolic act of scattering the ashes of a loved

one and the notion of the stillborn as part of the woman's body that makes it, therefore, hers to dispose of according to her wishes.

11 The prosthetic belly is a feature in contemporary films about pregnancy. In the comedy film *Knocked Up*, about Ben (Seth Rogan) and Alison (Katherine Heigel) who have one date and unprotected sex which results in a pregnancy, it is not only the belly that is prosthetic but the genitals as well, and the film is unusual in its prosthetic representation of a baby's head crowning. In *Baby Mama*, where a high-powered professional Kate (Tina Fey) pays a surrogate Angie (Amy Poehler) to carry her embryo, the prosthetic belly is a prop used by Angie who fakes a pregnancy in order to be paid for surrogacy.

12 I use the term 'ambivalent' in the *OED* sense of 'entertaining contradictory emotions (as love and hatred) towards the same person or thing', which suggest equivalence rather than a passivity. When applied to pregnancy, as Caroline Lundquist (2008) suggests, it is a significant but often disregarded part of pregnant embodiment.

Chapter 4

1 Sawchuk describes the journey through the inside of the body in *Fantastic Voyage* (1966, Fleischer, USA) by considering the interior body as a bioscape. She notes that *Life* magazine (1962) had already described the internal landscape in their series on the human body. In the December issue of that year, artist Arthur Lidov illustrated the journey of the sandwich through the body. The backgrounds of his stylized colour paintings are landscapes of hills and valleys, coral reefs under the sea and the sky.

2 The bioscape has also evolved to include many things including the aesthetic of imaging microscopic life forms such as bacterium and cells in both animals and plants by magnification. This aesthetic depends on taking the internal object and transforming the scale so that it becomes a distinct image – a hyperreal image – removed from its original context. The Olympus BioScapes digital imaging competition which brings together art and microscope imagery has been in existence for over a decade, and its subject matter includes animal fibroblasts and microscopic plants (www.olympusbioscapes.com).

3 Sawchuk mentions films that rely on the transposition of scale for their narrative purpose, including *Honey, I Shrunk the Kids* (1989, Joe Johnston, USA/Mexico), *Toy Story* (1995, John Lasseter, USA) and *The Borrowers* (1997, Peter Hewitt, UK/USA). This fascination with anatomical scale is also seen in films from the same era such as *Big* (1988, Penny Marshall, USA).

4 Joyce suggests that imaging such as MRI, particularly of the brain, can equate the visualization or photographic image with the person to indicate not only health but also to 'reveal one's identity' (2008: 2). This suggests that parts of the body can reveal something about the individual without this being connected to, say, gender.

5 The breast and breast milk have significance in Greek mythology, explains Marilyn Yalom (1997). The Amazonian warriors supposedly cut off their

left breast so that they could wield a sword effectively while Zeus allowed his son, Hercules, to latch onto Hera's breast so that by drinking her milk he could become immortal despite his own mother's mortal status. Yalom notes that, according to myth, Hera's spurt of breast milk created the Milky Way (20–3). The association of Christ and the breast, she explains, emerges in the thirteenth century when the Virgin Mary's breast milk is seen as 'spiritual nourishment' (46). She makes the observation that the link between blood and milk comes from the work of early physicians such as Hippocrates who believed that blood became breast milk (206). This association of blood and breast milk is also illustrated by Leonardo da Vinci in his – otherwise accurate – anatomical drawings, which show breast milk coming from the spinal cord made from blood that has been fed with sperm in *The Hemisection of a Man and Woman in the Act of Coition* (c. 1490–2, held at the Royal Collection Trust).

6   Bruno's 2014 *Surface: Matters of Aesthetics, Materiality, and the Media* tackles the subject of materiality in the arts as well as film.

7   This brings Meyers work, as she says, into dialogue with Latourian notions of interconnectedness in the social environment where technology is intrinsically bound to a social and cultural matrix and with the Deleuzian (1993) notion of interconnectedness as a 'fold', wherein each fold has an effect on the whole, despite its spatial position.

8   Martin explores the way in which metaphors of production – the body as a machine that needs to be fixed – mimic gender inequalities in the childbirth process where male practitioners take ownership of the female body (1987: 54–67). Martin also describes the metaphors that describe the anthropomorphism of the sperm and the egg (1991).

9   The technocratic model is taken from the work of Robbie E. Davis-Floyd (1994). He describes the way childbirth (in the United States), and the physical processes of the female body, is broken down into stages with certain rules and time constraints (first stage and second stage of labour). He explains that if these constraints are broken, there must be technocratic interventions in the form of drugs, obstetrical instruments or operations. In this way, the reproductive body can be managed if it does not perform within these constraints. Davis-Floyd, in turn, takes his inspiration from the One-Two Punch model (itself a mechanical metaphor) of modern technology by Peter C. Reynolds (1991) whereby the natural bodily process is transformed by creating technology to replace it (1125–40). Another model – the holistic model – by contrast, prioritizes the embodied experience of the pregnant woman, where the woman is trusted to birth with the help of female practitioners such as midwives and doulas rather than male obstetricians.

10 Jansson notes that contemporary tourism is driven by the 'hyper-realities of the mediascape' where the physicality of geography and landscape has been replaced by representation. This representation can take the form of mediated texts used to market and advertise landscapes which in turn produce both real and 'phantasmagoric visions of the world' (2002: 432).

11 Kroløkke relates these touristic metaphors to Orvar Löfgren's (2002: 7) notion of touristic locations as 'cultural laboratories'. Löfgren writes that vacationing

in tourist locations does not only mean being on holiday, but it can also be an expression of identity in relation to the landscape: a way of imagining and then reclaiming space, but also a way of exploring otherness.

12 Quinlivan explains that her analysis of breath in the cinema provided a counterpoint to the work of Marks and Sobchack as, she argues, each scholar prioritizes the image over the soundtrack.

13 Han's research is based on ethnographic research with pregnant women and their male partners between October 2002 and January 2004, in Michigan, USA.

14 Beugnet's work on French cinema intersects with the work of Jenny Chamarette (2012), which speaks to the importance of phenomenology and film.

15 Theidon also catalogues cases of *susto* that are not specifically related to pregnancy, such as the embodied reaction of adults and children who were witnesses to assassination and torture or who were chased by soldiers (2013: 162). Theidon also notes that *susto* is not something that exists in one geographical area and is not exclusive to Peru but is seen as an embodied reaction to trauma, especially the circumstances of war, in other parts of the world (44). Her work is based on testimonies taken in 1995 after the Shining Path – *Sendero Luminoso* – war had finished; therefore, the testimonies (from the Ayacucho region in the Peruvian highlands that suffered during the war) are based on the long-term effects on the community and on individuals. Other embodied symptoms of trauma might include *iquyasqa*, a 'profound, bone-penetrating exhaustion' or *llakis*, 'painful memories that keep passing through the heart' (48). Later in the film, Fausta explains that her brother died from being caught by lost souls because he had not kept to the edges of the path when walking. Although there is no evidence of *susto* in relation to her brother, the fact that they keep an x-ray of his stomach suggests that they think that *susto* might have also been transferred to him. See also Carolina Rueda's (2015) sociopolitical analysis of the film, where she places the fictional narrative in the context of historical facts through the lens of Walter Benjamin's phantasmagoria.

16 Barrow's (2013: 198) essay engages directly with the criticisms that Llosa has had about the content of her films, explaining that issues to do with womanhood and femininity are not universal and must pay attention to context. Her essay also deals with the problematics of a film industry that is fragmented nationally but functioning globally, or transnationally, which leads to an unevenness in who gets funding to tell their own stories. As she points out, Llosa is not the only filmmaker who makes films about Peru who is based outside of the country. It may be, although Barrow does not say this, that as a female film director, Llosa is being held to greater account than some of her filmmaking colleagues.

17 This problematizes Michel Chion's (1994) notion of *acousmêtre* whereby the voice of a character originates off-screen so that the mouth and lips are not seen and the power of the voice is in the unseen narrator (129–37) and Ian Garwood's (2015) 'materiality of the voice-over' in the three-dimensional

soundscape (99–138). It is perhaps closer to how Mary Ann Doane (1980) describes the internal monologue as the body 'manifest[ing] its inner lining' (41).

18 A duologue indicates an interaction, which has equal narrative weight between two characters; the term is more usually used in theatre to describe a two-handed performance or for a significant dialogue between two characters. I have used the term here as it expresses the weight of the communication between the two women that the term 'dialogue' cannot fully express.

19 Sigmund Freud (2001) notes the close relationship between mourning and melancholia. He describes the 'reaction to the loss of someone who is loved, contain[ing] the same painful frame of mind, the same loss of interest in the outside world' as not only the loss of a person but of 'some abstraction which has taken the place of [a loved person], such as one's country, liberty, an ideal, and so on'. He suggests, nevertheless, that mourning is a relationship to the world while melancholia is the relationship with one's ego (243).

20 White (2015) also explains that 'Fausta is not simply an allegorical figure of a violated Peru. Making her body host to the food source native to Peru, she could be said to have a rhizomatic relationship with the nation. As the potato grows and sprouts, it counters Fausta's positioning as an empty vessel symbolizing a violated indigenous culture. Instead the tuber serves an apotropaic [protecting against evil or harm] function – it is meant to deflect a would-be attacker by overwhelming him with disgust' (192).

21 There is an important implication here about where the potato is physically placed. Although it may be overly technical to highlight, the potato is understood to be in her vagina and, possibly, growing into her uterus. If this is the case, and the narrative suggests that it is infecting the uterus, care should be taken to site the potato accurately. Hart (2015) explains that this is part of an ongoing magical realism trope that Llosa had introduced in *Madeinusa* (2006), but he says that 'the potato is actually growing in Fausta's womb and – although we do not see this – she has to cut out the sprouts' (170). Hart demonstrates the difficulty of analysing what is happening in the body, as he reverts to a discussion on how the potato represents the gendered focus of magical realism 'as a magic formula designed to thwart the violence that men visit on women's bodies', rather than the importance of what is happening inside the body (170). I take Hart's point that this should be read as magical realism, even though he places it in the 'womb' not the vagina, and Rojas's (2017) observation that the potato is a metaphor, but the physical position of the potato is important to the lived body experience. Placing it in the uterus would be physically excruciating, and the body would try to expel it, meaning that the medical intervention would be more immediate and critical.

22 Rojas (2017) also explains that Perpetua uses different past tenses to describe her experiences, emphasizing the reinterpretation and reliving of the past (300).

23 The washing of clothes, Theidon (2013) says, is meant to ease the journey of the soul to heaven (59).

24 Paul A. Schroeder Rodríguez (2016) describes the 'hands and arms, connected like rhizomes under the surface of the cotton sheet [that] functions as a metaphor of private-social memory and identity' (287).

25 The intergenerational memory that Marianne Hirsch (1997, 2012) calls 'postmemory' – which describes the memories formed by second and third generation in relation to events that they were not part of – sits uncomfortably here. The memory that Fausta embodies is her own, as is her narration.

26 It was the director's aim to evoke the cinema of the 1960s and 1970s. Although the film was set in Texas and much of the filming was done in that state, filming also took place in Louisiana.

27 Director David Lowery was an editor before he was a director, which may explain the attention to storytelling and character building through editing.

28 *Apio verde* means green celery in Spanish. The term is used in a version of the song *Happy Birthday*, as in 'apio verde to you'. It is also a reference to the way abortions were carried out whereby celery is introduced into the vagina causing an infection, which results in an abortion. Adriana hears this from the second doctor she sees at the abortion clinic halfway through the film. The title has no translation in English.

29 The film is based on a case that was taken to the Chilean Senate in 2012 as the law to allow therapeutic abortion was discussed. The proposals for change were rejected. A measure of how sensitive this subject matter is in Chile is the fact that Morales Brucher was unable to secure a distributor because of its controversial subject matter. The laws on abortion were changed in 2017 when the Chilean Senate approved abortion on the grounds of an unviable foetus. The Chilean National Congress approved the law of 'abortion under three circumstances', No. 21.030 in 2017, becoming law in 2018, reinstating reproductive rights that were revoked by Augusto Pinochet in 1989. The three circumstances are: when the woman's life is in danger, when the foetus is unviable and when the pregnancy is a result of rape. There is, however, an ongoing uncertainty as to how abortion will be provided or accessed.

Chapter 5

1 Marks's conversation is about objects that are assigned significance depending on where they are, who is looking at them and the different pasts that they conjure for the spectator. She gives an example of how '[o]bjects that travel along paths of human diaspora and international trade encode cultural displacement' (2000: 78). She also describes people who have been treated as commodities or 'transnational objects' in human trafficking, relating this to 'objects that are created in cultural translation and transcultural movement' (78). Her critical discussion is about intercultural cinema and diasporic filmmakers, but I think that her way of describing a recollection-object is particularly pertinent to my discussion.

2 Taylor (2008) suggests that this miscorrelation results in the notion of bonding being used to justify the increase in use of scan equipment, to prevent women from having abortions and the commercial use of the ultrasound image.

3 Deleuze relates the recollection image to his work on other kinds of image – the perception image, the movement-image and the time-image – as well as to the recollection image in Bergsonian attentive recognition. Deleuze uses the term to articulate the relationship between the image and the virtual image (1989: 45–6). This points to Deleuze's much longer conversation in his Cinema 1 and Cinema 2 books. Although I have taken his lead in understanding off-screen space as an Elsewhere, I acknowledge that this book cannot address the complexity of his broader discussion.

4 This discussion of memory is part of a much wider discussion about memory and memorializing, which I am not able to address in detail in this book. Assman responds to Maurice Halbwach's (1992) notion of collective memory to argue that there are different ways of remembering. The importance of Assman's work is that he separates collective memory into cultural memory (which he says is institutionalized) and communicative memory (which he says is not institutionalized).

5 Paul Connerton (1989) talks more broadly about social memory and the ritualistic, habitual and institutional way memory is inscribed. He notes how oral history is transformed in the action of recording it through writing as the narrative is moved from the body to the page (75). In his discussion of social memory, Connerton differentiates between two forms of social practice: *incorporating*, where gestures or bodily actions exist only when the person is present or the action is taking place, and *inscribing*, when the person or action is over or not present but is recorded in some way (72–3).

6 The politics of memory has an extensive scholarship that comes out of Holocaust studies and is not limited to the work of Rothberg and Silverman. The importance of Holocaust studies is that collective and individual recollections and interpretations of memory have been, and are still being, collected from successive generations.

7 The reminiscence bump has been investigated by Ashok Jansari and Alan J. Parkin (1996) who conducted experiments on groups of people aged thirty-six to sixty (85–91). Their findings suggest that there is a difference in the way older people remember. They found that there is some evidence to show that the older age group can recall events in the past more easily because they are able to contain or put aside recent events – something that younger age groups find more difficult to do. Jansari and Parkin emphasize, however, that the reminiscence bump is present across age groups. Gillian Cohen and Stephanie Taylor (1998) urge caution when talking about reminiscence as often assumptions are made about certain age groups, arguing that research can reinforce the stereotype that older people are 'living on the past' and not connected to the contemporary (601–10). They note that both young and old reminisce, and the question about how often and about what is likely to be heavily influenced by differences in lifestyle, health status, gender, personality and time constraints. They also talk about the way negative reminiscences are sometimes masked by positive ones and that this can result in negative reminiscences going unrecorded in ethnographic studies.

8 Marks acknowledges Deleuze's use of the terms 'recollection image' and 'memory image' which they both take from the work of Bergson who writes about memory and temporality in his 1911 work *Matter and Memory* (2004).

Bergson established, in his studies of aphasia, that memory can exist despite the brain's inability to transmit this memory through speech.

9   Its opening sequence has been much lauded by critics for its narrative brevity and emotional punch (Bradshaw (2009); Ebert (2009); and French (2009)).

10 The *BMJ* prints film reviews of medical relevance written by medical journalists, medical staff and others. Such reviews have tackled issues around euthanasia, ageing and bereavement such as Gonzalo Casino's review of *The Sea Inside/Mar adentro* (2004, Alejandro Amenabar) which deals with the issue of euthanasia (2004).

11 Importantly, as Richard Neupert (2014) observes, the Pixar production house is known for using the aesthetic of digital animation (as opposed to animated drawn images) to represent embodied emotions (219). As Neupert explains, early digitalized images were not able to represent the human form with enough authenticity or believability, but Pixar began to create narratives that used non-human objects such as lamps and cars. Emotions were attributed to these digital images by animating them to mimic human movement (215–24). Representing emotions, Neupert explains, distracts the spectator from the artifice of the inanimate constructed image. Replicating humanly recognized bodily movements as emotion may explain how some of the imagery in the film relies on gestures rather than dialogue.

12 There are many revolutionary heroes in Cayetana's lucid dreams. Simón Bolívar fought for the liberation of Peru, Bolivia, Colombia, Venezuela and Ecuador against Spain in the early nineteenth century. Juan José de San Martín was an Argentinean who fought against the Spanish at the same time as Bolívar. Francisco Bolognesi Cervantes was a colonel in the Peruvian army in the mid- to late nineteenth century who died in his last military battle, which was fought in Arica on the border with Chile. He refused to surrender and said he would fight until the last shot/cartridge – *hasta quemar el último cartucho*. The fighting was chaotic on both sides, and he was killed along with most of the other Peruvian soldiers. Túpac Amaru, a supposed descendent of the last Inca leader, led an uprising against the Spanish in the late eighteenth century and was killed, as Cayetana describes, by having his legs and arms roped to four individual horses who were then ridden in different directions. His body was then quartered and decapitated. José Olaya, a fisherman, showed great courage when he swam across the sea with covert messages for the liberation soldiers. When captured he was tortured but refused to speak. For more, see Benjamin Keen and Keith Haynes (2009).

13 Sarah Barrow (2018) takes Karen Lury's (2010) lead to read *The Bad Intentions* as part of the trend in Latin American films for using a young protagonist to 'revisit a nation's troubled past marked by political violence' (166). Seen alongside the film *Paper Dove/Paloma de papel* (2003, Dir Fabrizio Aguilar, Peru), Barrow explains how each film uses childhood to progress the narrative through generic convention such as the fairy tale and fantasy to frame the coming of age of both the main characters and the national story. Each film, Barrow suggest, is also a way for filmmakers to come to terms with their childhood experiences in areas of conflict. Barrow says, *The Bad Intentions*

'emphasizes the links between birth and death [. . .] while also stressing the intense intertwining of the personal with the political as the girl approaches adolescence' (174).

14. There are many beliefs about death, the afterlife, immortality and reincarnation. Tony Walter (2001), in his empirical research in the UK, divides the belief in reincarnation into three areas: modern, postmodern and kin-based.

15. Ross Carey (2016) points out that this sequence in the film was 'so provocative' that it appears in Taste of Cinema's list of the top twenty controversial scenes in cinema. He argues that it is the reason that prevents this 'largely misunderstood film's chances of being perceived as a classic'. Although this might also be the reason why the film has attracted so little scholarly attention, as Carey says, the film is now being revaluated, mainly in reviews, as worthy of critical attention.

16. The opening to Richard Wagner's Die Walküre (1856, first performed as a cycle of four parts in 1876) is played by the Wiener Philharmoniker and conducted by Georg Solti in 1962.

17. Laurence E. MacDonald (2013) describes the technical sound bridge that connects this death of one person and the life of another. He mentions the way the music drops out immediately before the birth but does not explicitly mark this moment (with the foetus still in the uterus) as the moment of reincarnation (468).

18. MacDonald describes this as 'a five-tone motif for strings' (2013: 468).

Chapter 6

1. Brinkema does not use an accent when she uses the term *mise n'en scène*, but I have included the accent to maintain clarity and uniformity.

2. The OED also suggests the notion of being 'a little bit pregnant' to describe partial commitment.

3. Gina Zavota (2020), in a Derridean reading of the film, explains the importance of written language as a different form of communication than uttering language. This Derridean notion of 'arche-writing' where the spaces and gaps have meaning, she argues, is confirmed by the character Ian when he realizes that 'reading' the heptapods signs involves paying attention to their negative space.

4. Fleming and Brown open up a fascinating discussion of how to understand the speculative future in a time when there are no humans. McTaggart's essay emphasizes how the past, present and future are always shifting, as the present moves into the past and the future becomes the present (A-series), and how events are understood in relation to where each fit into a fixed timeline (B-series). As the key component of time, he suggests, is change, the B-series appears in opposition to the A-series which suggests that time is unreal.

McTaggart offers the C-series as atemporality where the direction of time is not proscribed, although an order still exists. Patricia Pisters (2012) offers the term 'neuro-image' as a way to understand how the language of cinema and the use of technology describe this speculative future.

5. Mamula's essay goes into more detail about the formal language of the film, explaining how the film is self-referential using, for example, mise en scène to evoke the spectacle of cinema on screen, even returning to the black-and-white and silent eras of film. She also argues that Villeneuve aligns the heptapods' language with cinema so that the main protagonist is being taught to 'see, think and experience *cinematically*' (543; emphasis in original).

6. As Amanda Alfaro Cordoba (2018) explains, the use of languages in the film is critical to understanding how difficult it is to translate Kaq'chikel, the predominant language in the film, as it is more visual that any translation can express.

7. Michelle Warren and Sonja H. Bickford (2020) read the film through the framework of Raymond Williams's *The Country and the City* (1973) to explain how the indigenous characters 'are inextricably tied to the market demands placed on them by the city (and by extension, the consumers from even beyond Guatemala' (11). They explain that María's body is treated like a rural field and her foetus/baby is the crop, 'harvested from her in the city and sold as a consumable good [. . .] much like the coffee produced on the plantation and exported to the city to sell' (16).

8. The film is in Spanish and Kaq'chikel, but my translations are of the French subtitles.

9. In Guatemala, abortion is severely restricted for cases where the mother's life is at risk. Edgar Kestler and Vinicio Mora (2018) explain that 'community beverages' and/or large doses of analgesics are sometimes administered for unwanted/unplanned pregnancies, and that many people go on to seek the services of someone in the community to perform an illegal abortion.

FILMOGRAPHY

A Girl Like Her (2011), [Film] Dir. Ann Fessler, USA: Ann Fessler.
Aborto (1965), [Film] Dir. Pedro Chaskel, Chile: Cine Experimental de la Universidad de Chile.
Abuelas: Grandmothers on a Mission (2012), [Film] Dir. Noemi Weis, Canada/Argentina: Women Make Movies.
Ain't Them Bodies Saints (2013), [Film] Dir. David Lowery, USA: Universal Home Entertainment.
Alias María (2015), [Film] Dir. José Luis Rugeles, Colombia: Cineplex.
Alien (1979), [Film] Dir. Ridley Scott, USA/UK: Twentieth Century Fox Film Company.
Aliens (1986), [Film] Dir. James Cameron, USA/UK: Twentieth Century Fox.
Amores Perros (2000), [Film] Dir. Alejandro González Iñárritu, Mexico: Optimum Releasing.
Apio verde (2013), [Film] Dir. Francesc Morales Brucher, Chile: Efecto Moral Films.
Arrival (2016), [Film] Dir. Denis Villeneuve, USA/Canada: Entertainment One.
Baby Mama (2008), [Film] Dir. Michael McCullers, USA: Universal Pictures.
Beautiful Sin (2014), [Film] Dir. Gabriela Quirós, Costa Rica/USA: Azul Films.
Bella (2006), [Film] Dir. Alejandro Gomez Monteverde, USA/Mexico: Lionsgate.
Big (1988), [Film] Dir. Penny Marshall, USA: Twentieth Century Fox Film Company.
Birth (2004), [Film] Dir. Jonathan Glazer, USA/UK/Germany/France: Entertainment Film Distributors.
Bonnie and Clyde (1967), [Film] Dir. Arthur Penn, USA: Warner Home Video.
Breathless/À bout de souffle (1960), [Film] Dir. Jean-Luc Godard, France: Optimum Home Entertainment.
Captive/Cautiva (2003), [Film] Dir. Gaston Biraben, Argentina: Primer Plano Film Group.
Carrie (1976), [Film] Dir. Brian de Palma, USA: United Artists.
Casa de los babys (2003), [Film] Dir. John Sayles, USA/Mexico: IFC Films.
Dead Ringers (1988), [Film] Dir. David Cronenberg, Canada/USA: Twentieth Century Fox Film Corporation.
Demon Seed (1977), [Film] Dir. Donald Cammell, USA: MGM, USA.
Devil's Backbone/ El espinazo del diablo (2001), [Film] Dir. Guillermo del Toro, Spain/Mexico/France/Argentina: Sony Pictures Classics.
El colombian dream (2005), [Film] Dir. Felipe Aljure, Colombia: Fondo Mixto de Promoción Cinematográfica.
Eraserhead (1977), [Film] Dir. David Lynch, USA: Mainline Pictures.

Fantastic Voyage (1966), [Film] Dir. Richard Fleischer, USA: Twentieth Century Fox Home Entertainment.
From Girl to Mother/De niña a madre/ (2005), [Film] Dir. Florence Jaugey, Nicaragua: Camila Films.
Fuck My Wedding/ Que pena tu boda (2011), [Film] Dir. Nicholás López, Chile: Uncork'd Entertainment.
Gestation/ Gestación (2009), [Film] Dir. Esteban Ramírez, Costa Rica: Cinetel.
Godsend (2004), [Film] Dir. Nick Hamm, USA/Canada: Lion Gate Films.
Grace (2009), [Film] Dir. Paul Solet, USA/Canada: Leomax Entertainment.
Honey, I Shrunk the Kids (1989), [Film] Dir. Joe Johnston, USA/ Mexico: Buena Vista Pictures.
How to Lose Your Virginity (2013), [Film] Dir. Theresa Shechter, USA: Women Make Movies.
Ixcanul (2015), [Film] Dir. Jayro Bustamente, Guatemala/France: Twin Pics.
Jane: An Abortion Service (1995), [Film] Dir. Kate Kurtz and Nell Lundy, USA: Women Make Movies.
Jennifer's Body (2009), [TV Film] Dir. Karyn Kusama, USA: 20th Century Fox.
Junebug (2005), [Film] Dir. Phil Morrison, USA: Eureka Entertainment.
Juno (2007), [Film] Dir. Jason Reitman, USA: Fox Searchlight Pictures.
Kept and Dreamless/Las mantenidas sin sueños (2005), [Film] Dirs. Martín de Salvo and Vera Fogwill, Argentina/France/Netherlands/Spain: INCAA and Four Film.
Knocked Up (2007), [Film] Dir. Judd Apatow, USA: United International Pictures.
Labor Pains (2009), [Film] Dir. Laura Shapiro, USA: First Look International.
Las Libres: The Story Continues (2014), [Film] Dir. Gustavo Montaña, USA/Mexico/Argentina: At Dusk Media.
Let it be Law/Que sea ley (2019) [Film] Dir. Juan Solanas, Argentina/France Uruguay: Caramel Films.
L!fe Happens (2011), [Film] Dir. Kat Coiro, USA/Canada: Lionsgate.
Lion's Den/Leonera (2008), [Film] Dir. Pablo Trapero, Argentina/South Korea/Brazil/Spain: Halycon Releasing.
Look Who's Talking (1989), [Film] Dir. Amy Heckerling, USA: TriStar Pictures.
Look Who's Talking Too (1990), [Film] Dir. Amy Heckerling, USA: Columbia TriStar Home Entertainment.
Look Who's Talking Now (1993), [Film] Dir. Tom Ropelowski, USA: TriStar Pictures.
Madeinusa (2006), [Film] Dir. Claudia Llosa, Peru/Spain: Dogwoof.
Maria Full of Grace/María llena eres de gracias (2004), [Film] Dir. Joshua Marston, Colombia/USA/Ecuador: Fine Line Features.
Misconceptions (2008), [Film] Dir. Ron Satlof, USA: E1 Entertainment.
Moon (2009), [Film] Dir. Duncan Jones, UK: Sony Pictures Classics.
Music on Hold/Música en espera (2009), [Film] Dir. Hernán Golfrid, Argentina: Argentina Video Home.
My Foetus (2004), [Film] Dir. Julie Black, UK: Bivouac Productions.
My Life Without Me (2003), [Film] Dir. Isabel Croixet, Canada/Spain: Alliance Atlantis Home Video.
Never Rarely Sometimes Always (2020), [Film] Dir. Eliza Hittman, USA/UK: Focus Features.

October Baby (2011), [Film] Dir. Andrew Erwin and Jon Erwin, USA: Christian Art Media.
One Child Nation (2019), [Film] Dir. Nanfu Wang and Jialing Zhang, USA: Amazon Studios.
Orphan (2009), [Film] Dir. Jaume Collet-Serra, USA/Canada/Germany: Optimum Releasing.
Pan's Labyrinth/El laberinto del fauno (2006), [Film] Dir. Guillermo del Toro, Mexico/Spain/USA: The Criterion Collection.
Paper Dove/Paloma de papel (2003), [Film] Dir Fabrizio Aguilar, Peru: Luna Llena Films.
Persona (1966), [Film] Dir. Ingmar Bergman, Sweden: The Criterion Collection.
Precious (2009), [Film] Dir. Lee Daniels USA: Future Film.
Preggoland (2014), [Film] Dir. Jacob Tierney, Canada: Film Rise.
Prevenge (2016), [Film] Dir. Alice Lowe, UK: Gennaker, Western Edge Pictures (Front Row Filmed Entertainment).
Pulp Fiction (1994), [Film] Dir. Quentin Tarantino, USA: Miramax.
Quinceañera (2006), [Film] Dir. Richard Glatzer and Wash Westmoreland, USA: Sony Pictures Classics.
Reservoir Dogs (1992), [Film] Dir. Quentin Tarantino, USA: Miramax.
Revolutionary Road (2008), [Film] Dir. Sam Mendes, USA/UK: DreamWorks.
Roma (2018), [Film] Dir. Alfonso Cuarón, Mexico: Netflix .
Rosemary's Baby (1968), [Film] Dir. Roman Polanski, USA: Paramount Pictures.
Rosita (2005), [Film] Dir. Barbara Attie and Janet Goldwater, USA: Bullfrog Films.
Saved! (2004), [Film] Dir. Brian Dannelly, USA/Canada: United Artists.
Stephanie Daley (2007), [Film] Dir. Hilary Brougher, USA: Liberation Entertainment.
Supernatural (2006–2019), [TV series] Warner Bros. Television.
The Back-Up Plan (2010), [Film] Dir. Alan Poul, USA: CBS Home Entertainment.
The Bad Intentions/Las malas intenciones (2011), [Film] Dir. Rosario García-Montero, Peru/Argentina/Germany/France: 3C Films Group.
The Blonds/Los Rubios (2003), [Film] Dir. Albertina Carri, Argentina: Primer Plano Film Group.
The Book of Life (2014), [Film] Dir. Jorge R. Guttiérez, USA: Twentieth Century Fox.
The Borrowers (1997), [Film] Dir. Peter Hewitt, UK/USA: Fabulous Films.
The Brood (1979), [Film] Dir. David Cronenberg, Canada: Anchor Bay Entertainment.
The Brothers Solomon (2007), [Film] Dir. Bob Odenkirk, USA: Sony Pictures Releasing.
The Fly (1986), [Film] Dir. David Cronenberg, USA/UK/Canada: Twentieth Century Fox.
The Handmaid's Tale (1990), [Film] Dir. Volker Schlöndorff, USA/Germany: MGM/UA Home Entertainment.
The Milk of Sorrow/La teta asustada (2009), [Film] Dir. Claudia Llosa, Peru/Spain: Dogwoof Pictures.
The Motherhood Archives (2013), [Film] Dir. Irene Lusztig, USA: Women Make Movies.

The Mothers of the Plaza de Mayo/Las madres de la Plaza de Mayo (1985), [Film] Dir. Susana Blaustein Muñoz and Lourdes Portillo, Argentina: First Run Features.
The Next Life (2011), [Film] Dir. Fan Jian, Japan/China/UK: Films Transit International.
The Return of Dracula (1958), [Film] Dir. Paul Landres, USA: MGM/UA Home Entertainment.
The Sea Inside/Mar adentro (2004), [Film] Dir. Alejandro Amenábar, Spain/France/Italy: Fine Line Features.
The Silent Scream (1984), [Film] Dir. Jack Duane Dabner, USA: American Portrait Films.
The Switch (2010), [Film] Dir. Josh Gordon, USA: Lionsgate Home Entertainment.
The Tingler (1959), [Film] Dir. William Castle USA: Columbia TriStar Home Video.
The Uterus (2017), [Film] Dir. Pedro Antoniutti, Brazil: Volante.
The Uterus Part 1 (2010), [TV] Prod. Wellington Chiu and Nicole Wright, USA: Highpockets.
The Wild Bunch (1969), [Film] Dir. Sam Peckinpah, USA: Warner Home Video.
Too Young To Be A Dad (2002), [Film] Dir. Éva Gárdos, USA/Canada: Warner Home Video.
Tourists/Touristas (2009), [Film] Dir. Alicia Scherson, Chile: Tiger Releases.
Toy Story (1995), [Film] Dir. John Lasseter, USA: Buena Vista International.
True Blood (2008–2014), [TV series] HBO.
Undertow/Contracorriente (2009), [Film] Dir. Javier Fuentes-Léon, Peru/Colombia/France Germany: Axiom Films.
Unplanned (2020), [Film] Dir. Chuck Konzelman and Cary Solomon, USA: Soli Deo Gloria Releasing.
Unpregnant (2020), [Film] Dir. Rachel Lee Goldenberg, USA: HBO Max.
Up (2009), [Film] Dir. Pete Docter and Bob Petersen, USA: Walt Disney Studios Motion Pictures.
Uterus Independence Day (2019), [TV] Series 1, episode 6 of *New Yorkers in LA*, Dir. Kalya Baken, USA: Messy Bun Productions.
Ventre Livre: Freeing the Womb (1994), [Film] Dir. Ana Luiza Azevedo, Brazil: Women Make Movies.
Virgin Tales (2012), [Film] Dir. Mirjam von Arn, France/Germany/Switzerland/USA: Women Make Movies.
Waitress (2007), [Film] Dir. Adrienne Shelly, USA: Fox Searchlight.
Way Down East (1920), [Film] Dir. D.W. Griffith, USA: Film Detective.
What to Expect When You're Expecting (2012), [Film] Dir. Kirk Jones, USA: Lionsgate.
Who Says It's Easy?/¿Quién dice que es fácil?(2007), [Film] Dir. Juan Taratuto, Argentina: Primer Plano Film Group.
4 Months, 3 Weeks, 2 Days/4 luni, 3 saptamani si 2 zile (2007), [Film] Dir. Cristian Mungui, Romania/ Belgium: Artificial Eye.

REFERENCES

Ahmed, S. (2004), *The Cultural Politics of Emotion*, Edinburgh: Edinburgh University Press.
Albites, E. B. and Gomez, L. (2017), 'Trauma y Aislamiento en "La teta asustada" de Claudia Llosa/Trauma and Isolation in Claudia Llosa's "The Milk of Sorrow"', *Iberoamericano (2000–)* 17 (65): 93–106.
Alvaray, L. (2012), 'Are We Global Yet? New Challenges to Defining Latin American Cinema', *Studies in Hispanic Cinema* 8 (1): 69–86.
Anderson, P. and M. Ángel del Arco, eds (2015), *Mass Killings and Violence in Spain, 1936-1952: Grappling with the Past*, New York and London: Routledge.
Anker, S. and S. Franklin (2011) 'Specimens as Spectacles: Reframing Fetal Remains', *Social Text* 29: 103–25.
Arnold, S. (2013), *Maternal Horror Film: Melodrama and Motherhood*, Basingstoke, Hampshire and New York: Palgrave Macmillan.
Arredondo, I. (2014), *Motherhood in Mexican Cinema, 1941-1991: The Transformation of Femininity on Screen*, Jefferson, NC: McFarland and Company Inc.
Assman, J. (2011), 'Communicative and Cultural Memory', in P. Meusburger, M. Heffernan and E. Wunder (eds), *Cultural Memories: The Geographical Point of View*, 15–28, Dordrecht Heidelberg, London and New York: Springer.
Atwood, M. (1985), *The Handmaid's Tale*, Toronto: McClelland & Stewart.
Ayres, S. and P. Manjunath (2016), 'Pregnancy Denied, Pregnancy Rejected in Stephanie Daley', *Law, Culture and the Humanities* 12 (1): 132–54.
Barad, K. (1998), 'Getting Real: Technoscientific Practices and the Materialization of Reality', *Differences: A Journal of Feminist Cultural Studies* 10 (2): 87–128.
Barad, K. (2007), *Meeting the Universe Half-Way: Quantum Physics and the Entanglement of Matter and Meaning*, Durham, NC: Duke University Press.
Baraitser, L. (2014), 'Time and Again: Repetition, Maternity and the Non-Reproductive', *Studies in the Maternal* 6 (1), 1–7.
Barker, J. M. (2009), *The Tactile Eye: Touch and the Cinematic Experience*, Berkeley: University of California Press.
Barrow, S. (2013), 'New Configurations for Peruvian Cinema: The Rising Star of Claudia Llosa', *Transnational Cinemas* 4 (2): 197–215.
Barrow, S. (2018), 'Growing Pains: Young People and Violence in Peru's Fiction Film', in G. Maguire and R. Randall (eds), *New Visions of Adolescence in Contemporary Latin American Film*, 165–81, New Directions in Latino American Cultures.
Battersby, C. (1998), *The Phenomenal Woman: Feminist Metaphysics and Patterns of Identity*, Cambridge: Polity Press.

Bazin, A. (1960), 'The Ontology of the Photographic Image', trans. H. Gray, *Film Quarterly* 13 (4): 4–9.
Beckman, L. J. (2016), 'Abortion in the United States: The Continuing Controversy', *Feminism and Psychology* 27 (1): 101–13.
Belej, C. and A. L. Rey (2013), 'Feminism and Women's History in Academic Institutions in the Southern Cone: Argentina, Brazil, Chile, and Uruguay', *Journal of Women's History*, 25 (4): 265–74.
Benjamin, W. (1968), *Illuminations*, trans. H. Zohn, New York: Schocken.
Benson-Allott, C. (2015), 'Dreadful Architecture: Zones of Horror in *Alien* and Lee Bontecou's Wall Sculptures', *Journal of Visual Cultures* 14 (3): 267–78.
Bergson, H. ([2011] 2004), *Matter and Memory*, trans. N. M. Paul and W. S. Palmer, New York: Dover Publications Inc.
Besse, M., N. M. Lampe and E. S. Mann, (2020), 'Experiences with Achieving Pregnancy and Giving Birth Among Transgender Men: A Narrative Literature Review', *Yale Journal of Biology and Medicine* 93: 517–28.
Betterton, R. (2014), *Maternal Bodies in the Visual Arts*, Manchester: Manchester University Press.
Beugnet, M. (2007), *Cinema and Sensation: French Film and the Art of Transgression*, Edinburgh: Edinburgh University Press.
Bildhauer, B. (2005), 'The Secrets of Women (c.1300): A Medieval Perspective on Menstruation', in A. Shail and G. Howie (eds), *Menstruation: A Cultural History*, 65–75, Basingstoke: Palgrave Macmillan.
Bobel, C., I. T. Winkler, B. Fahns, K. A. Hasson, E. A. Kissling and T. A. Roberts, eds (2020), *The Palgrave Handbook of Critical Menstruation Studies*, Palgrave Macmillan. Available on-line https://doi.org/10.1007/978-981-15-0614-7 (last accessed 22 February 2021).
Boltanski, L. (2013), *Foetal Condition: A Sociology of Engendering and Abortion*, Oxford: Wiley.
Bordwell, D. (1997), *Narration in the Fiction Film*, London: Routledge.
Bordwell, D., J. Steiger and K. Thompson (2002), *The Classical Hollywood Cinema: Film Style and Modes of Production*, Abingdon, Oxon: Routledge.
Boswell, P. A. (2014), *Pregnancy in Literature and Film*, Jefferson, NC: McFarland and Company Inc.
Bradshaw, P. (2009), 'Review of *Up*', *Guardian*, 9 October. Available on-line: www.theguardian.com/film/2009/oct/09/up-review (last accessed 11 October 2020).
Braidotti, R. (2013), *The Posthuman*, Malden, MA: Polity Press.
Brinkema, E. (2014), *The Forms of the Affects*, Durham and London, Duke University Press.
Brinkema, E. (2015), 'Introduction: A Genreless Horror', *Journal of Visual Culture* 14 (3): 263–6.
Bruno, G. (1992), 'Bodily Architectures', *Assemblage* 19: 106–1.
Bruno, G. (2002), *Atlas of Emotions: Journeys in Art, Architecture and Film*, London and New York: Verso.
Bruno, G. (2014), *Surface: Matters of Aesthetics, Materiality and Media*, Chicago and London: University of Chicago Press.
Burch, N. (1973), *Theory of Film Practice*, trans. H. R. Lane, New York: Praeger.
Burton-Carvajal, J. (2006), 'Marginal Cinemas and Mainstream Critical Theory', in C. Grant, and A. Kuhn (eds), *Screening World Cinema: A Screen Reader*, 17–35, New York: Routledge.

Campbell, S. (2006), 'History of Ultrasound in Obstetrics and Gynecology' [lecture], *OBGYN.net International Federation of Gynecology and Obstetrics*, Washington DC, USA.

Canessa, A. (2012), *Intimate Indigeneities: Race, Sex, and History in the Small Spaces of Andean Life*, Durham: Duke University Press.

Cannold, L. (2000), *Who's Crying Now? Chosen Childlessness, Circumstantial Childlessness and the Irrationality of Motherhood*, Melbourne: University of Melbourne.

Carey, R. (2016), 'The 20 Most Controversial Movie Scenes of All Time', *Taste of Cinema*, 1 April. Available on-line: http://www.tasteofcinema.com/2016/the-20-most-controversial-movie-scenes (last accessed 11 October 2020).

Casino, G. (2004), 'Film Reopens Euthanasia Debate in Spain', *BMJ* 329 (7470): 864.

Casper, M. J. and L. J. Moore (2009), *Missing Bodies: The Politics of Visibility*, New York: New York University Press.

Castillo, D. (2019), 'Trafficked Babies, Exploded Futures: Jayro Bustamante's Ixcanul', in J. G. Menjívar and G. E. Chacón (eds), *Indigenous Interfaces*, 119-40, Tuscon: The University of Arizona Press.

Chamarette, J. (2012), *Phenomenology and the Future of Film: Rethinking Subjectivity Beyond French Cinema*, Hampshire and New York: Palgrave Macmillan.

Chambers, Amy C. (2020), 'The (Re)birth of Pregnancy Horror in Alice Lowe's Prevenge', in A. Pierse (ed.), *Women Make Horror: Filmmaking, Feminism, Genre*, 209-21, New Brunswick: Rutgers University Press.

Chanan, M. (2006), 'Latin American Cinema: From Underdevelopment to Postmodernism', in S. Dennison and S. H. Lim (eds), *Remapping World Cinema: Identity, Culture and Politics in Film*, 38-54, London: Wallflower Press.

Chard, T. and J. G. Grudzinskas, eds (1994), *The Uterus*, New York: Cambridge University Press.

Chion, M. (1994), *Audio-Vision: Sound on Screen*, trans. C. Gorbman, New York: Columbia University Press.

Clough, P. (2010), 'The Affective Turn: Political Economy, Biomedia, and Bodies', in M. Gregg and G. J. Seigworth (eds), *The Affect Reader*, 206-28, Durham: Duke University Press.

Clover, C. J. (1992), *Men, Women and Chainsaws: Gender in the Modern Horror Film*, London: British Film Institute.

Cohen, G. and S. Taylor (1998), 'Reminiscence and Ageing', *Ageing and Society* 18 (5): 601-10.

Coleman, F. (2017), 'Deleuzian Spectatorship', in K. L. Hole, D. Jelača, E. A. Kaplan and Patrice Petro (eds), *The Routledge Companion to Cinema and Gender*, 322-31, New York: Routledge.

Connerton, P. (1989), *How Societies Remember*, Cambridge and New York: Cambridge University Press.

Cooper, S. (2013), *The Soul of Film Theory*, New York: Palgrave Macmillan.

Cordoba, A. A. (2018), 'Can Maria Speak?: Interpreting *Ixcanul/Volcano* (2015) from a Decolonial Perspective', *Studies in Spanish and Latin American Cinemas* 15 (2): 187-202.

Cosentino, O. (2018), 'Feminism and Intimate/Emotional Labour', *Mediático*, 24 December. Available on-line: https://reframe.sussex.ac.uk/mediatico/2018

/12/24/special-dossier-on-roma-feminism-and-intimate-emotional-labor (last accessed 09 November 2020).

Creed, B. (1993), *The Monstrous Feminine: Film, Feminism, Psychoanalysis*, London and New York: Routledge.

Curiel, O. (2016), 'Rethinking Radical Anti-Racist Feminist Politics in a Global Neoliberal Context', trans. M. Borzone and A. Ponomaroff, *Meridians: Feminism, Race, Transnationalism* 14 (2): 46–55.

Currie, G. (1999), 'Cognitivism', in T. Miller (ed.), *A Companion to Film Theory*, 105–22, Oxford: Blackwell Publishers.

da Vinci, L. (c. 1490–92), *The Hemisection of a Man and Woman in the Act of Coition* [pen and ink], reproduced in M. Clayton and R. Philo, *Leonardo da Vinci: Anatomist*, London: Royal Collection Publication.

Davis-Floyd, R. E. (1994), 'The Technocratic Body: American Childbirth as Cultural Expression', *Social Science and Medicine* 38 (8): 1125–40.

de la Mora, S. (2019), 'Roma: Reparation versus Exploitation', *Film Quarterly* 72 (4): 46–53.

de Lima Costa, C. (2007), 'Unthinking Gender: The Traffic in Theory in the Americas', in M. L. Feminías and A. A. Oliver (eds), *Feminist Philosophy in Latin America and Spain*, New York: Rodopi.

Deamer, D. (2016), *Deleuze's Cinema Books: Three Introductions to the Taxonomy of Images*, Edinburgh: Edinburgh University Press.

Deleuze, G. ([1983] 1986), *Cinema 1: The Movement Image*, trans. H. Tomlinson and B. Habberjam, London: The Athlone Press.

Deleuze, G. ([1985] 1989), *Cinema 2: The Time-Image*, trans. H. Tomlinson and R. Galeta, London: The Athlone Press.

Deleuze, G. (1993), *The Fold: Leibniz and the Baroque*, trans. T. Conley, London: The Athlone Press.

Deleuze, G. ([1968] 1995), *Difference and Repetition*, trans. P. Patton, New York: Columbia University Press.

Doane, M. A. (1980), 'The Voice in the Cinema: The Articulation of Body and Space', *Yale French Studies* 60: 33–50.

Donald, I. (1955), *Practical Obstetric Problems*, London: Lloyd Duke.

Drescher-Burke, K. M., J. Krall and A. Penick (2004), *Discarded Infants and Neonaticide: A Review of the Literature*, Berkeley: National Abandoned Infants Assistance Resource Center, University of California at Berkeley.

Duden, B. (1993), *Disembodying Women: Perspectives on Pregnancy and the Unborn*, trans. L. Hoinacki, Cambridge: Harvard University Press.

Ďurovičová, N. and K. Newman, eds (2010), *World Cinemas, Transnational Perspectives*, New York, Oxon: Routledge.

Dyer, R. (1990), *Now You See It: Studies on Lesbian and Gay Film*, London and New York: Routledge.

Ebert, R. (2007), 'A Trail of Blood: Review of *Stephanie Daley*', *Roger Ebert*, 31 May. Available on-line: www.rogerebert.com/reviews/stephanie-daley-2007 (last accessed 11 October 2020).

Ebert, R. (2009), 'Review of *Up*', *Roger Ebert*, 27 May. Available on-line: www.rogerebert.com/reviews/up-2009 (last accessed 11 October 2020).

Edelman, L. (2004), *No Future: Queer Theory and The Death Drive*, Durham: Duke University Press.

Elsaesser, T. and M. Hagener (2010), *Film Theory: An Introduction Through the Senses*, New York: Routledge.
Ettinger, B. L. (1995), *The Matrixial Gaze*, Leeds: Feminist Arts and Histories Network.
Fannin, M. (2014), 'Placental Relations', *Feminist Theory* 15 (3): 289–306.
Farrimond, K. (2017), *The Contemporary Femme Fatale: Gender, Genre and American Cinema*, New York: Routledge.
Fischer, L. (1992), 'Birth Trauma: Parturition and Horror in Rosemary's Baby', *Cinema Journal* 31 (3): 3–18.
Fischer, L. (1996), *Cinematernity: Film, Motherhood, Genre*, Princeton: Princeton University Press.
Fleming, D. H. and W. Brown (2018), 'Through a First-Contact Lens Darkly: Arrival, Unreal Time and Chthulucinema', *Film-Philosophy* 22 (3): 340–63.
Foster, G. M. (1987), 'On the Origin of Humoral Medicine in Latin America', *Medical Anthropology Quarterly* 1 (4): 355–93.
Frampton, D. (2006), *Filmosophy*, London and New York: Wallflower Press.
Francis, M. (2019), 'Roma: A Bibliography', *Film Quarterly* 72 (4): 61–2.
Fraser, N. (1996), 'Equality, Difference, and Radical Democracy: The United States Feminist Debates Revisited', in D. Trend (ed.), *Radical Democracy: Identity, Citizenship, and the State*, 196–208, New York: Routledge.
French, P. (2009), 'Review of *Up*', *Guardian*, 11 October. Available on-line: www.theguardian.com/film/2009/oct/11/up-disney-pixar-film-review (last accessed 30 October 2020).
Freud, S. ([1920] 1991), 'Beyond the Pleasure Principle', in J. Strachey and A. Richards (trans.), *On Metapsychology: The Theory of Psychoanalysis; Beyond the Pleasure Principle, The Ego and the Id, and Other Works*, 275–38, Harmondsworth: Penguin.
Freud, S. ([1918] 2001), 'Mourning and Melancholy', in J. Strachey (trans.), *The Standard Edition of the Complete Psychological Works of Sigmund Freud Vol XIV (1914-1916), On The History of the Psycho-analytic Movement Papers on Metapsychology and Other Works*, 237–58, London: Vintage.
Garcia, J., L. Bricker, J. Henderson, M-A. Martin, M. Mugford, J. Nielson and T. Roberts (2002), 'Women's Views of Pregnancy Ultrasound: A Systematic Review', *Birth* 29 (4): 225–50.
Garwood, I. (2015), *The Sense of Film Narration*, Edinburgh: Edinburgh University Press.
Getino, O. and F. Solanas (1970–1971), 'Toward a Third Cinema', *Cinéaste* 4 (3): 1–10.
Goldie, P. (2000), *The Emotions: A Philosophical Investigation*, Oxford: Oxford University Press.
Grant, M. (2004), '"Ultimate Formlessness": Cinema, Horror and the Limits of Meaning', in S. J. Schneider (ed.), *Horror Film and Psychoanalysis: Freud's Worst Nightmare*, 177–87, Cambridge: Cambridge University Press.
Grosz, E. (1994), *Volatile Bodies: Towards a Corporeal Feminism*, Bloomington, Indiana: Indiana University Press.
Guneratne, A. R. and W. Dissanayake, eds (2003), *Rethinking Third Cinema*, New York: Routledge.

Halbwachs, M. (1992), *On Collective Memory*, trans. L. A. Coser, Chicago and London: The University of Chicago Press.
Hammer, P. J. (2001), 'Bloodmakers Made of Blood: Quechua Ethnophysiology of Menstruation', in E. P. Renne and E. van de Walle (eds), *Regulating Menstruation: Beliefs, Practices, Interpretations*, Chicago and London: The University of Chicago Press.
Han, S. (2009), 'Making Room for Daddy: Men's "Belly Talk" in the Contemporary United States', in M. C. Inhorn, T. Tjørnhøj-Thomsen, H. Goldberg and M. la Lour Mosegaard (eds), *Reconceiving the Second Sex: Men, Masculinity and Reproduction*, 305–26, New York and Oxford: Berghahn Books.
Harrington, E. (2018), *Women, Monstrosity and Horror Films: Gyneahorror*, Abingdon: Routledge.
Hart, S. M. (2015), *Latin American Cinema*, London: Reaktion Books.
Hartouni, V. (1997), *Cultural Conceptions: On Reproductive Technologies and the Remaking of Life*, Minneapolis: University of Minnesota Press.
Hawthorne, N. (1983), *The Scarlett Letter: A Romance*, New York: Penguin Books.
Heath, S. (1976), 'Narrative Space', *Screen* 11 (21): 68–112.
Hirsch, M. (1997), *Family Frames: Photography, Narrative, and Postmemory*, Cambridge, MA and London: Harvard University Press.
Hirsch, M. (2012), *The Generation of Postmemory: Writing and Visual Culture After the Holocaust*, New York: Columbia University Press.
Inhorn, M. C., T. Tjørnhøj-Thomsen, H. Goldberg and M. la Lour Mosegard, eds (2009), *Reconceiving the Second Sex: Men, Masculinity and Reproduction*, New York and Oxford: Berghahn Books.
Iordanova, D., D. Martin-Jones and B. Vidal, eds (2010), *Cinema at the Periphery*, Detroit, MI: Wayne State University Press.
Isenberg, R. (2014), 'Award Winning Tico Director Esteban Ramirez Takes on Third Feature Film', *Tico Times*, 29 March. Available on-line: www.ticotimes.net/2014/03/29/director-ramirez-takes-on-third-feature-film (last accessed 28 October 2020).
Jacobs, H. A. (1861), *Incidents in the Life of a Slave Girl*, Boston: Thayer and Eldridge.
Jansari, A. and A. J. Parkin (1996), 'Things That Go Bump in Your Life: Explaining the Reminiscence Bump in Autobiographical Memory', *Psychology and Aging* 11 (1): 85–91.
Jansson, A. (2002), 'Spatial Phantasmagoria: The Mediatisation of Tourism Experience', *European Journal of Communication* 17 (4): 429–43.
Joyce, K. A. (2008), *Magnetic Appeal: MRI and the Myth of Transparency*, Ithaca and London: Cornell University Press.
Jülich, S. (2015), 'The Making of a Best Selling Book on Reproduction: Lennart Nilsson's A Child is Born', *Bulletin of the History of Medicine* 89 (3): 491–525.
Keen, B. and K. Haynes (2009), *A History of Latin America, Volume 1: Ancient America*, Boston: Houghton Mifflin.
Kermode, M. (2006), 'Girl', *Sight and Sound* 16 (12): 20–4.
Kern, L. (2013), Review of *Ain't Them Bodies Saints*, Film Comment March-April,

Kestler, E. and V. Mora (2018), 'Unintended Pregnancy, Induced Abortion, and Unmet Need for Effective Contraception in Twenty-First Century Indigenous Mayan Populations of Guatemala', in D. A. Schwartz (ed.), *Maternal Deaths and Pregnancy-Related Morbidity Among Indigenous Women of Mexico and Central America: An Anthropological, Epidemiological, and Biomedical Approach*, 531–52, Springer e-book. Available on-line: https://doi.org/10.1007/9 78-3-319-71538-4 (last accessed 30 October 2020).

King, J. (2000), *Magical Reels: A History of Cinema in Latin America*, second edition, New York: Verso.

Kirwan, J. (2005), *The Non-Rational and the Irrational in the History of Aesthetics*, New York: Routledge.

Kristeva, J. (1981), 'Women's Time', trans. A. Jardine and H. Blake, *Signs* 7 (1): 13–35.

Kristeva, J. (1982), *The Powers of Horror: An Essay on Abjection*, trans. L. S. Roudiez, New York: Columbia University Press.

Kroløkke, C. (2010), 'On a Trip to the Womb: Biotourist Metaphors in Fetal Ultrasound Imaging', *Women's Studies in Communication* 33 (2): 138–53.

Kroløkke, C. (2011), 'Biotourist Performances: Doing Parenting During the Ultrasound', *Text and Performance Quarterly* 31 (1): 15–36.

Kukla, R. (2005), *Mass Hysteria: Medicine, Culture, and Mothers' Bodies*, New York and Toronto: Rowman and Littlefield Publishers, Inc.

Kusumastuti, F. (2019), 'Polysemy in and of the Science Fiction Film *Arrival* (2016)', *Research in Social Sciences and Technology* 4 (1): 73–91.

Laine, T. (2013), *Feeling Cinema: Emotional Dynamics in Film Studies*, New York and London: Bloomsbury.

Lam, C. (2015), *New Reproductive Technologies and Disembodiment: Feminist and Material Resolutions*, Farnham, Surrey: Ashgate.

Latimer, H. (2009), 'Popular Culture and Reproductive Politics: *Juno*, *Knocked Up* and the Enduring Legacy of the Handmaid's Tale', *Feminist Theory* 10 (2): 209–24.

Latimer, H. (2013), *Reproductive Acts: Sexual Politics in North American Fiction and Film*, Montreal: McGill University Press.

Leach, E. (1966), 'Virgin Birth', *Proceedings of the Royal Anthropological Institute of Great Britain and Ireland, 1966*: 39–49.

Lifton, R. J. and E. Olson (2004), 'Symbolic Immortality', in A. C. G. M. Robben (ed.), *Death, Mourning and Burial: A Cross Cultural Reader*, 32–9, Malden MA and Oxford: Blackwell Publishing.

Löfgren, O. (2002), *On Holiday: A History of Vacationing*, Berkeley and London: University of California Press.

Lugones, M. (2007), 'Heterosexualism and the Colonial/Modern Gender System', *Hypatia* 22 (1): 186–209.

Lundquist, C. (2008), 'Being Torn: Towards a Phenomenology of Unwanted Pregnancy', *Hypatia* 23 (3): 136–55.

Lury, K. (2010), *The Child in Film: Tears, Fears and Fairy Tales*, London: I. B. Tauris.

MacDonald, L. E. (2013), *The Invisible Art of Film Music: A Comprehensive History*, second edition, Toronto and Plymouth, UK: The Scarecrow Press, Inc.

Maher, J. (2002), 'Visibly Pregnant: Towards a Placental Body', *Feminist Review* 72: 95–107.
Mamula, T. (2018), 'Denis Villeneuve, Film Theorist; Or, Cinema's Arrival in a Multilingual World', *Screen Dossier* 59 (4): 542–51.
Marcantonio, C. (2019), 'Roma: Silence, Language, and the Ambiguous Power of Affect', *Film Quarterly* 72 (4): 38–45.
Marks, L. U. (2000), *The Skin of the Film: Intercultural Cinema, Embodiment, and the Senses*, London: Duke University Press.
Marshall, H. (1996), 'Our Bodies Ourselves: Why We Should Add Old Fashioned Empirical Phenomenology to the New Theories of the Body', *Women's Studies International Forum* 19 (3): 253–65.
Martin, D. and D. Shaw, eds (2017), *Latin American Women Filmmakers: Production, Politics, Poetics*, London and New York: I. B. Tauris.
Martin, E. (1987), *The Woman in the Body: A Cultural Analysis of Reproduction*, Boston, MA: Beacon Press.
Martin, E. (1991), 'The Egg and the Sperm: How Science has Constructed a Romance Based on Stereotypical Male–Female Roles', *Signs: Journal of Women, Culture and Society* 16 (3): 485–501.
Martin, M. T., ed. (1997), *New Latin American Cinema, Volume 1: Theories, Practices, and Transcontinental Articulations*, Detroit: Wayne State University Press.
Maseda, R. (2016), 'Indigenous Trauma in Mainstream Peru in Claudia Llosa's *The Milk of Sorrow*', *Dissidences* 6 (11), Article 13.
Maseda, R. (2020), 'Songs of Pain: Female Active Survivors in Claudia Llosa's *The Milk of Sorrow*', in A. D. Plat and S. N. Silberman (eds), *Violence: Probing the Boundaries Around the World*, 38–55, Boston: Brill/Rodopi.
Massumi, B. (2002), *Parables for the Virtual: Movement, Affect, Sensation*, Durham and London: Duke University Press.
McClintock, M. (1971), 'Menstrual Synchrony and Suppression', *Nature* 229: 244–45.
McLaughlin, J. (2003), 'Risky Professional Boundaries: Articulations of the Personal Self by Antenatal Screening Professionals', *Journal of Health Organization and Management* 17 (4): 264–79.
McLelland, R. (2013), 'Cautionary Whales?: Adolescence and Genre in *Juno* and *Push*', *Mosaic: A Journal for the Interdisciplinary Study of Literature* 46 (2): 105–21.
McTaggart, J. M. E. (1908), 'The Unreality of Time', *Mind* 17 (68): 457–74.
Merleau-Ponty, M. (1968), *The Visible and The Invisible*, trans. A. Lingis, Evanston: Northwestern University Press.
Metz, C. (1974), *Film Language: A Semiotics of the Cinema*, trans. M. Taylor, New York: Oxford University Press.
Meyer, C. L. (1997), *The Wandering Uterus: Politics and the Reproductive Rights of Women*, New York: New York University Press.
Meyer, M. L. (2005), *Thicker than Water: The Origins of Blood as Symbol and Ritual*, New York: Routledge.
Meyers, S. (2010), 'Invisible Waves of Technology: Ultrasound and the Making of Fetal Images', *Medicine Studies* 2 (3): 197–209.
Mills, C. (2011), *Futures of Reproduction: Bioethics and Biopolitics*, New York: Springer.

Mitchell, L. M. (2001), *Baby's First Picture: Ultrasound and the Politics of Fetal Ultrasound*, Toronto, ON: University of Toronto Press.
Mitchell, W. J. T. (2005), *What Do Pictures Want: The Lives and Loves of Images*, Chicago and London: The University of Chicago Press.
Moi, T. (2001), *What Is a Woman? And Other Essays*, Oxford: Oxford University Press.
Moore, L. J. (2009), 'Killer Sperm: Masculinity and the Essence of Male Hierarchies', in M. C. Inhorn, T. Tjørnhøj-Thomsen, H. Goldberg and M. la Lour Mosegaard (eds), *Reconceiving the Second Sex: Men, Masculinity and Reproduction*, New York: Berghahn Books.
Morgan, L. M. (1997), 'Imagining the Unborn in the Ecuadoran Andes', *Feminist Studies* 23 (2): 322–50.
Mulvey, L. (2006), *Death 24X A Second: Stillness and the Moving Image*, London: Reaktion Books Ltd.
Naficy, H. (2001), *An Accented Cinema: Exilic and Diasporic Cinema*, Princeton and Oxford: Princeton University Press.
Neupert, R. (2014), 'Melancholy, Empathy and Animated Bodies: Pixar vs. Mary and Max', in D. Roche and I. Schmitt-Pitiot (eds), *Intimacy in Cinema*, 215–24, Jefferson, NC: McFarland and Company Inc.
Nicolson, M. and J. E. E. Fleming (2013), *Imaging and Imagining the Fetus: The Development of Obstetric Ultrasound*, Baltimore: The John Hopkins University Press.
Nilsson, L. (1965), 'Drama of Life Before Birth', *Life Magazine* 58 (17): 54–71.
Nilsson, L., A. I. Sunberg, A. Macmillan and B. Wirsén (2010), *A Child Is Born: The Drama of Life before Birth in Unprecedented Photographs. A Practical Guide for the Expectant Mother*, London: Jonathan Cape.
Oliver, K. (2012), *Knock Me Up, Knock Me Down: Images of Pregnancy in Hollywood Films*, New York: Columbia University Press.
O'Neill, D. (2009) 'Up with Ageing', *BMJ* 339, 14 October. Available on-line: https://doi.org/10.1136/bmj.b4215 (last accessed 20 November 2020).
Pagán-Teitelbaum, I. (2012), 'Glamour in the Andes: Indigenous Women in Peruvian Cinemas', *Latin American and Caribbean Ethnic Studies* 7 (1): 71–93.
Palmer, J. (2009a), 'Seeing and Knowing: Ultrasound Images in the Contemporary Abortion Debate', *Feminist Theory* 10 (2): 173–89.
Palmer, J. (2009b), 'The Placental Body in 4D: Everyday Practices of Non-Diagnostic Iconography', *Feminist Review*, 93 (1): 64–80.
Palou, P. Á. (2018), 'Broken Memory, Voice and Visual Storytelling', *Mediático*, 24 December. Available on-line: https://reframe.sussex.ac.uk/mediatico/2018/12/24/special-dossier-on-roma-broken-memory-voice-and-visual-storytelling (last accessed 9 November 2020).
Patrick-Weber, C. (2020). *The Rhetoric and Medicalization of Pregnancy and Childbirth in Horror Films*, London: Lexington Books.
Pedwell, C. and A. Whitehead (2012), 'Affecting Feminism: Questions of Feeling in Feminist Theory', *Feminist Theory* 13 (2): 115–29.
Petchesky, R. P. (1987), 'Fetal Images: The Power of Visual Culture in the Politics of Reproduction', *Feminist Studies* 13 (2): 263–92.
Pick, Z. (1993), *New Latin American Cinema: A Continental Project*, Austin: University of Texas Press.

Pisters, P. (2012), *The Neuro-Image: A Deleuzian Film-Philosophy of Digital Screen Culture*, Stanford, CA: Stanford University Press.
Platt, T. (2001), 'El feto agresivo: Parto, formación de la persona y mito-historia en Los Andes', *Anuaria de Estudios Americanos* 58 (2): 633–78.
Podalsky, L. (2011), *The Politics of Affect and Emotion in Contemporary Latin American Film: Argentina, Brazil, Cuba, and Mexico*, New York: Palgrave Macmillan.
Pollock, G. (2006), 'Femininity: Aporia or Sexual Difference', in B. Ettinger, *The Matrixial Borderspace*, Minneapolis and London: University of Minnesota Press.
Pomerantz, J. R. and E. A. Pristach (1989), 'Emergent Features, Attention and Perceptual Glue in Visual Form Perception', *Journal of Experimental Psychology: Human Perception and Performance* 15 (4): 635–49.
Porter, T. and H. Gavin (2010), 'Infanticide and Neonaticide: A Review of 40 Years of Research Literature on Incidences and Causes', *Trauma Violence and Abuse* 11 (3): 99–112.
Quijano, A. (2000), 'Colonialidad del poder, eurocentrismo y América Latina', in E. Lander (ed.), *La colonialidad del saber: eurocentrismo y ciencias sociales. Perspectivas latinoamericanas*, 201–46, Buenos Aires: CLACSO.
Quinlivan, D. (2012), *The Place of Breath in Cinema*, Edinburgh: Edinburgh University Press.
Remez, R. E. and E. Rubin. (1992), 'Acoustic Shards, Perceptual Glue', *Hoskins Laboratories Status Report on Speech Research* 111/112: 1–10.
Reynolds, P. C. (1991), *Stealing Fire: The Atomic Bomb as Symbolic Body*, Palo Alto, CA: Iconic Anthropology Press.
Richard, D. E. (2018), 'Film Phenomenology and the "Eloquent Gestures" of Denis Villeneuve's *Arrival*', *Cinephile* 21 (1): 41–7.
Roberts, J. (2012a), *The Visualised Foetus: A Cultural and Political Analysis of Ultrasound Imagery*, London: Routledge.
Roberts, J. (2012b), '"Wakey Wakey Baby": Narrating Four-Dimensional (4D) Bonding Scans', *Sociology of Health and Illness* 34 (2): 299–314.
Roberts, J., F. E. Griffiths and A. Verran (2017), 'Seeing the Baby, Doing Family: Commercial Ultrasound as Family Practice', *Sociology* 51 (3): 527–42.
Roberts, J., F. E. Griffiths, A. Verran and C. Ayre (2015) 'Why Do Women Seek Ultrasound Scans from Commercial Providers During Pregnancy?', *Sociology of Health and Illness* 37 (4): 594–609.
Robson, S. (2010), 'Fetal Ultrasound Screening and Diagnosis 10 Years Hence', *Prenatal Diagnosis*, 30 (7): 696–8.
Rødje, K. (2015), *Images of Blood in American Cinema: The Tingler to the Wild Bunch*, Farnham: Ashgate.
Rojas, A. (2017), 'Mother of Pearl, Song and Potatoes: Cultivating Resilience in Claudia Llosa's *La teta asustada/The Milk of Sorrow*', *Studies in Spanish and Latin American Cinemas* 14 (3): 297–314.
Rosewarne, L. (2012), *Periods in Pop Culture: Menstruation in Film and Television*, Lanham, MD and Plymouth: Lexington Books.
Rothberg, M. (2009), *Multidirectional Memory: Remembering the Holocaust in the Age of Decolonization*, Stanford, CA: Stanford University Press.

Rueda, C. (2015), 'Memory, Trauma, and Phantasmagoria in Claudia Llosa's "La teta asustada"', *Hispania* 98 (3): 452-62.
Sadlier, D. J., ed. (2009), *Latin American Melodrama: Passion, Pathos, and Entertainment*, Urbana and Chicago: University of Illinois Press.
Sandelowski, M. (1994), 'Separate but Less Unequal: Fetal Ultrasonography and the Transformation of Expectant Mother/Fatherhood', *Gender and Society* 8 (2): 230-45.
Sapphire (1996), *Push,* New York: Vintage.
Sawchuck, K. (2000), 'Biotourism, Fantastic Voyage, and Sublime Inner Space', in J. Marchessault and K. Sawchuk (eds), *Wild Science: Reading Feminism, Medicine and the Media*, 9-23, London: Routledge.
Sayed, A., ed. (2016), *Screening Motherhood in Contemporary World Cinema*, Bradford, ON: Demeter Press.
Schroeder Rodríguez, P. A. (2016), *Latin American Cinema: A Comparative History*, Oakland, CA: University of California Press.
Seigworth, G. J. and M. Gregg, eds (2010), *The Affect Theory Reader*, Durham and London: Duke University Press.
Shaviro, S. (1993), *The Cinematic Body: Theory Out of Bounds*, Minneapolis and London: University of Minnesota Press.
Shaw, D. (2018), 'Children of Women? Alfonso Cuarón's Love Letter to His Nana', *Mediático*, 24 December. Available on-line: https://reframe.sussex.ac.uk/mediatico/2018/12/24/special-dossier-on-roma-alfonso-cuarons-love-letter-to-his-nana (last accessed 9 November 2020).
Shildrick, M. (1997), *Leaky Bodies and Boundaries: Feminism, Postmodernism and (Bio)ethics*, London, and New York: Routledge.
Silverman, M. (2013), *Palimpsestic Memory: The Holocaust and Colonialism in French and Francophone Fiction and Film*, New York and Oxford: Berghahn.
Slifkin, M. (2013), Review of *Ain't Them Bodies Saints*, *Film Comment* July-August: 66.
Sobchack, V. (1992), *The Address of the Eye: A Phenomenology of Film*, Princeton, NJ: Princeton University Press.
Sobchack, V. (2000), 'A Violent Dance: A Personal Memoir of Death in the Movies', in S. Prince (ed.), *Screening Violence*, 110-24, London: The Athlone Press.
Sobchack, V. (2004), *Carnal Thoughts: Embodiment and Moving Image Culture*, Berkeley: University of California Press.
Stadler, J. (2017), 'Embodied Epistemology: *Arrival* and the Language of Cinema', *Film-Philosophy Conference*, 5 July, Lancaster University.
Steiner, K. L., D. B. Pillemer, D. K. Thomsen and A. P. Minigaan (2014), 'The Reminiscence Bump in Older Adult's Life Story Transitions', *Memory* 22 (8): 1002-09.
Stevens, E. P. (1973), '*Marianismo*: The Other Face of *Machismo* in Latin America', in A. M. Pescatello (ed.), *Female and Male in Latin America*, 90-101, Pennsylvania: University of Pittsburgh Press.
Stormer, N. (2000), 'Prenatal Space', *Signs* 26 (1): 109-44.
Studlar, G. (1990), 'Reconciling Feminism and Phenomenology: Notes on Problems, Texts and Contexts', *Quarterly Review of Film and Video* 12 (3): 69-78.

Subero, G. (2016), *Embodiments of Evil: Gender and Sexuality in Latin American Horror Film*, London: Palgrave Macmillan.
Taylor, J. S. (2008), *The Public Life of the Fetal Sonogram: Technology, Consumption and the Politics of Reproduction*, Piscataway: Rutgers University Press.
Teichert, E. P. (2019), '*Pañuelazo*: Visual Strategies of the Legal Abortion Campaign in Argentina' [conference presentation] *Latin American Studies Association Conference*, 25 May, Boston.
Theidon, K. (2013), *Intimate Enemies: Violence and Reconciliation in Peru*, Philadelphia: University of Pennsylvania Press.
Thoma, P. (2009), 'Buying Up Baby', *Feminist Media Studies* 9 (4): 409–25.
Thomas, S. (2014), '"Yo No Soy Invisible": Imaginative Agency in *Las malas intenciones*', in C. Rocha and G. Seminet (eds), *Screening Minors in Latin American Cinema*, 53–68, New York: Lexington Books.
Thompson, C. K. (2014), *Picturing Argentina: Myths, Movies, and the Peronist Vision*, Amherst and New York: Cambria Press.
Tonkin, L. (2017), 'A Sense of Myself as Mother: An Exploration of Maternal Fantasies in the Experience of Circumstantial Childlessness', *Studies in The Maternal* 9 (1): 1–21.
Tyler, I. (2000), 'Reframing Pregnant Embodiment', in S. Ahmed, S. Kilby, J. Lury, C. McNeil and B. Skeggs (eds), *Transformations: Thinking Through Feminism*, 288–302, New York: Routledge.
Tyler, I. (2001), 'Skin-Tight: Celebrity, Pregnancy and Subjectivity', in S. Ahmed and J. Stacy (eds), *Thinking Through The Skin*, 69–84, New York: Routledge.
Tyler, I. (2009), 'Against Abjection', *Feminist Theory* 10 (1): 77–98.
Tyler, I., R. Coleman and D. Ferreday, (2008), 'Methodological Fatigue and the Politics of the Affective Turn', *Feminist Media Studies* 8 (1): 85–99.
van Dijck, J. (2005), *The Transparent Body: A Cultural Analysis of Medical Imaging*, Canada: University of Washington Press.
Vargas, A. S. (2016), 'Trailer: 'Apio verde' is a harrowing call to arms for reproductive rights in Chile', *Remezcla* 22 June. Available on-line: https://remezcla.com/film/trailer-apio-verde-francesc-morales-abortion-chile (last accessed 8 October 2020).
Vertovec, S. (2009), *Transnationalism*, New York, Oxon: Routledge.
Vostal, S. L. (2005), 'Masking Menstruation: The Emergence of Menstrual Hygiene Products in the United States', in A. Shail and G. Howie (eds), *Menstruation: A Cultural History*, Palgrave Macmillan.
Walter, T. (2001), 'Reincarnation, Modernity, Identity', *Sociology* 35 (1): 21–38.
Walters, J. (2011), *Fantasy Film: A Critical Introduction*, New York and Oxford: Berg.
Warner, M. (1976), *Alone of All Her Sex: The Myth and Cult of the Virgin Mary*, New York: Knopf.
Warren, M. and S. H. Bickford (2020), 'Market Demands and the Perpetuation of Poverty: City versus Country in Jayro Bustamente's Ixcanul', *El Ojo Que Piensa* 20: 11–19.
Weatherford, D. J. (2020), 'Populating the Margins: Hope and Healing in Claudia Llosa's *La teta asustada*', *Diálogo* 23 (1): 85–99.

Weir, L. (2006), *Pregnancy, Risk and Bio-Politics: On the Threshold of the Living Subject*, New York: Routledge.
White, P. (2015), *Women's Cinema, World Cinema*, Durham and London: Duke University Press.
Williams, R. (1973), *The Country and the City*, London: The Hogarth Press.
Wilson, H. C. (1992), 'A Critical Review of Menstrual Synchrony Research', *Psychoendocrinology* 17 (6): 565–91.
Wright, P. (2007), *Iron Curtain: From Stage to Cold War*, Oxford and New York: Oxford University Press.
Yalom, M. (1997), *The History of the Breast*, New York: Ballantine Books.
Young, I. M. (2005), *On Female Body Experience: 'Throwing Like a Girl' and Other Essays*, Oxford and New York: Oxford University Press.
Zaner, R. M. (1971), *The Problem of Embodiment: Some Contributions to the Phenomenology of the Body*, The Hague: Martinus Nijhoff.
Zavota, G. (2020), 'Given (No) Time: A Derridean Reading of Denis Villenueve's Arrival', *Film-Philosophy* 24 (2): 185–203.
Ziomkiewicz, A. (2006), 'Menstrual Synchrony: Fact or Artifact', *Human Nature: An Interdisciplinary Biosocial Perspective* 17 (4): 419–32.
Županović, M. (2019), 'Ambiguity of the Trauma Narrative in Claudia Llosa's The Milk of Sorrow', *Interdisciplinary Description of Complex Systems* 17 (2-A): 294–303.

INDEX

Page numbers followed with "n" refer to endnotes.

A Girl Like Her (2011, Fessler) 32
abjection 12, 13, 25–9
abortion 7–8, 22, 30, 32, 77, 78, 187 n.20, 198 n.9
  laws 8, 180 n.6, 181 n.9, 194 n.29
Aborto (1965, Chaskel) 5
absence on screen 43–5
Abuelas: Grandmothers on a Mission (2012, Noemi Weis) 32
adolescence 188 n.1
aesthetics 49–53. *See also* emotion
agential realism 42, 94, 186 n.12
  Barad, Karen 94
Ain't Them Bodies Saints (2013, Lowery) 90, 91, 93, 96, 97
  biotourist narrative 106–15
Alien (1979, Scott) 24, 26
Alvaray, Luisela 10
Americas
  abortion in 7–8
  foetal personhood 8–9
  gender and sexualities 9
  pregnancy 9–10
  reproductive rights 7–8, 10
Apio verde (2013, Morales Brucher) 90–3, 96, 115–24
  biotourist narrative 115–24
Arnold, Sarah 22, 33
Arredondo, Isabel 31
Arrival (2016, Villeneuve), pregnant embodiment in 155, 157–67
ARTs. *See* Assisted reproductive technologies (ARTs)
Assisted reproductive technologies (ARTs) 19
Assman, Jan, communicative memory 127

authentic exoticism 168
Ayres, Susan 87

Baby Mama (2008, McCullers) 19
The Back-Up Plan (2010, Poul) 20
The Bad Intentions (2011, García-Montero) 128, 196 n.13
  recollection-object 138–46
Barad, Karen
  agential realism 94
  intra-action 6, 42–3, 45–6, 48, 62, 66, 73, 79, 94, 96–7, 108, 110, 112, 116, 122–3, 139
Baraitser, Lisa 159
Barker, Jennifer M. 47, 96
Barrow, Sarah 99, 196 n.13
Battersby, Christine 27, 52, 156
Bazin, André 58
Beautiful Sin (2014, Quirós) 31
Beckman, Linda J. 8
Belej, Cecelia 9
belly talk 97
Benson-Allott, Caetlin 24
Beugnet, Martine 11, 97
bioscape 38, 190 n.2
  foetus in 116
  Sawchuck, Kim 4, 38, 88–90, 92–4, 98, 103, 106, 110, 116, 119, 123, 124, 174, 176, 190 n.2
  of uterus 88, 90, 92, 94, 103, 106, 116, 123–4, 176
biotourism
  defined 89
  Krøløkke, Charlotte 4, 92
  qualities of 90

Sawchuck, Kim 12, 88–96, 123, 189 n.4
  uterus and foetus 90–6
Birth (2004, Glazer) 128
  recollection-object 146–54
The Blonds/Los Rubios (2003, Carri) 32
Bordwell, David 44
Boswell, Parley Ann 17, 18
Braidotti, Rosi 45, 52
Breathless/À bout de souffle (1960, Godard) 18
Brinkema, Eugenie 51, 169–70
  horror genre 24
  mise n'en scène 2, 4, 5, 12, 26, 45, 50, 51, 68, 69, 71, 74, 97, 108, 130, 135, 147, 154, 155, 157, 158, 162, 164, 166, 168, 170, 172, 174–6, 198 n.5
The Brood (1979, Cronenberg) 24
The Brothers Solomon (2007, Odenkirk) 20
Brown, William 157
Bruno, Giuliana 93, 95
Burch, Noël 45

Canessa, Andrew 9
Captive/Cautiva (2003, Biraben) 32
Carey, Ross 197
Carrie (1976, De Palma) 24
Casa de los babys (2003, Sayles) 21
Casper, Monica J. 91
Castillo, Debra A, authentic exoticism 168
Chanan, Michael 10–11, 181 n.13
Clough, Patricia 52
Clover, Carol J. 26–7
Coleman, Rebecca 51
collaborative coding
  as perceptual glue 40–3
  Roberts, Julie 12, 35–7, 40–3, 55, 56, 58, 60–4, 66, 73, 80–3, 88, 176
collective memory 125, 127, 195 n.4
communicative memory 127
complicitous communication 50

conceptual narrative 16, 41, 46, 57, 58, 67, 77, 81
Connerton, Paul 127
  social memory 195 n.5
Cooper, Sarah 177
corporeality 97, 105–8, 122, 165
corporeal sensibility 92–3
Creed, Barbara 5
Curiel, Ochy 9

Deamer, David 39
Deleuze, Gilles 186 n.16
  Elsewhere 38–9, 43, 44, 55, 58, 65, 71, 86, 88, 176, 195 n.3
  off-screen space 1, 12, 38–40, 43–5, 51, 53, 55, 56, 65, 74, 77–9, 81, 84, 86, 88, 130, 154–6, 158, 170, 174–6, 195 n.3
  recollection image 195 n.3, 195 n.8
  third synthesis of time 157
de Lima Costa, Claudia 9
Demon Seed (1977, Cammell) 24
documentary films 12, 29–32
Duden, Barbara 43, 48–9, 158
Ďurovičová, Nataša 11

El colombian dream (2005, Aljure) 22
embodied response 150, 152
emotion 49–53
emotional closeness 75
emotional intra-action 62, 112
empathy 50
Eraserhead (1977, Lynch) 22
Ettinger, Bracha L., matrixial gaze 46–7

Fantastic Voyage (1966, Fleischer) 89, 190 n.1
fantasy 91
female subjectivity 28
femininity 31
feminist theory 52–3
Ferreday, Debra 51
fertility 30
  rights to 31
fetishized foetus 93

film-philosophy 37, 38, 177
Fischer, Lucy 2, 23
Fleming, David H. 157
Fleming, John E. E. 6
The Fly (1986, Cronenberg) 24–5
foetal narrative 97
foetal objects 49
foetal personhood 8–9
foetal rights 31
foetal scan 41
foetal ultrasound 4, 6, 35–7, 42, 49, 57
foetus 21, 22, 41, 45–7, 90–1, 168
  in bioscape 116
  biotourism 90–6
  presence-absence of 169
Foster, George M. 7
Frampton, Daniel 50, 177
Fraser, Nancy 9
From Girl to Mother/De niña a madre (2005, Jaugey) 30–1

gender and sexual difference 9
gentleness of the frame (Sobchack) 4, 39, 43, 44, 55–6, 58, 69, 77, 121, 122, 130, 176
Gestation/Gestación (2009, Ramírez) 55, 57, 59
  collaborative coding 73
  narrative negotiations 70–9
Grace (2009, Chan) 22
Grant, Michael 26
Grosz, Elizabeth 52
gynaehorror 23

Halbwach, Maurice, collective memory 195 n.4
Hammer, Patricia J. 7
Han, Sallie 97
haptic hearing 97
Harrington, Erin, gynaehorror 23
holistic model 191 n.9
Hollywood cinema 16, 17
horror film 22–4, 26, 116. *See also* melodrama
How to Lose Your Virginity (2013, Shechter) 30

interconnectedness 47, 93, 94, 191 n.7
intergenerational memories 127, 194 n.25
interobjectivity 50
intra-action (Barad) 6, 42, 43, 45–6, 48, 62, 66, 73, 79, 94, 96–7, 108, 110, 112, 116, 122, 123, 139
in-vitro fertilization (IVF) 19, 31
Iordanova, Dina 10
IVF. *See* in-vitro fertilization (IVF)
Ixcanul (2015, Bustamente), pregnant embodiment in 155, 167–74

Jane: An Abortion Service (1995, Kurtz and Lundy) 30
Jansson, André 95
Janus-faced technology 41–2
Junebug (2005, Morrison) 19
Juno (2007, Reitman) 55, 57, 58, 188 n.1
  narrative negotiations 59–70

Kept and Dreamless/Las mantenidas sin sueños (2005, de Salvo and Fogwill) 18
Kern, Laura 107
Kristeva, Julia
  abjection 25–7
  'Women's Time' 28
Kroløkke, Charlotte 38, 39, 88, 89, 93, 95, 96, 123
  biotourism 4, 92
Kukla, Rebecca 45
Kusumastuti, Fenty, polysemy 157

Labor Pains (2009, Shapiro) 19
Laine, Tarja 49–50, 176–7
Las Libres: The Story Continues (2014, Montaña) 30
Latin American Cinema 10–11, 181 n.13
Leach, Edmund 31
Let It Be Law/Que sea ley (2019, Solanas) 29
L!fe Happens (2011, Coiro) 21
Lifton, Robert J. 128
Lion's Den/Leonera (2008, Trapero) 18–19

Llosa, Claudia 17, 99, 192 n.16, 193 n.21
Look Who's Talking (1989–93, Heckerling, Ropelowski) 21, 90–1, 183 n.3
Lugones, María 9

McLaughlin, Janice 185 n.8
McLelland, Rachel 188 n.1
McTaggart, John M. Ellis, unreality of time 157, 159, 197 n.4
Mamula, Tijana 158
Manjunath, Prema 87
Maria Full of Grace/María llena eres de gracias (2004, Marston) 18
marianismo 31
Marks, Laura U. 47, 194 n.1
 distanciation and objectification 36
 recollection object 4, 12, 38, 125–9, 131, 132, 136–9, 143, 144, 146, 147, 149, 151–4, 176
Marshall, Helen 53
Martin, Deborah 29
Martin, Emily 91, 95
Martin-Jones, David 10
masculinity 31
Massumi, Brian 50
maternal melodrama 23
maternity 23
matrixial gaze 46–7
mediated experience 95
melodrama 23
memory 125–7
memory image 195 n.8
menstruation 25, 27–8, 75, 79, 184 n.13–14, 189 n.7
Merleau-Ponty, Maurice 44
metaphorical space, uterus as 45, 57, 86, 90, 110
methodological fatigue 51
Metz, Christian 44
Meyer, Cheryl L. 5
Meyers, Sonia 94
The Milk of Sorrow/La teta asustada (2009, Llosa) 89–93, 95
 biotourist narrative 97–106

Mills, Catherine, sympathetic imagination 45–6, 58, 186 n.18
miscarriage 131–3, 135–7
Misconceptions (2008, Satlof) 20
mise n'en scène (Brinkema) 2, 4, 5, 12, 26, 45, 50, 51, 68, 69, 71, 74, 97, 108, 130, 135, 147, 154, 155, 157, 158, 162, 164, 166, 168, 170, 172, 174–6, 198 n.5
Moi, Toril 26
Moore, Lisa Jane 28, 91
Morgan, Lynn 8–9
mortality 139
The Motherhood Archives (2013, Lusztig) 30
The Mothers of the Plaza de Mayo/ Las madres de la Plaza de Mayo (1985, Muñoz and Portillo) 32
multi-sensory process 36
Mulvey, Laura 159
Music on Hold/Música en espera (2009, Golfrid) 20
My Life Without Me (2003, Croixet) 21

narrative space
 collaborative coding (Roberts) 12, 35–7, 40–3, 55, 56, 58, 60–4, 66, 73, 80–3, 88, 176
 Elsewhere (Deleuze) 38–9, 43, 44, 55, 58, 65, 71, 86, 88, 176, 195 n.3
 gentleness of the frame (Sobchack) 4, 39, 43, 44, 55–6, 58, 69, 77, 121, 122, 130, 176
 intra-action (Barad) 6, 42, 43, 45–6, 48, 62, 66, 73, 79, 94, 96–7, 108, 110, 112, 116, 122, 123, 139
 mise n'en scène (Brinkema) 2, 4, 5, 12, 26, 45, 50, 51, 68, 69, 71, 74, 97, 108, 130, 135, 147, 154, 155, 157, 158, 162, 164, 166, 168, 170, 172, 174–6, 198 n.5
 off-screen space (Deleuze) 1, 12, 38–40, 43–5, 51, 53, 55, 56, 65, 74, 77–9, 81, 84, 86, 88, 130, 154–6, 158, 170, 174–6, 195 n.3

premises for perception
(Sobchack) 4, 12, 35, 38, 55,
56, 58, 61, 65, 71, 73, 75, 79,
80, 86, 88–90, 94, 110, 112,
120, 123, 138, 152, 174, 176
recollection object (*see* recollection object)
neonaticide 189 n.8
Neupert, Richard 196 n.11
Never, Rarely, Sometimes, Always (2020, Hittman) 22
Nicolson, Malcolm 6
Nilsson, Lennart 49
non-fiction, pregnancy as 29–33
'not-yet' born child 158

October Baby (2011, Erwin and Erwin) 22
off-screen space (Deleuze) 1, 12, 38–40, 43–5, 51, 53, 55, 56, 65, 74, 77–9, 81, 84, 86, 88, 130, 154–6, 158, 170, 174–6, 195 n.3. *See also* on-screen space
Oliver, Kelly 5, 17–19, 21, 22
O'Neill, Desmond 128–9
on-screen space 40, 44, 45, 58, 60, 65, 155, 156, 171, 174, 176
out-of-field (*hors-champ*). *See* off-screen space (Deleuze)

Patrick-Weber, Courtney 23
Pedwell, Carolyn, feminist study 52–3
perceptual glue 60, 62
  collaborative coding as 40–3
Petchesky, Rosalind 47
  fetishized foetus 93
phenomenology 12, 35, 37, 53, 175–7, 186 n.16
Platt, Tristan 9
Podalsky, Laura 10–11, 181 n.13
Pollock, Griselda 47
polysemy 157
post-national 182 n.16
Preggoland (2014, Tierney) 19
pregnancy. *See also* narrative space; uterus
  Americas 9–10
  centrality of 19
  comedy films and 21
  disparate characters 20
  documentary films for 29–32
  embodied experience of 23, 30, 51, 56
  foetal personhood and 9
  genre 2, 15–33
  horror film and 22–4, 26
  and human rights 31
  lived body experience 155–6, 158
  mediated experience 95
  as non-fiction 29–33
  and pregnancy loss 128
  and reproduction 3, 4, 16, 17, 30
  and reproductive rights 7, 8, 10
  termination of 8
pregnant embodiment 155–7
  in *Arrival* (2016, Villeneuve) 155, 157–67
  in *Ixcanul* (2015, Bustamente) 155, 167–74
premises for perception (Sobchack) 4, 12, 35, 38, 55, 56, 58, 61, 65, 71, 73, 75, 79, 80, 86, 88–90, 94, 110, 112, 120, 123, 138, 152, 174, 176
prosthetic belly 190 n.11
psychoanalytic theory 22–3

Quijano, Aníbal 9
Quinceañera (2006, Glatzer and Westmoreland) 20
Quinlivan, Davina 96–7

recollection 127
recollection image 128, 195 n.3, 195 n.8
recollection object, Marks, Laura U. 4, 12, 38, 125–9, 131, 132, 136–9, 143, 144, 146, 147, 149, 151–4, 176
reincarnation 150, 151
reminiscence bump 127, 195 n.7
reproductive rights 7–8, 31
Revolutionary Road (2006, Mendes) 19
Rey, Ana Lía 9

Richard, David Evan 157
rights to fertility 31
Roberts, Julie 39, 47, 48, 57, 88, 89, 91, 123
  collaborative coding 12, 35–7, 40–3, 55, 56, 58, 60–4, 66, 73, 80–3, 88, 176
  connectivity of the placenta 187 n.24
  uterus as metaphorical space 45, 57, 90
Rødje, Kjetil 27
Rosemary's Baby (1968, Polanski) 22, 23
Rosewarne, Lauren 27–8
Rosita (2005, Attie and Goldwater) 31
Rothberg, Michael 127

Sapir-Whorf hypothesis 157
Saved! (2004, Dannelly) 20
Sawchuck, Kim 189 n.4
  bioscape 4, 38, 88–90, 92–4, 98, 103, 106, 110, 116, 119, 123, 124, 174, 176, 190 n.2
  biotourism 12, 88–96, 115–24, 189 n.4
scan photograph 57–8
Seigworth, Gregory J. 51
self-reflective intra-action 123
shared subjectivity 38, 47
Shaviro, Steven 50
Shaw, Deborah 29
Shildrick, Margrit 52
The Silent Scream (1984, Dabner) 5, 47, 187 n.18
Silverman, Max 127
Slifkin, Meredith 107
Sobchack, Vivian 4, 37, 39–40, 45, 51–2, 57, 186 n.16
  embodied viewing 55
  gentleness of the frame 4, 39, 43, 44, 55–6, 58, 69, 77, 121, 122, 130, 176
  interobjectivity 50
  phenomenology 35, 177
  premises for perception 4, 12, 35, 38, 55, 56, 58, 61, 65, 71, 73, 75, 79, 80, 86, 88–90, 94, 110, 112, 120, 123, 138, 152, 174, 176
social memory 195 n.5
social relationship formation 128
somatic talk, touch and the belly 96–8
sperm 92
Stadler, Jane 157
Stephanie Daley (2006, Brougher) 55, 57, 59, 79–88
Stevens, Evelyn P. 31
Stormer, Nathan 49
Studlar, Gaylyn 53
sublime 189 n.4
susto 98, 99, 104, 105, 192 n.15
The Switch (2010, Gordon) 20
sympathetic imagination 45–6, 58, 73, 86, 186 n.18
sympathy 50, 58

targeted regulation of abortion providers (TRAP) 8
Taylor, Janelle 126
technocratic model 191 n.9
Teichert, Erika 29
Theidon, Kimberley 98
Thomas, Sarah 139
Thompson, Currie K. 16
Too Young to Be a Dad (2002, Gárdos) 21
Tourists/Touristas (2009, Scherson) 18
transforming anatomy into landscape 90, 123
transforming internal space 92
transposition of scale 90–1, 123
Tyler, Imogen 51, 156
  abjection 25–6
  elasticity of pregnant subjectivity 50

ultrasound scan 4, 6, 41–3, 45–8, 94
  history of 180 n.3
ultrasound transducer 46
Undertow/Contracorriente (2009, Fuentes-Léon) 19
Unplanned (2019, Konzelman and Solomon) 22

Unpregnant (2020, Goldenberg) 20
Up (2009, Docter and Petersen) 128
  recollection-object 128–37
Uprichard, Emma 160
uterus 4–6, 21, 32, 38, 41, 90–1,
  114–15. *See also* narrative space
  bioscape (Sawchuck) 4, 38, 88–90,
    92–4, 103, 106, 110, 116, 119,
    123–4, 174, 176, 190 n.2
  biotourism 90–6 (*see also*
    biotourism)
  cartography 93, 95, 97
  collaborative coding (Roberts) 12,
    35–7, 40–3, 55, 56, 58, 60–4, 66,
    73, 80–3, 88, 176
  Elsewhere (Deleuze) 38–9, 43,
    44, 55, 58, 65, 71, 86, 88, 176,
    195 n.3
  as the frame 45–9, 56, 58, 176
  intra-action 112
  materiality 47
  as metaphorical space 45, 57, 86,
    90, 110
  mise n'en scène (Brinkema) 2, 4,
    5, 12, 26, 45, 50, 51, 68, 69, 71,
    74, 97, 108, 130, 135, 147, 154,
    155, 157, 158, 162, 164, 166,
    168, 170, 172, 174–6, 198 n.5
  off-screen space (Deleuze) 1, 12,
    38–40, 43–5, 51, 53, 55, 56, 65,
    74, 77–9, 81, 84, 86, 88, 130,
    154–6, 158, 170, 174–6, 195 n.3
  premises for perception
    (Sobchack) 4, 12, 35, 38, 55,
    56, 58, 61, 65, 71, 73, 75,
    79, 80, 86, 88–90, 94, 110,
    112, 120, 123, 138, 152,
    174, 176

van Dijck, José 41–3, 185 n.6
Vargas, Andrew S. 116
Ventre Livre: Freeing the Womb (1994,
  Azevedo) 31
Vertovec, Steve 11–12
Vidal, Belén 10
virgin birth 31
virginity 31, 184 n.19
Virgin Tales (2012, von Arn) 30
voice-over 69, 70, 103, 108, 109

Weir, Lorna 127–8
*What to Expect When You're
  Expecting* (2012, Jones) 21
White, Patricia 17
Whitehead, Anne, feminist
  study 52–3
*Who Says It's Easy/¿Quién dice que es
  fácil?* (2007, Taratuto) 20
WMM. *See* Women Make
  Movies (WMM)
womb 4–5, 25, 30, 49
Women Make Movies
  (WMM) 29–30
'Women's Time' (Kristeva) 28

Young, Marion 26, 37, 156

Zavota, Gina 197 n.3

www.ingramcontent.com/pod-product-compliance
Lightning Source LLC
Chambersburg PA
CBHW062215300426
44115CB00012BA/2066